From That Terrible Field

CIVIL WAR LETTERS OF
JAMES M. WILLIAMS,
TWENTY-FIRST ALABAMA INFANTRY VOLUNTEERS

"I call this poor camp home, and I hail it with joy again! I marched away from it to the battlefield of Shiloh, and it seemed like home when I came back from that terrible field, weary, wet, and heart-sick . . . "

Lt. Col. James M. Williams, Mobile, March 1864

From That Terrible Field

Civil War Letters of
JAMES M. WILLIAMS,
*Twenty-first Alabama
Infantry Volunteers*

EDITED BY

John Kent Folmar

10|8|02

Scott -

All the Best,

Your Obt. Svt.,

John Kent Folmar

The University of Alabama Press
Tuscaloosa & London

Library of Congress Cataloging in Publication Data
Williams, James M 1837–1903.
  From that terrible field.

  Bibliography: p.
  Includes index.
  1. Williams, James M., 1837–1903. 2. Alabama
Infantry. 21st Reg., 1861–1865—Biography. 3. United
States—History—Civil War, 1861–1865—Personal narra-
tives—Confederate side. 4. United States—History—
Civil War, 1861–1865—Regimental histories—Alabama
Infantry—21st. I. Folmar, John Kent, 1932–
II. Title.
E551.5 21st.W54 1981   973.7'82 [B]   80-27672
ISBN 0-8173-0068-6   AACR1

To Mother

CONTENTS

MAPS AND ILLUSTRATIONS

PREFACE

A number of years ago, while I was teaching U.S. history at University Military School in Mobile, Alabama, a young student asked me if I would like to see his great-grandfather's Civil War letters. I expected to find a few letters written in the unintelligible prose of the "I take my pen in hand" genre. Instead, I found, in a large black box, with the name Powell Williams in wooden block letters on the top, the James Madison Williams letters, papers, documents, and ambrotypes. The bulk of the collection consisted of over two hundred letters written by a literate, artistic, observant, and fascinating "northern rebel" (whose penmanship, by the way, was superb).

I soon determined that Williams was a sufficiently prominent officer in the Confederate army to deserve study in his own right. Beyond his historical importance, however, is his importance as an observer and reporter of many facets of the Civil War era. The officer corps of that war consisted overwhelmingly of nonprofessional citizen-soldiers at the middle levels of command. Williams, as one such soldier, can help us understand how troops functioned when led by men not educated to the profession of arms. He also shows the range of mobility (and its limits) within that profession: the extent to which a man of ability but not of military education could rise in the chain of command. Mobility, however, is not just institutional, but social, as well. Williams, after all, was an Ohioan who had moved south just three years before the war. How such an "immigrant" could become so attached to Southern values so soon, how he could actually decide to fight for the Confederacy against the region of his birth, and how he was viewed by long-time Southerners help reveal in microcosm both the fluid social structure of the United States in the late antebellum period and also the pervasiveness of secessionist sentiment in the deep South during those years.

Wartime social, economic, political, and military conditions in the Confederate seaport, Mobile, also fell under Williams's observation. While those conditions rarely involved great battles, they are nevertheless historically important. The tedium of garrison duty is also a part of army life, and it should not be overlooked in comprehending the military experience. When battle did come, moreover—the fight at Shiloh in 1862, the two combats below Mobile in 1864—Williams's often prominent role adds to our understanding of them. His controversial service in the Battle of Mobile Bay, furthermore, reveals the impact of command disapproval and popular outcry on the system of military justice. In fact, his whole career—in combat, camp, and fort—not only is a part of his personal story, but also is intimately connected to the history of his regiment, an outfit about which no unit history has been published. In the absence of such a formal unit history, one must look to the Williams letters to find out about the attitudes and experiences of the common soldiers of the Twenty-first Alabama Regiment, Volunteers.

I identified most of the people (military and civilian), ships, and military locations. If I was not absolutely convinced that I had the correct indentification, I did not attempt to provide it. I did not correct spelling errors; fortunately, Williams had an uncommon writing ability. Duplicative portions of letters and some letters in their entirety were deleted from the manuscript. Ellipses are used when letters were fragmented or torn, as well as to indicate excisions.

I am indebted to many people who helped make this project possible. At California State College, Pennsylvania, I am grateful for the encouragement and assistance of Nancy Z. Nelson, Vice-President of Academic Affairs. William L. Beck, Director of Library Services, helped make research resources conveniently available to me. The Faculty Scholarship Committee provided needed travel funds.

For their important research and archival aid, I wish to express my appreciation to Elaine Everly, Director, Navy and Old Army Branch, Military Archives Division; Dale E. Floyd, Staff Assistant, National Archives; Milo B. Howard, Jr., Director, Alabama State Department of Archives and History; Caldwell Delaney, Director, City Museum of Mobile; and Jane M. McDonald, Museum Staff, Fort Morgan Commission, Gulf Shores, Alabama. Other Mobilians who were helpful include Lucille S. Mallon and John H. Friend. William R. Armistead's willingness to share his knowledge of Mobile's Civil War sites and ordnance was an essential part of the project.

I am particularly indebted to Dr. Richard J. Sommers, Archivist-Historian, U.S. Army Military History Institute, Carlisle Barracks, Pennsylvania, who read and critiqued the entire manuscript. My son, Tramel Lee, assisted with the cartographic chores.

My special gratitude goes to Louise Williams Chamberlin and to her son, James Williams Chamberlin. Their kindnesses over the years have made this study a joy beyond imagination.

INTRODUCTION

One of five children, James Madison Williams was born October 5, 1837, in St. Clairsville, Ohio. His father, John Hugh Williams, had migrated to Ohio from Philadelphia in 1832, and married Eleanor Frances Anderson, the daughter of Hugh Anderson, a prominent local Democratic politician, skilled engraver, and merchant. A watchmaker and silversmith by trade, the elder Williams established a prosperous mercantile business over the next two decades. He also became prominent in the cultural and educational affairs of the community. He was an educated man, and he became interested in the Church of New Jerusalem. In 1852 he was ordained as a minister of the church. He regularly preached in St. Clairsville and eastern Ohio and debated the leading Protestant ministers of the area. Young James often accompanied his father to these meetings and played the melodeon. In addition, he received training in watchmaking from his father and grandfather.[1]

In 1855, James's father decided to sell out and move to Iowa. By 1856, the family was situated in the frontier prairie town of Homer, in newly formed Hamilton County. The Panic of 1857 proved to be disastrous to the family; suddenly the debts owed to the elder Williams could not be paid, and their financial situation became tenuous. With money almost nonexistent, he arranged for James, now twenty-one years of age, to go to Augusta, Georgia, for one year and work as a clerk in the firm of a fellow New Churchman, Henry J. Osborne. James agreed and departed for the deep South on July 21, 1858. There he immediately became acculturated to the Southern way of life. He sent money to his father and entered into the local social activities with gusto; for instance, he took dancing lessons, sang with a choral group, and joined a baseball club. He also became a member of a militia company, the Clinch Rifles. Much to the consternation of his family, his affinity for the North declined to the degree that in August 1859, he decided to stay in Augusta for another year. Osborne increased his salary to $800.00 per year in early 1860, and in May a cousin from Ohio asked if he was not trying to escape bachelorhood. That was indeed the case! He had fallen in love with Eliza Jane Rennison, a seventeen-year-old Augusta belle. About the same time, he made another momentous decision, when he wrote to James Conning, in Mobile, Alabama, asking for employment. Conning, who owned a nationally known company manufacturing silver, jewelry, and swords, answered Williams from New York that he would hire him as a bookkeeper for $950.00 per year beginning in November. Williams immediately informed his surprised family of his decision to marry "Lizzy" and to move to Mobile. He left Augusta on November 12, 1860, and arrived in Mobile on the 17th. After working for three weeks for Conning, he made a whirlwind trip to Augusta, arriving on the evening of December 13, marrying Lizzy, and

LIZZY AND JAMES WILLIAMS, 1860

departing for Mobile the following evening. He did not know, of course, that except for the war years, Mobile would be his home for the remainder of his life.[2]

Although sympathetic to the secession movement and the formation of the Confederate government, Williams did not immediately enlist in a military unit.[3] His beloved Lizzy was pregnant; however, in early August she suffered a miscarriage.[4] Then Williams joined a newly organized local militia company, the Washington Light Infantry, number two. During September, he was listed as a sergeant in a local newspaper recruitment advertisement.[5]

Williams enlisted for one year in the Twenty-first Alabama on October 4. The regiment was accepted into Confederate service on October 11, 1861, and immediately sent to the nearby training camp at Hall's Mill.[6] There Williams began his correspondence with Lizzy (sometimes spelled Lizzie), which continued for the duration of the war, except for the periods when they were together. He wrote to her as often as possible, even though he was never far from Mobile (except for the Shiloh and First Corinth Campaigns from March until July 1862).

Why did Williams write so often, and why did he preserve the letters and documents? Primarily, he loved his wife and enjoyed talking to her by writing. Secondly, he seemed to have a historical perspective of the events that he witnessed and helped shape. In August 1862, perhaps on that account, his colonel suggested that he collect data for a history of the regiment. His sense of humor, his writing and drawing skills, his literary style, his adoration of military life, and his enthusiasm for Southern independence all combine to illustrate the life of a Northern devotee for the "cause" as he progressed from private to field command.

Williams began his military career enthusiastically as first sergeant of Company A (Washington Light Infantry) at Hall's Mill encampment. Adjustment to the new life, especially administrative and training duties, was a full-time task, although it did not keep him from feeling lonely for his wife. On November 16, 1861, the regiment was ordered down the bay to Fort Gaines on Dauphin Island. There the regiment, whose function was to prevent a landing west of the fort, lived in tents until barracks were constructed.

Since his enlistment he had been critical of the incompetence and absenteeism of Company A's officers. Finally, in protest, he resigned his position, effective December 13, and joined the ranks as a private. He was very popular with the men in the company (and regiment) and was sure that he could be elected to a command position if a vacancy occurred.

His escapades while on picket duty on the sandy beach dunes were often humorous. He and the friends in his tent were soon operating a short-lived, unofficial post exchange which he named the "Bazaar." They thoroughly enjoyed eating and drinking together on their first Christmas Day. They began to learn how to fire the fort's big guns, and fishing and oystering in the Mississippi Sound occupied their free time. It was a pleasurable way to spend the early days of the war.

In February 1862, the Confederacy suffered a disastrous defeat when Forts Henry and Donelson, in northwestern Tennessee, surrendered. In order to meet this threat, in late February the Twenty-first was ordered back to Hall's Mill, where it was brigaded with other regiments pursuant to being sent to western Tennessee. By March 7, the regiment was at Fort Pillow, north of Memphis, on the Mississippi River. After a fortnight, it was sent to Corinth in northwestern Mississippi, where the western commanders were concentrating all available Confederate forces. There, in quick succession, Williams was elected junior second lieutenant and second lieutenant of Company A. In the absence of his two senior officers, he led the company in the Battle of Shiloh, April 6–7, in which the regiment and company suffered severe losses and in which he was commended for gallantry. A few days after the battle, while near Corinth, he was appointed regimental adjutant. The depleted regiment was soon placed on picket duty at nearby Monterey.

When the Twenty-first was reorganized in early May 1862, James was elected captain of Company A. He led the company in the fight at Farmington on May 10, with minor casualties. He soon became seriously ill and was forced to take a furlough home to Mobile. In consequence, he was not with the army when it withdrew from Corinth south to Tupelo. Although still weak, he returned to his command in early June, and again was ordered to picket duty near Saltillo. On July 26 the Twenty-first was ordered to join the Mobile "garrison" in the District of the Gulf, where it would remain, much to Williams's consternation, for the balance of the war. The company was initially assigned to artillery at Fort Morgan, where he commanded a battery.

Promoted to major in early October 1862, Williams and the regimental colonel, with four companies (the first battalion), were ordered to Oven Bluff and Choctaw Bluff, which were batteries in Clarke County, one hundred miles up the Tombigbee and Alabama rivers, respectively. His wife joined him near Oven Bluff for over six months. She became pregnant again and their first child, George Dixon, was born in Mobile in May 1863.

The next month, Williams was promoted to lieutenant colonel, and after a visit to his beloved family, was ordered back to Fort Morgan again, this time to command the second battalion of the Twenty-first. The regiment was temporarily reunited, although for over a year various companies were detached to posts and camps within the district's defenses. In November 1863, Williams moved his wife and little George down to be near him at Navy Cove, where they stayed for almost four months.

In early January 1864, when Admiral David Farragut decided to try to enter the lower bay via the Mississippi Sound, Williams was detached to command Fort Powell (at Grant's Pass), whose garrison included two companies of the Twenty-first. The Union flotilla bombarded Fort Powell from February 16 until March 1, 1864. After his successful defense, he received a furlough and moved his wife back to Mobile. He returned to Fort Powell and was in command on August 5, when Farragut's fleet ran past Fort Morgan's guns. That night, realizing that he could not defend the fort from the rear, he evacuated the garrison and blew up the magazine. Fort Gaines's garrison, including seven companies of the Twenty-first, surrendered on August 8.

Relieved of command pending an investigation, Williams sent his wife and son up the Alabama River to Prattville, near Montgomery. He was acquitted by a military tribunal in early September, but his superiors refused to return him to command. Finally, in early December, he was ordered to command the remnant of the Twenty-first in the defenses around Mobile. The regiment was at Blakeley and Spanish Fort on the eastern shore during the final days of the war in March and April 1865. In his last letter, dated March 22, from Spanish Fort, he wrote: "If the Yankees don't come this time I will be vexed—for I want to see them in front of my boys once more—"

With the evacuation of Mobile on April 12, the regiment retreated up the Mobile and Ohio Railroad with General Taylor's command. Resistance in Virginia and North Carolina having collapsed, the 210 soldiers in the regiment finally surrendered on May 4 at Cuba Station, Alabama, in Sumter County. The men of the Twenty-first Alabama were paroled at Meridian, Mississippi, on May 10.

Williams returned to Mobile by May 17, where he began to assist John A. King "with some work." After a visit to see his wife in Prattville, he returned to Mobile in July in an attempt to find a "situation." Despite hard times, he refused to accept two offers to return north.[7] Instead, he chose to remain in Mobile for the rest of his life. There, although he was unable to achieve great economic success, he maintained an active life in civic, veterans', and military affairs. In January 1866, he, with John A. King and George H. Bassett, formed a partnership in a steam laundry business. When it failed in early 1867, Williams became chief bookkeeper for M. Threefoot and Company. By 1869, he was bookkeeper for Kennedy and Lyons, another retail dry goods store. A venture with the Alabama Gold Life Insurance Company failed in the panic year, 1873. From 1876 until 1885, he was a clerk for the Mobile and Ohio Railroad Company. For the remainder of his working career he was associated with the Mobile County probate court, variously as recording, deputy, or assistant clerk.[8]

He was also prominent in the formation of the state militia when it was reorganized after November 2, 1872, and was the first major of the First Infantry Battalion of Volunteer Militia in Mobile. Twenty years later, in 1891, he was still Major and Inspector of Rifle Practice for the First Regiment Alabama State Troops.[9]

A founder of the Raphael Semmes Camp Number 11 of the United Confederate Veterans, the first such group established in Alabama, Williams remained an active member for over three decades. From 1895 to 1898 he was a brigadier general and commander of the First Brigade in south Alabama. When the Blue and Gray Veterans' Union was organized on July 4, 1890, at the battle site of old Fort Blakeley, he was named the Southern copresident. He was also a president of the Mobile camp of that organization.[10]

Williams also played an active role in a most unusual civic organization, the "Can't-Get-Away Club." Organized in 1839 and incorporated by the state legislature in 1854, it provided care and assistance for those afflicted with the deadly yellow fever, which frequented Mobile until 1897. These citizens refused to "get away" to safe locations. From 1884 through 1897, Williams was on the executive committee and served as first vice-president, second vice-president, and president of the organization.[11]

All the while, Williams's family grew larger. After the birth of George, Lizzy bore two daughters, Eleanor Frances and Eugenia; a son, Rennison Lee; and another daughter, Adelia. Their last child, a son, born in 1878, was named Powell.[12]

Williams resigned his position with the probate court in 1900 because of ill health. He died January 21, 1903, at the age of sixty-five, and was buried in an unmarked grave in Magnolia Cemetery only a few hundred feet from where he had served a generation earlier at Battery K in the Mobile defenses.

On January 22, 1903, the editor of the Mobile *Daily Register* wrote, in a brief column headed "Colonel Jas. M. Williams":

> James M. Williams who died yesterday was a courageous and ready soldier, a patriotic and earnest citizen and an honest man, a gentleman, in the fullest sense of the word. It would be well for the republic if every man were to mold his life to conform to the high ideals that inspired our friend who has gone to the other world.

From That Terrible Field

Civil War Letters of
James M. Williams,
Twenty-first Infantry Volunteers

"I call this poor camp home, and I hail it with joy again! I marched away from it to the battlefield of Shiloh, and it seemed like home when I came back from that terrible field, weary, wet, and heart-sick . . . "

I
Hall's Mill, Fort Gaines, and Camp Memminger: October 19, 1861 – February 28, 1862

CAMP NEAR HALLS MILL, OCT. 19, 1861[1]

Dear Lizzy:

Sitting down to write you a love letter carries me back to old times, and it seems as if you were away off in Augusta and I lonely and impatient in Mobile; I cant call on you to come and join me as I used to but instead, I can promise to come to see you often

We are comfortably fixed already— my tent is floored and having but three men in it is very comfortable— I will receive a desk to-day when I can write more comfortably than I do now on a camp stool— there is nothing worthy of note in camp yet— all well but one man, who trifled with a nest of yellow jackets and was so badly stung that he is unfit for duty and I have just given him a furlough to go home till he is better— Sergeant Chester was chased by the same enemy but more fortunately escaped   Send me all the news by sergeant Chester when he returns— I dont know of anything that I need except a watch— I am almost sure that my watch has not been fixed yet, and you will please go to the store and get them to send me a common silver watch for camp use— if my own is in order I would rather have it   Mr. Chester will bring it down.[2]

One of these days I intend to bring you and Mrs. Turner down to the Camp it would amuse you to look through it but as it is possible that we will not be permanently located for a few weeks you will have to be patient—[3]

I will certainly come to see you the last of the month—

Williams

CAMP NEAR HALL'S MILL — [SATURDAY] OCT. 26 [1861]

Dear Lizzie—

There will be a letter for you sunday— it is rather a rough looking dirty letter to be sure but I hope you will receive it well— I am the letter in question— I will

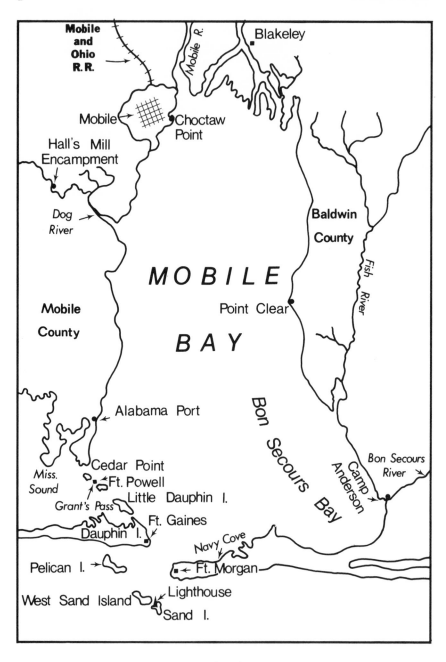

MOBILE BAY AREA

leave the camp in time to get home late Sunday evening and will stay in town three days— I am well and think that the rough work and rough fare will agree with me as it used to do

Williams

CAMP GOV. [MOORE]⁴ [NOVEMBER ? 1861]

Dear Lizzie—

. . . Mr. Turner also [wishes] to be remembered all around to the folks—⁵ the red caps are the gayest and, I flatter myself, the most admired of anything of the kind in Camp   Mr. Turner and myself wore them constantly and some of the boys already are changing the name of our mess to "Red Top" mess— but we won't have it so— we are the original and only "Pine Top Mess" and will bear no other name

The camp has been regularly organized and we have parade every evening—
. . .

Williams

You naught[y] girl worked at the shirt till midnight—when you might as well have taken your time— it don't matter if I should not get it for a week yet

CAMP GOV. MOORE NOV 12TH 1861

Dear Lizzie:

You must begin to think that I have forgotten you entirely— but if you knew how I am driven from pillar to post and back again all day long— from reveille at a quarter before six in the morning to tattoo at nine at night— You would not be cross with me. I have had beside all my duties as first sergeant the additional troubles of instructor and with the exception of one or two days have drilled the company for four hours daily— I tell Mr Turner that if your folks would like to come to see us he must urge you to do so now while you have bright moonlight nights— or you might come in a little party some day stay over night— in my tent which we will give up to you,   it is very comfortable, and furnished with two standee's such as are used on steamboats— holding four all together

Drum beats for guard mounting— Turner will leave before I can come back to my desk again— love to all—

Williams

CAMP GOV. MOORE. Nov. 13, 1861.

My dear Lizzie:

The letter which I sent you by sergeant Turner was cut short by the call for guard-mounting and I did not have time to finish it before he left. still I can't say that you missed anything very interesting for beyond the daily routine of camp life there is nothing to interest us in the acting, or you in the story.— this afternoon we have had some little excitement   a report has come to camp that we are to be sent to Fort Gaines day after to-morrow,   whether it is so or not I don't know, but I am inclined to believe it— I do not like to leave our present camp in which we have at last made ourselves comfortable, and our really beautiful parade ground which we won from the piney woods with many a strong stroke of axe and pick. but if the defence of Mobile requires that we should go there I am more than willing

Nov. 16th There's the letter as it was cut off by the disorder in the camp which I told you about when you came the next day = the thing then a rumor is now an accomplished fact: we have marched away to Dog river—[6] made our camp on its banks for one night. loaded the Steamer Clipper with ourselves and baggage— steamed down to Fort Gaines pitched our tents by moonlight on the parade ground—and this morning we realized that we were away from our piney woods shelter, as the North wind swept over us flapping our tents like sails and filling them with sand and dust— we slept well last night for I was determined to have our bunks put up at once— and rather than wait till morning for the wagons we carried them and our bed-clothing all the way from the landing on our shoulders: we will have to move in a day or two a few hundred yards— the regiment which is here is exchanging places with us, and will leave for our camp Moore to-day. I think I will have no difficulty in obtaining a furlough at the end of this month— for by that time the history of Lincoln's armada will be finished— if it comes here I hope we will be able to repulse it— if it does not we will have no alarms before two or three months at least for the enemy could not organize another expedition in less time.[7] we will be camped west of the fort and outside of its walls   we will always have a picket guard down the island several miles and if you should at any time fail to hear from me when you expect to— you must imagine that I am absent from Camp on that duty.

There is only one thing that I dislike in our position here that is the water is bad— we will make it up into coffee and drink plenty of that— and a little good whiskey added will keep us right = The post of danger is the post of honor, and I am glad that the defence of Mobile is not left to North Alabamians but to Mobile's own soldiers.[8]

Oh how I would liked to have gone home with you. It seemed to me that I could not leave you till the last minute and though I knew that I had no permission to go home with you and might be reprimanded if I did so, I nearly did it any-how. When I reported myself to Capt Jewett[9] that evening I told him how you had tempted me to go home with you— he said that I should have gone and it would have been all right— and took occasion to compliment you— by asking where you came from— and if you was a sample of the Augusta ladies he said they were beautiful women—

You are no "sample," darling, you are the only one for me in the whole world. You are all that is good and lovely— and when this war is over I will go back to you again, never no *never* more to leave you unless to the call of my country in her hour of danger— I love my wife and I love my country— and though the latter calls me to leave you darling it can never make me forget you— we are now perhaps permanently stationed and I want you to send me the ambrotype you gave me long ago when you first began to acknowledge your love; there might be better pictures but none could please me so well as that and I must have it at once— do not forget to send it by the very first opportunity

I think that I am certain of promotion to a Lieutenancy before very long. there are no vacancies yet, but will be as a matter of course before very long— do not say anything about that though till it happens. You know that if I am promoted it is a great honor, for I have no money or influential friends to find me a position, but win it by making myself worthy of the position— We have not heard from Lieut Whiting—[10] I understand he is quite sick. I hope he will be able to join us soon—

Give my love to all. Mrs Wyatt— Mrs Wainwright in particular.[11] Fort Gaines is a better place than I thought and is capable of making a strong defence. our regiment will doubtless operate on the island to prevent a landing of the enemy beyond the fort =

I am called off again—

Williams—

FORT GAINES—SUNDAY NOV 17, 1861

My dear Lizzie:

A good sea bath has made me feel like a new man— the water is cold and to warm ourselves after coming up from the water we ran up and down the smooth beach— it would have been a funny sight to have seen us— three lean men and one fat one capering in the sunshine dripping and naked: but no one was there to enjoy the spectacle unless spy glasses bore on us from the walls of Fort Morgan or the decks of one of Lincoln's vessels which lies in sight to the left of the light house but far beyond[12] Yesterday there were three of the enemy's fleet in sight— to-day but the one = I hope they will never come nearer, but if they do come we are prepared here to give them a memorable welcome— if we dont the ladies of Mobile should never smile on us again or acknowledge us for husbands brothers sons or lovers anymore— I hardly think they will make any attack upon the two strongholds that defend the approach to Mobile. Changing the subject abruptly I want you to send me either two pairs of woolen socks or send some yarn and a needle to darn those I have. they no longer keep my toes in confinement as the[y] used to do, but let them out incontinently— You may send them by Mr Chester when he goes to town— or in a few days I suppose there will be some kind of an express to this regiment from town— . . .

Enough of camps and wars   it will all be over one of these days and then I'm
going back to the "dearest girl in the world" with a light heart and a will to make
her happy. we will have that little cottage which we have so often talked of and
our dreams will be at last realized—

There is something solemn in the roar of the waves as they beat upon the
beach of our island, and to-night as I write they are the only thing to break the
silence that reigns over the fort and camp: I think of those majestic lines of
Byron which you know I love—
"Roll on thou deep and dark blue ocean— roll!
Ten thousand fleets sweep over thee in vain"[13]
and I think of the fleet which now hovers somewhere over our southern waters =
if it is destined for the attack of Mobile? there is no answer— but still the splash
of wave succeeding wave warns us that time is moving on moment by moment to
solve the great question.
      Mr Bassett sends his regards to you—[14] and charge you Lizzie not to forget to
send me the picture I say. once more good night
                                        Williams
I commenced my letter this morning and have had no chance to finish it before
to-night at 10 o'clock

                                        FORT GAINES. NOV 22D, 1862 [FRIDAY]
"Dearest Girl in the world".
      Tommy Traddles himself never looked forward to the time of visiting the
dearest girl with more pleasure than I do, but here the resemblance ceases— he
was all patience, I am all impatience =[15] you might— no you *must* come down
on the [steamer] Bagaley which makes an excursion next Sunday   you would
like to see us in our new-camp I know, and the boat will be here long enough to
satisfy us with a kiss— and a few hours talk— you need not be affraid to come on
account of the class of excursionists that you will meet on the boat for since our
regiment has been here the best people of the city come down and I have no
doubt you will be satisfied— I expect to go home on a 48 hours visit the last of
the month— but I might be disappointed, so come down Sunday— You might
come down any time the boat comes, through the week but it generally stops but
a few minutes, so that you would be hurried off unless you bring a little party to
stay a couple of days— I will give up my tent to you if you will do that. it will
accomodate [you and your friends?] and if you are not affraid of the Yankee fleet
[you will?] enjoy yourselves for that time very well. . . .
      —last evening four vessels were in sight— to-day the atmosphere has been
hazy and we can see but one— day before yesterday a large vessel sailed within
three and a half miles of us; a gun was manned and she was watched but she
pulled off again before a shot was fired at her =

Sometimes I wish that they would come within range of our guns and give us battle. but that is only when I am tired and hungry and cross; but after a hearty dinner such as I have just had I would rather they would lie at anchor at a good safe distance of eight miles, as I believe they will.

If you come down Sunday you might go back on Tuesday afternoon

One of the Regulars here is to be shot next Friday.[16]

—*Williams*—

Love to all—

Don't let anybody read my letters Lizzie. I write them always in a hurry with constant interruptions and they won't bear inspections by any other than your partial eyes—

Good bye darling— come [soon?]

Washington Light Infantry
through the Post Office

FORT GAINES— Nov 30— [1861]

Dear Lizzy—

Im back again to Camp— glad I got home to see you but somehow I feel as tho' I hadn't been to see you at all, and would greedily snatch another furlough to go back by the same boat again if I could. I'm bound to come as soon as I possibly can—

I told Mr Conning to send you $30 or $35 and if that is not enough send to him for more— settle with Mrs Turner—

Good bye

Williams

FORT GAINES— DEC 3ᴰ, 1861

Dear Lizzie =

I see the smoke of the boat away over the bay, and I must write you a line as well as I can with my cold hands, to send by it; I have no news for you as usual— last night about eight o'clock we were startled by the boom of a canon over at Grant's pass and every body came out of tents listening and wondering what's-the-matter over there, is the enemy attempting a surprise? or have their gunboats slipped in to make an attack? a hundred excited questions were asked by every body to every body else— and then came the sound of a steamboat whistle blowing long and loud, we haven't heard what was the matter, but we suppose that one of our own boats was coming in and not making the proper signals to the fort was fired upon and then whistled to let them know who it was.

I said I had no news, and that is the best I have in place of it, it turning out to be nothing at all.— Five vessels were in sight this morning— but we have often seen as many as that— I sent you a letter by the boat I came down upon just to let you know that I was living and thinking of you still— and that's the object of this letter too.— Oh! Greenland and Shades of Sir John Franklin![17] but the North wind did come down upon us last night with a will! The tent strained and tugged at its pins like mad, and if I had not made them three feet long, and driven them in myself, might and main, I would have been unable to have slept for fear of being uncovered by the wind, and my imagination would have tortured me with visions of the tent blown out of its roots— shirts, drawers, jackets, caps, books, papers, tin cups, towels, stockings and blankets scudding before the wind and myself in scanty clothing in pursuit alone— for Bassett lay sick (he's well this morning however) and King and our darkey have gone to town—[18] but as I said I knew the tent was securely pinned to the ground— so I rolled in my blankets comfortably and after listening to the roar of the waves, and the "clipp", "clip", all around which told that somebody was out driving down tent pins in the cold— turned over to sleep again and tried to dream of you; but couldnt dream about anything—

Wouldn't you think I was satisfied to stay here now for a while after having a two days furlough— I'm not— I'm just as lonesome and just as anxious to see you again as I was last Thursday Morning when I went for Colonel Crawford to sign my furlough— well— well— well the war will be all over after awhile and then I'll go home with a light heart— till then, though it is hard to be seperated from you I can not rest easy by your side.— my country calls me— and my own self respect forces me to make the sacrifice— It is an unpleasant thought to me though that while we soldiers sacrifice everything for our country and our honor the mean spirited poltroons stay at home,— save their money— add more to it— live at their ease, and bask in the smiles of lovely women— and save their cowardly souls for the "better days a'coming" (they'll take care to live till then), and long years from now the hoary headed cowards will sit down among their grandchildren, and make heroes of themselves while they tell the stories of the revolution of 61.— who then will speak the names of the heroes that lie buried at Manassas— Columbus—[19] and all the other glorious fields consecrated, and yet to be consecrated by the blood of martyrs to Southern liberty? None! But their glory is none the less! as men they will soon be forgotten, but their deeds have gilded our whole nation already! . . .

I am perfectly well as usual, heart warm— fingers like icicles—

Williams

FORT GAINES. DEC 5, 1861

Dearest Lizzie =

Again the smoke of the steamboat in the bay invites me in your name to write a word, and again, thank fortune, it finds me with no bad news to report of our little band, who have in charge one of the chief defences of Mobile. Yesterday we distinctly heard some half hundred cannon shots which appeared to come from the [Mississippi] sound— it was doubtless an engagement between our gunboats and some of the enemy's fleet; you have heard all the particulars I suppose before this as we saw the gunboat "Florida" (or maybe t'was the "oregon") going up to town yesterday— I hope they came out well in the encounter what ever it was =[20] I thought I would grow unpopular after a while among our boys— but I believe it is the reverse, since we came from Hall's mills I have had very little chance to drill the men, our lieutenants having taken almost exclusive charge of that department— the boy's don't like it altogether and they grumble a great-deal particularly against poor Lieut. Whiting— But to-day I got charge of them for an hour, and put them through an exercise in skirmishing— firing and loading lying flat on the ground and kneeling— and when it was all over they went to their tents cheering and waving their hats— If I had exclusive charge of the drills for two months I would make them by far the best drilled company on the island— not excepting the regulars— who by the way are not perfectly taught by any means—

I know that you are not interested in this drill talk— don't show anybody this letter in which I display so much egotism in self praise—

I received the red cap and the letter which came with it— send on some more of the same sort— letters I mean— not red caps—

I forgot to take that silver watch back to Mr Connings— the first time you go down there leave it with them— Thank Mr Conning for me for the enclosure which you received—

Give my love to Taylor[21] and all the folks at your house— particularly Mrs Turner

Im affraid you can't read my hasty letters but it is little loss beside your time
Williams

FORT GAINES. DEC 7, 1861.
Dearest Lizzie:
Boat-day has come again and I must send you a letter by sergt. Cothran[22] who goes to town on furlough, a good officer and a good fellow he is by the way as ever wore three worsted bars on the arm— he will be first sergeant of the company on the fourteenth day of this month. for I have resigned the office; the resignation to take effect on the 13*th* at which date I will be a private in the ranks again— You will not be surprised at this move on my part, for you know how I have always grumbled to you about the way the Infantry has been managed and vowed to have as little to do with it as possible— I am convinced now that there is little or no chance for a vacancy among the commissioned officers and I'm not going to worry along with the first sergeancy any longer— I have been doing all the work and keeping up the company's drill as well as I could with the weight of incompetent officers like the [old?] man of the sea on my shoulders.— and it is to [be] shifted now for I *won't* put in the whole year as I have done the first two months of service— in the ranks I will shew the boys how to be good soldiers   I will have nothing to do with the management and will not be worried when everything goes wrong as I am now— To shew you how I have worked I will tell you what is the truth, that notwithstanding the fact that our commissioned officers are among the most ignorant in the regiment in military matters, I have managed to get the company into almost as perfect a drill as the very best in the regiment.

When I'm in the ranks again I'll have nobody to look after but myself. I'll not have half as much work to do as I have now and I will be contented and happy as a lord—

Good bye darling— excuse this cross letter this time— I won't write any more such

Jas. M. Williams 1st Sergt

FORT GAINES DEC 10, 1861 [TUESDAY]

Dear Lizzie:

The boys don't seem to be well pleased with my resignation, but can't help themselves, and are talking about a successor. Capt. Jewett has not come back yet but I think it is likely he will be on the boat to-day when it comes: I would not be surprised to find him angry with me for what I've done, but don't care very much— the weather is hot and we have just come off from a very hard drill of two hours and a quarter which has spoiled the mood for writing which possessed me this morning.

Yesterday one of the enemy's steamers came up on the west of pelican island and fired eight or ten shells in the direction of our pickets   they fell short I understand some five hundred yards, it is likely they were not expecting to succeed in shelling them out of their position, but only taking the range of their guns— Fort Morgan fired two or three shots as a challenge for them to come on if they felt like it, and the other blockader fired her guns also, so that for an hour we had quite a lively little cannonading at safe distances— which put me in mind of old country roosters all crowing without pitching in to fight it out[23] . . .

Dinner's ready— good bye—

Williams

DECEMBER 12TH. FORT GAINES— [1861]

Dear Lizzie:

Boat's coming again, maybe you're on it and will see me to-day, but if you don't I must write a line anyhow. we've had another cold storm from the north, dust and smoke have filled my tent for twenty four hours, and my eyes are sore as a consequence and face and clothes as dirty as they well can be, we were to have been inspected this morning by one of the high officials, but on account of the rough sea, I suppose, he did not come and instead of the inspection our colonel put us through a very severe drill; it was hard on account of the wind which blew so fiercely, drifting the sand in our faces while it penetrated with cold our thin blue uniforms, the knapsacks on our backs cap— sheaved our misery— My darling, I was very glad to get your little letter and the papers that came with it by the last boat. You must try and send me letters as often as you can for you do not know how it cheers me up to receive them, I am very— very— very homesick— or lovesick, I want to be with you, and when I can go home again I will be the happiest man in the world when I kiss my dear wife, . . .

I do *not* think Mrs Turner charged you too much considering the wild prices of provisions of every kind— it is no doubt as low as she can afford to board you
Williams

FORT GAINES. ALA. DEC 14TH [1861]

Dear Lizzie:

I'm in an unusual hurry this morning, just have gone through an inspection which did no credit to our officers, but the men and their arms: the men were in good order— arms all perfect— but the officer's displayed their ignorance as much as their worst enemy could desire: If captain Jewett comes home before night, (for he is expected by this day's boat) this will be my last day as orderly sergeant: . . .

I send a kiss for my darling and another good bye— Three of the enemy's vessels in sight—

James M. Williams

FORT GAINES ALA. DEC 15TH 1861. [SUNDAY]

My dear Lizzie—

The die is finaly cast. Captain Jewett, came back to camp again last night, had a long talk with me tried to persuade and drive me out of the resolution which I had taken and after all I told him that I would give him a final answer this morning— so this morning I sent my resignation back again to him— he will be very angry I suppose but it dont matter.— There I was interrupted and I take up my pen again two days after I wrote the above— the Captain was not so angry as I thought he would have been— and the unpleasant part of the operation is all over   I am a private in the ranks once more, and will no doubt hold that position for a long time as there is little or no prospect for promotion in this company—

I was going to ask you to come down next Thursday [December 19] but I learn that the boat will make its principal stop over at [Fort] Morgan on that day— so you had better wait a week longer when it will give this post the longest visit— you see they have arranged it so as to have a day at each fort alternately— last Thursday [December 12] they lay a long time at our wharf— next they will stop but a few minutes here and lay over at— Morgan— and so on

I could probably obtain a situation in one of the military offices in town, but I don't want to be seperated from the active field service which you know I love; I would not feel like a soldier If I was in town writing all the time, or superintending the loading of boats and carts— I must be where I can hear the click of arms, and the roll of the drums or I would not think that I was any better soldier than the cowardly stay-at-homes that I so heartily despise— There *is* a position that I will be glad to take if I can get it; and that is drill-master in the Confederate Service, but I don't know whether I can obtain it or not. I am not as you know much of a wire worker, and have no rich or influential relations to push me forward; and if I should be so fortunate will have nothing to thank for it but my own fitness for the post— If I conclude to apply for the office I have no doubt but I can obtain the very highest reccomendations from the colonel and lieutenant colonel—[24]

I hope for a letter from your sweet hand by this boat; you must think of me by every boat if possible and write, for you know that I would rather have a letter than anything you can send me, and next to that is word by somebody that you are well and cheerfull— "*Fall* in Infantry" I hear and I'm a private and must obey

Williams

FORT GAINES DEC. 20ᵀᴴ 1861. [FRIDAY]

Dear Lizzy;

I don't know what has become of the letter you sent last Tuesday, it has never appeared yet; I certainly expected to find it here to meet me on my return from my short visit to you: Hard as it has been to obtain furloughs heretofore it will be still more difficult, as new and more stringent orders have just been read to us on parade,— I do not expect to see Mobile again before St Valentine's day unless I am so fortunate as to receive a promotion, or so unfortunate as to get sick or a gun-shot wound— Yes! there *is* one more chance for me! but I am not sanguine enough to build up lively hopes on it— that is that the war may end, and all be speedily disbanded— Once more fancy pictures to my mind that return to civil life, and wife, and home! how my heart thrills responsive to every tap of the drum as our regiment files through Dauphin Street, and up Royal! and then we will be dismissed for the *last time* —

Right—FACE! = Arms!— PORT Break Ranks! MARCH!!!— May that day come soon! The clouds on the horizon are not so dark as they were, and maybe the glorious dawn of Peace and Southern Independence will break upon us suddenly! I go on the picket in the morning and the letter which you will doubtless send me by the boat will not reach me untill I return sunday Morning so that while I receive yours, you will be with this in your hand; I hope it will find you entirely well and over that little spell of the blues which had possession of you day before yesterday; you must fight the little indigo colored imps *right cheerfully*, and drive them out of their stronghold in the dear breast where I should reign supreme, and where with the exception of their occasional usurpations I believe I do reign always =

My tent is (and here is the inconvenience of being a popular man!) continually infested with visitors— when I feel like receiving them I call it company— but when I am busy with work— or I am writing a letter to the "dearest girl in the world" I think that they are nothing but *loafers.* = So far to-night, I have remarkably escaped their persecutions   I buttoned up my tent and wrote away without listening to anybody; while I have been writing I verily believe, that twenty men have peeped in but seeing me apparently deeply absorbed in writing each has gone off about his business; I mention this more as a curious circumstance worthy of record than anything else, for I don't know that it has-ever occurred before that I have written even a short letter in peace and quite = It seems to me that whereever I go I can never get rid of the "P-salm-" singers— they are in full blast with a Prayer meeting a few rods off; it is some poor consolation to me that if all are rewarded according to their deeds, I will be able to say that I like a good boy was writing to my darling while they were making night hideous with their horrid nasal twang butchering bad music, and insulting the Most High with hypocritical and "impious prayers!— Confound the whole set of P-salm singing "brethren" and "sistern" too, If it had not been for them I would never have been soldiering here on Dauphin Island, they were for years preaching abolitionism from every Northern pulpit, and these same canting rascals that follow us here to camp with their confounded cliques— and howling meetings would have been preaching the same doctrine if they lived on the other side of Mason and Dixons line.— I often wonder how our P-salm singers will stand fire— not Hell fire for they seem to handle that very familliarly— but Lincoln's fire; maybe that when the fiery day of trial comes they will be as good soldiers as the rest of us, but if I had to go off with a few men on a dangerous expedition to-night I'd rather take an old granny than any of them— Give me a jolly good "sinner" to stand by me when the hour of danger comes! . . .

Only two of the enemy's vessels are in sight to-day— one sailing vessel lies beyond Sand island, and the other a large steamer is beyond Pelican Island

Good Bye—
Williams

Fort Gaines, Dec 24th [Tuesday, 1861]

A Merry Christmas! I wish my darling! oh! that I had a furlough to share it with you to-morrow we would both get "tight" on eggnog wouldn't we? You think you wouldn't do you? but I say if I were home I'd make you take enough to exhillerate you for once in your life well! well! if I am *not* home with you I won't make a funeral of my Christmas, but will be as merry as can be, we have a merry party in the "Bazaar" mess and if we only receive a jug of good old rye whiskey by this boat, which we expect confidently, we will make the "welkin ring" to-morrow;— I like private life very well; have just been through my first tour of picket duty and had a jolly good time of it: for want of something better to write about, I will tell you its story— Saturday morning at 7½ o'clock we started for the last post of the picket— King one other man from the Infantry and myself— each carried his arms and equipments complete— a blanket with two ends tied to-gether thrown like a scarf over the right shoulder; a haversack filled with eatables, and a canteen full of water, an oil cloth covering, and water proof leggins tied to the blanket made a heavy load, under which we marched to the post of the advanced picket, which is between four and five miles down the island; arriving there we unloaded ourselves; and leaving everything behind started for a walk down the island, on a voyage of discovery. the island is very long and narrow and we followed it four or five miles below the post, finding nothing but the wreck of an old bell-buoy on which we wrote our names and the date of our visit, and turned our faces homeward— picking up shells on the way we got back to the picket station about half past two o'clock in the afternoon; as ravenously hungry as three bears; and made soon quite a cavity in each haversack; as soon as I was done eating I took my turn as look out on the top of a little sand hill and for the ballance of the afternoon watched the ships of the enemy with a spy glass, one of them lay at anchor directly off our post about three miles and I could distinctly see the man on the foremast and others on deck; night came and we made our coffee and then the watch commenced in earnest— we were posted down at the water's edge. to keep a look out for boats [from the blockading vessels], so that we would not have a Billy Wilson trick played on our regiment;[25] nothing came to alarm us and at the end of our first watch we thought to have a nap; there is a little shed in which the horse is kept and all the pickets from other companies were in there sleeping; but we were affraid of fleas and vermin, and preferred to sleep up on the roof, and so we did, soundly— at 1 o'clock it suddenly began to rain smartly, and we rattled off the roof in such a hurry and made such a racket in doing it that we frightened some of those inside till they got up and ran out in the rain to see what was the matter— it was time then for us to take the last watch and away we went down by the sea shore again; in the morning we sent our clothes home by a darkey who happened to come along and went to the "shell-banks" on the northern side of the island for oysters; we had as many oysters as we wanted and then were so lucky as to catch a sail boat which brought us around to the camp before a nice little wind; firing our muskets at a pair of ducks on the way— and landing under a heavy shower of rain our first tour was over— I send you the shells which will always remind me of my first day as picket— . . .

A Merry Chirstmas once more.

Williams

FORT GAINES, ALA. DEC 24, 1861.

Dear Lizzy:

Just after finishing my letter this morning we were startled by the cry that the *"Florida is going out to attack the blockaders!"*— I run up the sand hills and there was the glorious little steamer going out alone to meet the new vessels of the enemy! she stopped by the light-house and fired two shots as a challenge for them to come on! the black steamer which lay opposite came up swiftly and soon the cloud of smoke from her deck proclaimed that the ball was opened; fast replied the spunky little Florida knocking up the water all around her, and advancing steadily all the time; the Lincolnite backed slowly out; Oh! it was a glorious sight, and the music of the guns was a grand accompaniment. Boom! Boom! goes the Lincolnite! Bang! Bang! the Florida replied with her sharp rifled guns, the difference in the sound was so great that without looking at the vessels you could tell which had fired— The Florida has drawn off, and now lies over at [Fort] Morgan, I don't think she is hurt, as we could not see any of the enemys shells strike her, several burst above her high in the air; I hope and believe that Lincoln's steamer has not been so fortunate— The most magnificant scene I ever witnessed—![26]

> *In great haste*
> *Williams*

FORT GAINES, CHRISTMAS EVENING [1861]

Darling Lizzy:

Mr John-Sampson— with—the—gray—pants—and—blue-stripe—, belonging—probably—to—the—regulars, has never appeared before me to deliver the long looked for letter, which has been mentioned before by both of us; and I suppose it may be classed among the missing who never *do* turn up— I hope that Mr John Sampson derived as much pleasure from it as I lost; The little green box of eggs and cakes, and mince pie, and the sweet little letter, was more fortunate in its Voyage and was landed safely in tent No 1, just before last evening's parade; the mince pie was too tempting to keep over night, so we made away with it very soon; it represented Miss "Phe's" Kiss, you say, and our mess have unanimously voted that if Miss "Phoe's" Kisses are as sweet as the substitute, each member of the mess—including myself especially— would be glad to receive them every day.[27] Tell Miss "Phe" that though the pie was good I have not forgotten how she turned her back to the farewell of a poor soldier, bound for the war: and it is not altogether forgiven— I am sorry that Mr. Bassett was not here to taste the pie too— poor fellow he has been so unfortunate as to be off to town on a furlough— by which he has already lost the mince pie and a sight of the exciting engagement between the Florida and Lincoln's steamer— what more he will miss before he comes back no-body can guess— poor, poor fellow, I pity him! Apropos of the Lincoln steamer I might mention that like the evil spirit that was taken out of the house, and it swept and garnished; she returned early last evening with two more of the same sort. so that we have four of the sea-leaches sticking to us now—[28]

Christmas began this morning before daylight with me; two glasses of egg-nog came for each before we were out of bed, which took away our appetites for breakfast; then the reveille began to beat, when a large party of the infantry seized tin pans and every thing that would rattle or jingle about the quarters and we followed the band all through the regiment singing and tin-panning the tune of "Dixie"— it has been a long time since I have heard, or made so much racket.

The grand event of the day was a regimental mock parade which came off at ten-o'clock; all the companies turned out in full dress, with officers chosen from the privates in the ranks; one of the Infantry boys acted as colonel [Crawford], and imitated him very well, another of our men was dressed as a woman with a cocked hat, to represent the Major [29]— who is nicknamed "Nancy" you know— I, dressed in Lieutenant Cluis' uniform well stuffed out with Mrs Turner's pillows had command of our company—[30] King was lieutenant   every-thing went off in the best manner, the men all acted their parts seriously as though it were a real parade, and the colonel and the officers who took no part in the performance but that of spectators seemed to be very much amused— [Lt.] Colonel Ingersoll seemed to think that the burlesque of the Major was rather *too* severe and I think he sent word to him that he had better retire from the field; however he was there long enough for every-body to see, recognise, and laugh at the cariaca-ture;— The day has passed without anything serious happening to our regiment, a number are drunk, and there have been a few small fist fights, but nobody hurt— The regulars though have had at least one bloody row, and several are laid up with bloody heads, one of whom is reported to be dying to-night—

There has been a new order issued which prohibits all visitors from coming to this Island, besides reducing the number of furloughs,— so I am affraid that I can't see your sweet face as often as I have done, and must be content to write and receive letters; . . . see how faithfully *I* write now that I am a private in the ranks and have plenty of time once more!

I have made no application for an appointment as drill master, and am about out of the notion of doing so— I believe it is more to my interest to remain here with my old "infants"— I am such a pet of theirs that where ever there is a chance they will take care of me, and give me a good place unanimously.

I musn't close my letter without giving you a little description of our christmas dinner, Bob Wier[31] who presides over the "last chance mess" invited us to dine; and a grand dinner it was I tell you!—

Bill of Fare

Cold Turkey	Eggs	Sweet Potatoes	Another kind of cake
Roast Beef	Bread	Mince Pie	Sugar topped cake
Pigeon Pie	Rice	One kind of cake	Salt
Pepper	Vinegar	Pepper sauce	Turnips
Mustard	Jelly cake	Sugar	
	Sherry Wine	Port Wine	

Every one of the above dishes was there and more than I can eat or remember— then there were toasts all around—

my toast

"The last chance"— may the 'Bazaar mess' never fare worse than when they took the "last chance" for a Christmas dinner!

"Bob Wier's"
" *'The loved ones at home'*, missed to day more than ever—"

"King Cotton our support in peace and reliance in war" was given by some one in compliment to King, and John Cothran (who we always call Cotton) of our mess—

Then there were toasts to every one around the table and a little speech in acknowledgement from each,— we drank all our wine in toasts and got into the humor of toasting so that when it gave out we commenced on the pepper vinegar!

But I must stop— I have worried out your patience with the story of my Christmas— . . .

May this be the last Christmas that I spend away from your side!

Williams

Fort Gaines Dec 27th 1861.

Dear Lizzy:

I'm in a hurry this morning for certain, am on guard and have been excused for a few minutes from the Guard house, don't know but King and I will get *inside* of it before long, as a fool of sentinel has just reported us for running over his lines; we were determined to go outside whether or no, and the fool of a sentinel had to report us; . . .

Night before last we thought that the enemy were about to attempt a landing— the[y] had many boats prowling along the coast of the island, but if they had ventured ashore they would have stepped into a lively trap, sure as Fate!—

Good bye darling— Cothran says "Jim" get through with your writing in a *hurry* for I want to clean out this tent—"

Williams

Fort Gaines, Sunday Dec 29th 1861.

Dear Lizzy:

When the "Fool-Killer" comes to Dauphin Island he will find plenty of game, it really seems to me that all the imbecile old grannys in the country have been gathered together and put in command of this devoted 21st Regiment; officers of all ranks (with a very few exceptions) from those with your stars on their collars, down to the corporals in two bars of worsted, class the same— incompetent— conceited— childish— and indolent— It was on account of this state of things— particularly in our own company, that I resigned my petty office, as you know— and every day I am better pleased that I did so; I have just got off from a 24 hours tour of duty as sentry, which, as it was managed, was worse than a farce, in this, that a farce is a foolish play that amuses without "hurting" anybody— while *this*, tired down half a hundred men, and uselessly exposed them to the cold night air for hours— In the first place we were posted as sentries all around the camp, where we could not possibly do any good for ourselves or harm to the enemy.— at two o'clock last night there came two reports of cannon in the distance— *boom!*— *boom!* far away over the sea; I spoke to King to see if he had heard it, he had— a remark was made that we supposed some of the Lincoln fleet must have brought a vessell to by firing a couple of shots, and we thought no more of it— In a few minutes there came an order to *turn out the guard instantly and march them down the island;* the two superlative fools who were in command of us seemed to be very much excited, and ordered us to load our pieces and away we went some three miles down the beach as fast as we could paddle along— almost a "double-quick"— we poor privates tripped along briskly, for, not knowing what had caused the alarm, we imagined that the pickets must have sent word that the enemy's boats were landing, and we thought that our little party of thirty men would have the honor of the first shot at the invaders; well we arrived at the center picket post and found them all quiet, and they reported that all was quiet below at the advanced post, so we trudged back to camp, and all tired and heated as we were were posted around the camp again for two hours as soon as we returned— *Now* we found out what had caused the alarm— *What do you suppose it WAS? The two distant cannon shots which anybody but a d—d fool would have known were not near the island, but at least fifteen miles out at sea!* Well we came back as I told you after our wild goose chase, and presently along comes an officer— one of the highest officers on this Island he is too and to show you how childish and cowardly he is I will give you a specimen of his conversation with the officer of the guard— spitting all the time—

"Well Captain— (spits) so you had all your men down the island to night, what did you see?"

(The Captain explains that we heard two shots, and saw nothing) "Ah! I heard them when I was down (spits) at the (spits) Shell-Banks, and I came over to the pickets (spits) on the other side but they had'nt heard any firing (spits)— Ah— when I was coming by the Pelican— spit I heard somebody *whistling* out on it— I asked the pickets if they had been whistling but they said (spits) that they had not— If I had known whether it was any (spit) of our men or not I would (spit) have come up here and taken about a dozen men and gone to see who they (spit) were" Confound his cowardly soul! I say, if there was any-body "whistling" *out there, why did'nt he ride out like an OFFICER and a brave man AND SEE WHO IT WAS!*— But the fact of the matter is, there was nobody there at all— the sand hills on the beach are inhabited by rats, and every time we are on guard we hear them chiping all around, and if we were so easily alarmed as the high and mighty officer who made the rounds last night might report any night that we heard "whistling"

And would you believe that the old poltroon had almost a mind to take a dozen of us back again to the very same place from which we had just returned on our fool's errand!—

Lord save us from our friends— when the Lincolnites come, I will be more alarmed on account of the kind of Officers we have to manage the defence; than all other danger put to-gether—

But once more enough of this, you don't realize, or enter into the spirit of my military troubles and I can't say that I much desire that you should— . . .

Good bye— darling— I think of you allways— and love you more and more every day.

Williams

SEPTEMBER 7, 1862

This letter teaches me a lesson that I hope I will never forget— Maj Stewart afterwards was distinguished for cool and determined courage at the Battle of Shiloh

FORT GAINES. JANUARY 2D, 1861 [1862]

Dear Lizzy:

The devil was to pay last night among the blockaders, they were showing signal lights and rockets, fired a gun, and sailed about, from ten o'clock till daylight   our sentries were on the qui-vive and every few minutes we would hear the cry of the sentry whose post is up on the flagstaff "corporal of the guard— lookout!" which means, in military language, that the corporal must hasten to the lookout post to take the report of the sentry who is stationed there, and carry it to the "officer of the day"— Three times I got up and went to the top of the nearest sand hill to see what might be seen, but there was nothing more than the varicolored lights moving beyond "Sand Island"— and to bed I went again— during the night a boat arrived bringing the report of the occupation of Biloxi [Mississippi] by the Federalists, and the opening of the fight at Pensacola at 2 o'clock yesterday—[32] I have tried to get a furlough but can't do it, and don't know when I can get one, very likely it will not be this month, unless I should be so unfortunate as to get sick— which might not be so unfortunate after all for if I was not *too* sick I would by that means get a furlough for a week or ten days—

I am about to go into one of the regular companies for drill at the big guns on the fort. and will drill with them every day until I can handle them as familliarly as my musket. I have spoken for this priviledge to one of the captains and will begin to drill with his company in a day or two; and then when the fight comes here to fort Gaines I will not be a chaffing spectator from behind a sand hill or hid away with the infantry down in the piney woods, but can take a hand at the guns, and be in a position to see and assist in the battle,— The sergeant calls "Fall in for drill!" and I must go— maybe I will have time to finish my letter after it is over— well they called a little too soon, and we are dismissed again for a few minutes, or untill the drum beats— New-Year passed without any excitement or anything to distinguish it from any other day, we did not even have so much as a good dinner in the "Bazaar" mess,— It seems to me that if I were rich as our colonel and in command of his regiment I would have had a dinner for the whole regiment— but instead of that the old cove only gave us a very severe drill of two hours before dinner— confound his old baldheaded pate,— . . .

Let me give you a picture of all the officers that are left us now—
1st Captain Jewett— is selfish and conceited, and knows no more about drilling
a company than Frank Snow[33]
2d Lieut Cluis— is a good man— and is the best drillmaster we have, and he
knows no more than a corporal ought to know—
4th Nat Whiting is a booby whose skull is as thick as a buck-niggers— and is a
coward to boot—
5th 2d sergeant John F. Cothran is a very good soldier—
6th 3d sergeant Campbell[34] is as much of a booby as Nat Whiting— and more of
a coward   two corporals fill out the list of our officers— one is a tolerable good
soldier but a drunken dog— the other is a poor soldier— and half idiot I believe

Who would want to stay in such a company! I *don't*— don't mention it to any
one though— for I don't want the boys to know that I am going away untill I am
all *ready* to leave—

I have written to Mr Conning to give you some money as I can't get home
myself this month— Good Bye darling

Williams

Fort Gaines, January 4ᵀᴴ 1862

Dear Lizzie:

I am very tired and this will be a short letter,— was on guard last night and as
it was a damp watch I held, I don't feel very fresh or frisky this morning— it is no
joke to stand on the beach for two hours, and then have the good-for-nothing
sergeant at the guard tent to fall asleep and forget you for an extra hour, as was
my lot on the first relief last night— I went on at ten o'clock and if the scamp
had not fallen asleep, should have come off again at twelve; I marched the beach
through the salty fog and thought that it was the longest two hours that had ever
worried my patience away— and when relieved found it was one o'clock— at
four in the morning I assumed my post again and was so fortunate as to be
relieved at six— with the "rustiest" gun that has been seen since the famous
Van-Winkle picked up his!— Now if there is any kind of work that I dislike
more than another it is the cleaning of a dirty musket, and you will give me some
credit for attempting to write to you by this boat, when you know that I have
just laid the old fusee by, clean once more after scouring, burnishing— and
cursing for two hours and a half.— Well! the greasy job is done, and the musket
stands in the rack clean, inside and out, and ready at a minute's warning to do
justice to the deadly aim which my Western trained eye can give it.— I am
growing in good humor every time I look at it— There is hardly a night but our
sentries report seeing boats near shore, or men on the island, and I begin to feel
very sure that boats and men are visions called up by their own fears, for the
simple reason that I can't see any myself when I'm on guard— Last night I had a
chance to investigate one of these alarms,— about midnight the sentry whose
post was next to mine called me, and said that he had seen two men about two
hundred yards below him— and as he was the last sentinel but one, it could not

be any of our guard— he was evidently affraid to go to them, and though it is against the law for a sentinel to leave his post unless he is actually driven off by the enemy, I was determined to see if there really was two men down there, so I told him to walk back to my post and keep it so that if the officer of the guard came along he would not discover anything wrong, and I would go in search of the two men— away I went— after while I saw two dark objects before me, which on a near approach proved to be a pair of old pine stumps— I was not quite satisfied however and went a little further and saw two more black objects this time there was no mistake for they were walking— I came up to them and challenged and it turned out to be our other sentry and one of the pickets who had walked up from the picket station a mile and a half below us— and I believe that if all our little alarms were looked into at once they would all be explained as easily as this was,— While I was gone the officer of the day came along and the soldier that had exchanged posts with me was so frightened that he had to tell that we were both off of our proper posts— if he had kept his mouth shut the officer would never have known the difference— When he asked me about it I told him why I had gone off— he did not make any reply, So I suppose he thought it was all right, . . .

As to Bassett and King— they are bad boys and tell stories about me,— They make a pretence that I eat more than all the rest of the mess together— and threaten to have my rations cooked seperately— or to turn me out of the tent altogether— They have made me the cashier of the mess, and they nicknamed me "Judas"— because forsooth "Judas carried the bag"! Besides many other tricks too tedious to mention.

If either of them comes to see you I hope you will pull their hair *well*— that is if you can find any on their heads long enough to catch hold of— which I doubt.

This was to have been a short letter, but it ran away with me.

> *Good bye sweetheart—*
> *Williams*

FORT GAINES ALA, JANUARY 7TH 1862

My dear Lizzie:

The last boat brought, instead of the little letter from you, one from Mr. Conning notifying me that on his application Gen. Withers had detached me for thirty days that I might write up his books, and that the order would probably reach me by the same boat,— it did not come however, and I have been patiently waiting for to-day's boat to bring the little scrawl from the pen of the "great Mogul" which will restore me to the arms of my darling for a month; for fear that it should not come even to-day— I write this letter,— I was a little sick yesterday, ate no breakfast, but I drilled in the fore-noon rather than tell that I was ill; eat a very little dinner— and grew worse by degrees— evening drill came and I thought I would go through that too, and so I would but for an unfortunate circumstance that upset my calculations and my stomach,— next to me was our Russio-Frenchman (—you remember he brought you a letter once—) he had eaten garlic for dinner and a few whiffs of his breath did my business for me! I deserted the ranks in double-quick but had not got many steps before my little dinner came up,— I am all right this morning for it was nothing but a little indigestion which you know, happens to me once in a while.

Well I hope that when the boat comes to day I will be allowed to bear this letter myself—

Good Bye

Williams

FORT GAINES. JANUARY 8, 1862.

Dear Lizzie:

This is not "boat day," but I hear that it is in sight and is making us an extra visit so I begin a letter; how far I will progress with it before the sergeant will cry "Fall in!" for afternoon drill, the sequel will show.

After waiting anxiously since Saturday for the order that would release me from the durance of Dauphin Island it was a cruel disappointment to find that Gen Withers had returned Mr Conning's application endorsed "Not approved" and I was not a little gloomy for a while, in consequence, but what's the use of *fretting* over the fact that I am what I agreed to be when I stood up before the mustering officer on the fourth day of last October— a soldier— a soldier is necessarily compelled to stay at his post as long as he is able to perform his duties, and the sooner he makes up his mind to bear cheerfully his separation from wife and family and friends, the better for him, *so*— twelve hours after my disappointment finds me in a very good-humor, and my philosophy works so well that I think that it is not very hard after all to wait another month for my turn to see my sweet wife again!

The "Yanks" are booming away at something out to sea; I have been up on to the hill to see what may-be the matter but can see nothing but two of their vessels far out beyond the light house— they are firing signal guns— or maybe bringing to some vessel— This is no unusual occurrence here— every day, and nearly every night too— we hear their guns— when will they come in to try our mettle?— it may be tomorrow— it may be never!—

It is a singular life we lead— isn't it?— watching day after day— and night after night— not knowing when the blow will fall upon us— or if we ever will feel the weight of Lincoln's crippled hand,

We had an election to-day for sergeants and corporals to fill the vacancies that have existed so long— Sellers has my old place,—[35] and "Bob Wier" Mr. Turner's 5th sergeantcy—

Some very influential men are working to get me a lieutenancy in a fine country company, but there are two little "*ifs*" in the way of their success— The first is *if* the lieutenant will resign as he should, for he is so ill as to be unfit for service, and probably will never be any better— and secondly— *if* the men of the company can be made to conquer their prejudices and pride so as to vote for a man from the city of Mobile I may get the place,— As for myself I build very slightly on so small a structure, still *it* may be the seed which I have faith to believe is germinating somewhere, which will spring up and bear fruit— namely a commission— for your forlorn husband— to repay him for the hours stolen from you in poring over those "dry old military books" that you have condemned so many times. You must not mention, even there in town, that I have any such prospects in view, for these country fellows are so sensitive, that the least word from me or my friends that I was expecting to be called to an office in their company would ruin everything—

I have to mention that more strict orders were issued to-day about furloughs, so that hard as it has been to get off to town it will be still more difficult in future— it bears hard on you and I, but I know that it is right! and if I were the Commander I would have done it long ago

The boat which was the cause of this letter being written today did not stop here— so it lays by for to-morrow's regular boat— . . .

When the boat comes I invariably expect a letter— and almost invariably get one— but Saturday it missed— and— would you believe it?— if it had not brought Mr Conning's letter which told me that I would be allowed to come home by the next boat I should have almost been unhappy—

I send you the shield off my cap— give it to Taylor some time when you are down to the store and tell him to gild it— you can send it back in a letter when it is done—

Give my respects to Mrs Turner— no not my cold respects— but my warm regard—

Good bye

Williams

FORT GAINES JANUARY 10, 1862.

Dear Lizzie:

To-morrow's "boat-day" and as I am going on picket again in the morning I must write my letter to-night or not at all,— maybe you would not be so much disappointed by a miss of one opportunity for sending you a letter as I am, but I am fond enough to believe so,— I will be on the advanced post I believe, and it is a long weary walk, and a long weary watch which follows. You will maybe receive this while I am walking the lonely beach, alone— and you can imagine how I look as I tramp up and down the post, gun on my shoulder, watching seaward for landing boats, and landward for the "officer-of-the-day" and the "relief"— occasionally making a quick leap to escape a wave which comes up over the path— more than its fellows— I have to spend twenty four hours of each week in this duty, and although I have bragged some about the peculiar advantages of my new situation as a private,— I never have accomplished a tour of guard duty, but I have— (just a little—) regretted that I resigned my office,— but alls well that ends well, and as I went into the ranks, partly in a pet— partly to further my own ambitious projects, I am satisfied to abide cheerfully by the consequences of my venture,— I hear no more about the matter I spoke of in my last letter, the lieutenant who holds the office in question has gone home on a sick-leave for thirty days, and it is likely I may never hear of it any more.

Captain Jewett is playing us a pretty trick I think, since the 22d day of November he has been absent from his post, and now I hope he may *never* come back, I prefer for my captain Lieut. Cluis; who does and will *stay* here.

"Taps" are beat, (that is the signal to extinguish lights,) and I have barricaded my candle so as to hide the light from shining through the tent, as well as I can— as the moon shines on the outside and assists to make my little light invisible I hope that no one will notice that the "Bazaar" is laying itself liable to a night's lodging in the guard house,— Now my dear Lizzie don't you value this letter more than you did before you knew that I was writing it under such difficulties? if you don't, you should,— King and Bassett are gone, I hope King will be back soon, but at present the Bazaar contains but Cothran and myself— and it is more lonesome than it has been for a long time;— All day at intervals of perhaps thirty minutes to an hour the Yankees have been firing guns outside; it may be on account of the dense fog which has enveloped us.

We are all mad about our winter quarters,— we expected to have had them built for us long ago; but now an order has been sent to us to commence and build them ourselves, and they are located up among the stumps again, so that we will have to grub once more almost as much ground as we cleared at Hall's Mills. by the time they are finished the winter will be over nearly = and even then, I presume they will move us some-where and fill our houses with another regiment— . . .

I am very anxious to come and claim that kiss you promised in your letter, I know how ripe and sweet it is! save it for me when I do come,— for a whole year how I will have to kiss you five-hundred times a day when I go home! to make up for all that I lose now!— I will think twice before I leave you again Lizzie!— but if my country calls, my first thought will be for her— and the second will be that there are better days a'coming for me and my dear wife— much as I long to hear your voice, sweeter to me than that of any other— I do not regret, even to night, that I enlisted in the Confederate Service—

Good night

Williams

FORT GAINES, TUESDAY JAN 12, 1862.

Dear Lizzie:

Shades of Sir John Franklin! how cold it is! The stormy winds do "blow, blow, blow" as they do in the old sailor-song which one of our men often sings— on such a day as this what a misfortune it is to have nothing but bread and molasses for breakfast! that is all that cheered the board of the Bazaar this morning— very frugal, anti-scorbutic and cheerless was the repast!— For some cause our meat-ration did not quite hold out: we'll draw another to-day and doubtless have something good for dinner.

Your letter was sent down to the picket station so that I received it very soon after the boat came; we were, at the time listening to a heavy cannonading out to sea but could see nothing— the two Yankee ships which were in sight got under way and sailed in the direction of the firing— nothing unusual occurred while I was on the picket,— nothing unusual ever does occur on my watch, simply— (as I believe) because I am determined never to be frightened until I am *sure* there is danger— so when I see some dark object moving on the beach; before I run away and give the alarm I always go close enough to see what it is— and— so far— have met nothing more dangerous than one of our own men, or a stray cow— This last picket I amused myself by setting words to a little air that was "running in my head"— and as I paced the beach, for company I sang of my return "Home again":

Home from war!— and safe from harms!
  Lizzie! clasp me in your arms!
Soothe my weary head to rest,
  Pillowed on your snowy breast.

Lonely days and nights I spent,
  On the watch, or in the tent,
Yet how sweet it was to be,
  Thinking— dreaming— love, of thee!

Let me kiss the lips I love;
  No more from thy side I'll rove!
I'll forget the world for thee,
  More than all the world to me!

What do you think of that for a specimen? That is beach-side poetry—

Sellers, who was elected to the first sergeantcy a few days ago, has procured a substitute and is discharged from service,— my friend Cothran is first sergeant— and the other officers have advanced each one grade— Captain Jewett was here day before yesterday, and met a very cold reception— not a man, but one, went to his tent to shake hands with him— he was off again in an hour—

While on the picket Cothran and I went away down the island; some six miles beyond the "advanced post of the picket we "gathered shells" again, and as we did not "throw them one by one away" I send my collection to you in the carpet sack— There are some dirty clothes which you will, be so good as to have washed and send to me— send me all the flannel underclothes I have— that is if there are any at home; also send that gray "Georgia" suit— it is warm and will be a change of costume for me occasionally— I'm tired of looking blue and bob-tailed-gray by turns!— that Base ball shirt you may keep; it has shrunken untill its, originally skimpy proportions will no longer button over me, and if I wear it again I will be in danger of catching a nickname that would out-do "Judas"— "Cutty Sark"— I don't know if you have ever read [Robert Burns's poem] "Tam O'Shanter"? "Cutty Sark" being interpreted signifies "short shift"—

King is not back yet: I wish he would come— he's the life of the "Bazaar"—

. . .

Williams

FORT GAINES. WEDNESDAY NIGHT JAN. 15, 1862

My dear Lizzy,

I have made a resolution that I would never grumble any more about military matters in these letters, which should be devoted to love and cheerful narrative or sentiment, but, I swear to Mars! I can't help it! They are the safety-valves which may save me from a mutinous explosion when the pressure of my indignation runs too high, and you must be content to listen to my grievances regularly three times in each week, and bear the inflictions patiently even if they are incomprehensible to you.— Well, so much for preface— now for the quill from the fretful porcupine which has pierced me this time! You know that I came off guard only Sunday morning. I go on again to-morrow!

Put this and that to-gether and what conclusion do you come to? *Mine* is, that if the officers who command the regiment had ordinary common sense, or knew as much about the science of war as a school boy does of Geology they would never make a detail for guard, every day, of one fifth, or one sixth even,— of the effective strength of the regiment, unless under very pressing circumstances— no one pretends that we are in such a peculiarly dangerous situation now— yet out of a company whose morning report shows forty-seven men for duty— *nine* go on guard in the morning! of which I am one!— I never write an oath profanely— but this day I have orally cursed them for all that is bad and foolish in this world and the next!— so much for that safety valve! I feel better for taking you into my troubles again, and if the twenty-four hours duty was *over* I wouldn't care a Saving's-Bank-shin-plaster about it, at least for four or five days when my turn will come again. . . .

An amusing scene occured just now, which made Cothran and I pause from our letters for another laugh at our Irish neighbors the "Montgomery Guards" [Company B]— one of their sergeants was calling the eight-o'clock roll— he had got about half way down his alphabet and was among the O'Flannigan's and O'Flahertys when suddenly the rain began to fall briskly and we could hear them all scampering off to their tents— Apropos of tents, nobody who has not tried them knows what a comfort a tent is— you know that there has been some right cold weather— and you know that on this bleak island it is colder than in Mobile, yet we got through it very well— even comfortably— already I begin to look on a fire as a luxury that might easily be dispensed with; If I live comfortably in a tent without a fire, why can't I live in a warm room without one?

I believe that after I am done being solider, I'll be a philosopher! I have learned to submit my will and my personal comfort even— to men who are fools— and maintain cheerfulness— (for with all my peevish letters I tell you truly that I am cheerful and (almost) contented with my lot here)— and I have learned to look on things as luxuries— which once I thought the very necessaries of life: If I don't profit by my experience here and be a happier man all the rest of my life, it is because my memory of camp experience grows dim indeed— . . .

As to getting into the guard house for burning lights after "Taps" I don't believe I am in much danger even if I *did* tell you so (for I forget what I wrote) for

I always pin up an inner wall of blankets which effectually blockades the tell-tale lights which would show through the thin curtain; and as I often do the same trick to play cards till midnight; it is no great credit to me, after all, that I write my wife a letter under such difficulties! So for all your little admonition I will occasionaly write you a letter after "taps," and when I *do* go into the guard house for it, I will let you know—

The rain falls steadily now— I love to hear it pattering on the tent; it makes everything look comfortable and cozy inside— and is the finest music in the world to go to sleep by— my love to Mrs Turner and Mrs Wainright and all the *ladies*

Williams

FORT GAINES, JANUARY 17TH 1862 [FRIDAY]

Dear Lizzie:

This day it is just one month since I surprised you by an unexpected visit, and you surprised me by a bow in answer to the question, "is this Mrs Williams?": how funny it was to see that you did not recognize your own husband!— How serious it is now to think that probably half my probation has not yet passed; that all the long hours of absence must be duplicated before I shall see you again.

There is a little rascal in the company yclept Ward[36] one of whose pranks amused me very much when I heard of it last night from his own lips— He was down on picket guard and was so fortunate as to kill a fine duck: not being on very friendly terms with the men of his "mess", he concluded to make a present of the fowl to some of his friends— so he sent it up to Harry Gazzam in the "Jackson mess" and sent his "compliments" to his own mess![37] They were wroth; the "compliments" adding insult to injury, and determined to revenge themselves by turning him out of the tent; which they succeeded in doing by making application to the Lieutenant commanding— so, when Ward returned from picket he found himself moved out: it is hard to tell which party has the laugh on their side— it was diamond cut diamond— another man had saved a bottle of whiskey to comfort him on his tour of picket duty through the long and chilly night watches; he filled a pocket flask with the precious fluid and laid it on the shelf ready for use; while he was out, his comrades drank the liquor; and then filled the flask with molasses and water, which looked precisely like whiskey— our picket-man went on his post— five miles from camp— with the precious flask of sweetened-water in his breast pocket; and when the "officer of the day" made the rounds that night he invited him to drink with him; imagine the face of the officer when he tasted the sweet water and then fancy the astonishment of our picket-man in his turn! [He?] could not take it as a joke and came back next day in a rage!

Poor Lieutenant Whiting has been court-martialled for keeping some men on guard five hours, instead of two,— it was one of his blunders— the error of a block-head— I believe there was nothing done to him unless it was a slight reprimand from a superior officer—

I was on guard all last night which leaves me at liberty to rest to-day, I will not sleep any till night for I can't afford that the day of leisure which has been so hardly earned should be thrown away in sleep— There came no letter for me yesterday and I was cross in consequence all evening, and half made up my mind that I would not write to you by the next boat, by way of balancing accounts with you; but while I am so lonesome or homesick— neither word expresses my meaning— home-sick will do better— next to receiving a letter *from* you, my greatest [relief?] is to write one *to* you; so my spiteful resolution yielded to the yearnings of my heart for communion with my wife. "Wife." what a noble word that is to me! suggesting all that is good and beautiful patient, loving and unselfish in woman!

Cothran has taken quite a fancy to the guitar, and already plays the old fandango passably well,— I believe that I have forgotten till now— more shame to me— to acknowledge the present of the cabbage-head which accompanied your last letter; it was good, and as a rarity on the Bazaar table was greatly appreciated by us all, which means, at present, "Cotton" and myself— . . .

I have just finished reading that wonderful book "The Household of Bou-verie"[38] it was strange power over me, in its dreamy reachings into the mysteries of Fate, love, fascination, and evil: it is not without the interest of the drama, but its great beauty is the stream of fine thought, sometimes strange and weird, but always beautiful, which runs through [its pages?] maybe I have been so deeply impressed with this book because I [see?] it running into old channels of my own mind— accross [them?]

There is a rumor— I may have alluded to it before— that our [company?] and the [Mobile] Cadets [Company K] will be ordered to Mobile soon; what foundation there [is to?] it I don't know; but, I suspect, it is a slight and sandy one; I must say that I would not be pleased with the change— It would certainly restore me oftener to the side of my darling wife; but in all other respects the change would be disagreeable, I enlisted to fight the open enemies of my country, and not to prowl about the house of my friends, watching for the traitor's knife or torch! This may-be a very necessary duty, and a very noble one; so it is to amputate the shattered limbs of comrades who are wounded in battle; still it is a painful and unpleasant duty— I hope therefore, that we will not be added to the military police of Mobile— though it seperates me entirely from my wife for a time, I prefer to face the squadron of the enemy off Dauphin Island,— Most of our men look on the matter in a more favorable light, and would be glad to be quartered in the city on any terms.

 . . . I have a project which may bring me a furlough sooner than I expect; that is to *buy* somebody off, whose turn it is; and I might come up to take tea with you almost any day— when shall I come? fix the time, and if they don't charge me too high I'll buy a furlough— send the shield down when it is ready— "the infantry" is not lost entirely yet, and I am not ashamed to wear its badge on my cap; though if it continues to go down hill as fast as it has done, I soon will be; think of our magnificant company turning out on evening parade thirty-five strong![39] It's incompetent officers are the "Old man of the Sea" that has fastened on its shoulders, and cannot be shaken off— and what I fear most is that, if they ever *are* dislodged they will leave such a miserably attenuated skeleton of a company that I will not care to assume a command in it which belongs to me *now*, by right of superior fitness and the choice of the company; they will destroy the company and then its wreck will be put into my hands— . . .

What a long weary letter! I cant do better than turn over this [leaf] and close.

Love to all,
Williams

SATURDAY AFTERNOON: [JAN. 18, 1862]

. . . The day is beautiful— another schooner has run the blockade this morning; she is aground just outside of Fort Morgan but near enough to be protected by its guns.

Our winter-quarters are progressing finely, and will soon be ready to receive us.— I have just been informed by the gentleman who has been working to give me a lieutenancy in another company— that for the present at least he considers his efforts a failure so that "string to my bow" has snapped. I don't feel very much disappointed for you know I never build up strong hopes on uncertainties like that was.

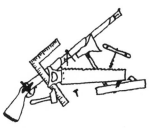

FORT GAINES, MONDAY EVENING
JANUARY 21ST, 1862

Dear Lizzie:

The last boat brought my clothes and another letter from you, as well as the letter from Mr. Procter [in Iowa] which you mentioned— and which I now send to you; it brings good news from home; perhaps you cannot imagine how deeply its contents affected me; the dark fog of war had settled between the friends I love, and me, for months, and its damp chill brooded over all my thoughts of father— mother, sisters and brothers like the gloom of death; To hear from them unexpectedly, and that all are well, is an inexpressible pleasure— I will try to reply by the same channel soon, and then they can rejoice at home too— at home? did I say? no not home— in any sense save one, that is; that there are all my heart-treasures but you my dear Lizzie— and if tis home where'er the heart is "even the country against which I stand in arms has some claim to the "dear and honored name of home."

The brave little Florida steamed out this evening to attack a big ship [the *Potomac*] of the enemy's fleet which came in closer than usual, as soon as our gun-boat started out, it raised all its sails, and we thought it was coming in to meet our champion, but, instead of that it showed it's heels, and ingloriously put out to sea! Hurrah! for the little boat that has chased a man-of-war!— as soon as the Florida came back, the Lincolnite came back too, and anchored in his old place—

I am a carpenter now; building our quarters— for a few days we all worked on the job, or rather three fourths of the company made a *pretence* of working, but really did nothing; the "boss" thought that this would never do— so he detailed a dozen to build the houses while the rest have to do all the guard duty &c until the work is done— I was one of the selected ones, so I ply the hammer and saw every day— the buildings progress rapidly— "our picked men" work like Trojans.

I do not intend to send my clothes to town regularly— I merely threw them in as I was sending the carpet sack any-way—

Love to all,

                                                                          Williams

Fort Gaines Wednesday evening
January 23d. 1862

Dear Lizzy,

King is back; and from his hand I have your letter: the scamp that he is to tell you that I could come home as well as he! I could go home *well* if I could go at all— he went home *sick* whatever story he may have told you about it: even those whose turn it is to receive furloughs can't go now; for, since the fleet has been reported in the [Mississippi] sound,[40] all furloughs have been prohibited entirely, except to those who are unable to perform their duties; even those who were all ready to embark for town, last Tuesday, had to remain; though they had washed their faces and put on their clean (God save the mark!) clothes, and were sauntering about with the precious little warrants in their pockets all morning— sergeant Wier— who was to have carried my letter, was one of the disappointed ones.

When you say that you are "going to get me off" do you mean to tease me, or do you really think that I would be glad to receive my discharge from service? Let me "define my position" as the politicians say— (for I don't entertain the least notion that either you or Mr. Conning could loosen the bond which holds me to service for nine months more; so it is not necessary to persuade you out of your little determination) I may blow hot and cold by turns on the subject of soldiering; and then too pining for my darling in every letter; until you might think that I would rejoice to be let out of the scrape— like one half of our regiment or more— more shame to them for it!— no! I rejoice that I am permitted to take up arms in this war, and if my discharge were to come to-morrow, I would mourn over it as a great misfortune— I hope and believe that I will be in the army until the war is over, and we have conquered a peace; I am certain that unless the war closes very soon I will not remain in the ranks, I can't be kept down; before long I must attain a position fitted to my talents; and you will yet see me placed where I can be useful to the cause— the ambition, which the true soldier always feels, gratified; and the path opened for a glorious career in the service of my country; or an honored death, and a grave that will not be forgotten!

The only trouble I have is, that I must be separated from you for a time at least; otherwise, I would never for a moment look back with a sorrow that is half regret.

It is very stormy to-night and the north-wind is colder and colder as the hours pass, the tent strains in the wind, but it can't blow down I'm sure, if there is any virtue in new ropes and tent pins driven four feet into the ground— The weather stopped our work on the building this morning— King and I were nailing shingles when the rain first came up. I am glad that you report yourself so hearty— I have never had to mourn but one change in you since our marriage, and that was, that Mrs. Williams was not so fat and plump as Miss Rennison I am rejoiced that Miss Rennison's fat and beautiful shoulders are coming back again! Oh! I wish I could go and see you again!

The gloves fit well, and will be a great comfort to me if I should be on guard such a night as this; I will prize them none the less that they were kit by the little fingers that so often I have clasped for hours— Patience— Patience! that little hand will yet lay lovingly in mine, while I tell of the events of the campaign; or listen to the story of your war-widowhood!

> Good bye
> *Williams*

THURSDAY MORNING— [JAN. 24, 1862]

. . . A schooner tried to run the blockade last night but was unfortunately run aground about a mile and a half from fort Morgan. The storm continues so severely that we cannot go to her assistance, nor can the enemy approach to take her; maybe they will try to take her to night if the wind goes down— I don't see how we can save her, but I have no doubt our men will burn her rather than let the enemy seize her valuable cargo of cotton.[41]

All our men have taken the shell fever, and they frequently make long tramps down the island in quest of them— of all the collections that I have seen mine is the best—

FORT GAINES, FEBRUARY 1, 1862.[42]

Dear Lizzie:

Your letter and the shawl which I had forgotten came to hand by the last boat.— I am on the building squad and have no time to write you a long letter— My project for raising a company— can hardly say that I have commenced operations yet for I have only started the talk a little by announcing that I am "in for the war", how many men of my own company will follow my lead I can't even guess, until I commence to take down names which I propose to do next week: and then we will soon see what prospects I have— at present I am certain it is better to talk about it until the leaven works— The fruit can't be plucked before it is ripe, and men do not make up their minds to such a step without time for consideration.

Your battle flag is very much admired.

> Good bye sweetheart
> Williams

FORT GAINES FEBRUARY 4, 1862

Dearest Lizzie:

I'm only going to write a line to-day; my fortunes begin to brighten at last; Lieutenant Mann tells me that he is going to resign as soon as we are paid off.[43] so that you see I am likely to have a commission at last; besides if we twelve months men are allowed to form new companies for the war I believe that I can easily raise a full company; indeed I have been offered about forty men already.

I hope to be in town to fit myself out as a lieutenant or maybe captain before six weeks   I am now doubly anxious for pay day to come!

Don't tell anybody what I say above.

> Williams

Your letter was received:

FORT GAINES SATURDAY FEB. 6. [1862]

Dear Lizzie:

I have the fortune lately to write you on a short allowance of time; what with building houses, and drilling on cannons, and talking with everybody about enlisting for the war, I have no extra time to spin out long letters;

As to the houses,— we are working at a great disadvantage on account of tardy and scant supplies of lumber, The company building is most finished, the house for the officers is framed, the kitchen is framed and roofed: The battallion of regulars will soon be moved over to [Fort] Morgan, and that we may be qualified to take their place we are now drilling at the big guns on the fort— . . .

I received your letter by the last boat,— Please send me that "Guitar Instructor" John Cothran wants the use of it, and as soon as you can have them mended send my shoes, . . .

> Williams

P.S. Buy me a quire of letter paper, put it into the guitar book and it will carry safely— I dont expect to see you again before I am made a lieutenant, which will be soon after pay day— I must go to town then for equipment— If you have some good boullion I will have you to embroider the bars on my collar.

FORT GAINES, FEBRUARY 7TH, 1862

My dear Lizzie:

Your little letter came by the last boat. I am glad that you keep such a flow of good spirits; and to please you better for a little while I can tell you to-day that I am not going in for the war just yet; orders have come permitting us to enlist for two years more, but they require us to remain under our present officers until the twelve months is out— and then we can form new companies; this don't suit me, and I will not put my name down for the extra two years until we are allowed to reorganize and elect new company officers— . . .

A little squad of our company has been drilling at the big guns on the fort for several days, and we will now each of us have to instruct a squad of the men in the same drill— this is a source of great satisfaction to me for when the fight comes, I can have a chance to pop at the Yank's with the heavy artillery— and— God hastening my little commission have the command of a gun or two to myself!

I am to make the grand rounds to-night with Lieut. Cluis, we will visit all the pickets— horseback of course— . . .

Good night.
Williams

FORT GAINES, SUNDAY EVENING
FEBRUARY 9TH 1862

Dear Lizzie:

The storm yesterday prevented the steamboat from making a landing at our wharf, so it put back to town— disappointing you and me in our hopes for letters We happily moved into our new quarters just in time to escape this storm— the worst we have yet experienced since we have been in the service; the house is very comfortable indeed— our Bazaar mess is all fixed up and our room looks like home— in the west end of the room are our bunks placed one above the other like shelves or the berths of a boat.— mine is the lowest, King's in the middle, and Cothran's above— in one corner we have a cupboard made of a box nailed against the wall   the lid services for a door   we find it very useful, and if we

have anything which we don't want every one to see we can lock it up.— we have plenty of shelves to keep everything handy— Here my candle burned out and could not make our little lamp burn so I had to lay my writing aside till this morning— and now it is so very cold that I will not hold out long   I will sometime finish my description of the interior of the Bazaar; and of the exterior I will only mention that our end of the building is surmounted by the battle flag and streamer; our boys— I mean our Bazaar boys— have a great affection for your flag, and take it out of my hands entirely, raising it early in the morning, and lowering it after evening parade. . . .

Charge the cold weather for this short letter and dont scold me any more; my heart is as warm to you as ever it was, but my fingers are too cold to write much of it down; so good-bye— be a good girl— and I will come to see you as soon as I can.

Williams

TUESDAY FORT GAINES. FEBRUARY 11 1862.

Dear Lizzie:

Last night I received your letter and the guitar book, and sent you a letter by the same boat: The camp talk now is all about an order which has come for four companies of this regt. to go to Mobile, what four will be selected I cant say; but I have reason to believe that we will not be of the number; I dont wish to be a city policeman and did not enlist for that purpose.— The bad news from the western seat of war has thrown quite a gloom over our spirits, but we are so far from discouraged that we long for the day when the enemy's fleet shall come within range of our guns, that in sinking them, we may revenge our losses in Tennessee,—[44] every day I have greater confidence than ever in the strength of our fortifications, and every day, under the skilful hands of the engineers they grow stronger and more formidable;— let them come to meet the defeat that awaits them at the entrance to Mobile bay! Since the storm the weather has been fine, the days are bright and pleasant, and the nights clear and cold; our boys all seem to think that our quarters are not so warm as the tents were, and complain more of cold than they ever did before; but I think it is because the last was a more severe trial than we had ever experienced in our tent life; . . .

Nearly all the companies have moved into their new quarters; and the tents which are still standing look forlorn and deserted, straining and flapping their empty curtains in the wind— I will be glad when they are pulled down and packed away in the store-house; the life has gone out of them, and they remind me of the dead;

It is painful to see my old home deserted, even though it is only a tent— God grant that this war will bring to me no greater desolation in heart or hearth! . . .

Williams

Infantry Quarters—

FORT GAINES. FEBRUARY 14. 1862. [FRIDAY]

Dear Lizzie,

From all accounts we have from town I conclude that you are much more alarmed at the threatening aspect of affairs than we are here in the fort; the fact is we are not alarmed in the least; so far as I can see; the men talk about the expected attack, and all are busily preparing for the struggle should it come; but there are no signs of nervousness or fear; I was amused very much to-day to hear Lieut. Cluis tell how he came away from town— he says he went there cheerful and hopeful in his spirits, but heard so much gloomy talk that he began to get frightened himself— and it has taken him all day to throw off the influence of the city croakers; In a few days we will know whether or not there is any cause for us to fear an immediate attack; if we are attacked I feel that we are able to beat the enemy off— and I mean to prove myself a man worthy of you my dear wife; . . . I dont want to fight as a private soldier, when I know that I am fitted to lead others by study as well as by nature;— a soldier who has no ambition is not a good soldier; it is a noble thing to fall fighting in the ranks, but it is nobler to win a higher place and fall at the head of the column— chief among a hundred men!— when my fate meets me let me hold an honorable post, and die doing it honor!

"Never say die" is a saying that I have disregarded without a cause— my pulse is strong and vigorous yet, and the enemy has only three or four ships in sight. Even should he come with an hundred I would be a fool to give up for dead. I mean to live through a score of fiercer battles than any that ole-Dabe [Lincoln] is likely to offer us here: and we will decorate the mantle piece of the little cottage that we are one day going to live in with the fragments of bomb shells, that for all their evil mission never did me any harm! . . .

I am glad that you sent the shoes   I was beginning to feel the want of them; they were waiting dry for me when I came in soaking wet from the picket through the rain— I say that I was soaking wet; it was only my feet that were in that condition, my body being cased in oil cloth from head to foot; I never go on picket without carrying my oil cloth cloak— capcover & cape, and leggins— so that no matter how hard it rains I only have my face and feet wet— At last the money has come, and the quartermaster has commenced paying off the regiment— the Infantry will take its turn probably to-morrow.

It seems that you expected us to come to town; we did not expect to go— and not many of us desired to go— one of the officers told me that if our company wished to go they could easily get permission; but I am glad that we all had pride enough to keep us at this post in preference to taking that of the city police.

Dont forget that this is Saint Valentine's day. sacred to love's sweet correspondence; how could I forget such a day thinking of you? every day of my life since I have known you has been dedicated to *love*, and many, and many a letter have I written you in that time, each one of them was a "Valentine" if it expressed the deep, steadfast love I have for you,— my dear Lizzie— but on this day while I live, I mean you shall have your formal valentine; and while young lovers, all over the loving lands of Christendom, are billing and cooing— my sweetheart shall have a homely souvenir of the time— tried love that is *better, deeper, truer* than all fleeting fancies that agitate the bosoms of youth— and maid.

I might have given you an orthodox Valentine in verse; but my muse has either not recovered from the effects of exposure on the beach side, when he favored you with a few lines from the picket post; or in excessive modesty has not ventured to effuse again, because you never so much as mentioned the last; by which I conclude it must have been very bad.

Just here I was called out suddenly to receive my pay and came back with it in my pocket— queer interruption— but it is the way of the world! money and love!— Cupid and Mammon! they *will* get mixed up, and go to-gether! I send you enclosed $40

Valentine
Feb. 14. 1862

[FEB 17, 1862]

Confound the whole tribe of borrowers! I've been waiting for my ink-bottle for an hour; while the gentleman who borrowed it this morning is composing an epistle at his elegant leisure, though I sent him word to bring it home that I might write some letters in time for the boat if it should come to-day, (we are wrapped up in such a dense fog that we cant see whether it is coming or not—) once more, confound borrowers! and all who encourage them in their evil habits by lending to them, of which I am one, and the whole Bazaar mess another— I believe that half our effects are continually in pawn for the good opinion of our neighbors— every day we make a resolution that we neither borrow nor lend, but no attempt is made to carry it out persistently, and I begin to see that if we cannot reform we will soon be added to the list of borrowers ourselves by reason of having lost all our property— it was on this account that we named our mess the Bazaar— a "Bazaar" is, according to [Joseph E.] Worcester [*A Dictionary of the English Language*]— "an Eastern market place"— "a collection of retail shops"— now the Bazaar is a place of general resort, it is to the infantry what the bar-room is to a country village,— every body comes in without knocking at the door, feels at perfect liberty to sit or loll on the beds, smokes, squirts tobacco juice over floor and carpet, and goes away when ready and not before— not dreaming that any one has been imposed upon—. as to the retailing of trifles it is really and *truly* a Bazaar— here are to be found (—price one— thankee) nails, sand paper— neats-foot-oil— writing paper and envelopes— pins, needles, and thread, buttons, fish hooks— whiskey— stomach bitters— and ink bottles— in short all the little articles of necessity or luxury which a soldier requires— we have a constant stream of customers and they all continue to patronise the Bazaar which proves that its goods give general satisfaction; both as to quality and price— The Bazaar long may it wave!

My ink has come home; an envelope has been furnished for our friends letter— out of the Bazaar stock, of course— so I will turn over the leaf and begin my letter—

FORT GAINES, FEB. 17, 1862. [MONDAY]

Dear Lizzie:

. . . You know that we are expecting the Lincoln fleet here to-day— indeed we do not know that it is not here now, for the fog has prevented our view of the blockaders all day— I am not affraid that they will take our forts, for I believe we can whip them; but I am a little alarmed lest they should run some of their gun boats through in the night or fog, and give you a warming in Mobile in spite of our vigilance— it would be a melancholy sight for us to see some morning six or eight of their craft between us and Mobile! For the purpose of preventing them from going through Grant's pass, the pass will be stopped up and yesterday about an hundred of us went over to little Dauphin island for that purpose; when we went up to the northern point of the island we found a narrow channel between this and the other island; and we had no means of crossing but by riding four or five at a time on the tress of a wagon, while two more mounted each of the

mules, or as a few did— strip off shoes stockings pantaloons, and wade through, carr[y]ing clothes in our arms— we infantry men however did not cross in either of these ways but waited until a boat was brought which carried us over in better and more comfortabl[e] style— we did not work more than an hour, when we were forced to desist by a drenching rain; King and I enveloped ourselves in our oil cloths and started home; but as we had come prepared for a feast with oyster knives; we would not go home without it, came around by some oyster beds, forked them out with sticks and litterally filled ourselves with the delicious contents of the enormous shells— you would have thought it a funny sight if you had been there to see us raking them out and eating in a deluge of rain!— and then the walk home which followed— it rained and poured by turns until we reached once more the friendly shelter of the Bazaar— a party went out to day, which has been even more unfortunate than we were; for it has rained on them too, in coming back a boat load of them was capsised, and I just now saw half a dozen of them coming in in their shirt-tails— . . . Lieut. Mann has not gone to town yet as a matter of course— being no boat—

There is not the least alarm manifested by the soldiers here, all seem anxious that the fleet may come, confident that we can drive them back in disgrace.

Good bye

I hope to see you before the first of March—

Williams

FORT GAINES [FEB. 19, 1862]
WEDNESDAY MORNING

Dear Lizzie:

That [shirt] was a beautiful present, Everybody admires it very much; and it would amuse you to have seen our boys looking at the pretty faces on the buttons and chosing sweethearts. I am delighted beyond bounds— we had no boat for a whole week, which is the reason you got no letters— and we haven't got her yet, for since yesterday she has been aground off a half mile from the wharf— I am in a great hurry this morning, am just going off the picket— good girl you are— What I found about Lieut. Mann's movements has happened, he will not resign now, until the present excitement is over—so I can't come to town until the fight is over or we are satisfied that there will be none—

Williams

FORT GAINES, THURSDAY FEB. 20. '62.

Lizzie:

I've just returned from picket, had a hearty and relishing breakfast of fat pork, bread, molasses and coffee; and am just enough fatigued to enjoy this, my day of rest,— After I have finished this letter I'll clean my gun; then submit my person to the same or a similar operation, and as the day is promising, then I'll dress up in my new shirt and gray suit walk down to the boat— if it comes— to the admiration, doubtless, of all who behold! once more I must tell you what a fancy I have taken to that shirt, when I came home this morning, the first thing I did was to take it out of my knapsack to look at it— I have fallen in love with all the pretty faces on the buttons— the very thing you cautioned me against— I couldn't help it!

There is a rumor that we are to be moved away from this fort, and our place supplied with artillery men; and I am disposed, for once, to believe the rumor— where we will be placed I can't say or imagine— it may be at Mobile— Hall's Mill— North Alabama or devil-knows-where— . . .

King and I went oystering yesterday while we were off duty— the tide was in, and we had to go in "belly deep" to find them, we brought out more than we could eat; and sat down on the beach and made a glorious dinner, which was suddenly cut short— or rather adjourned, by a rain storm which made us take shelter in a deserted house not far off, where we finished discussing the oysters which we mannaged to carry with us in our flight.

We took advantage of a lull in the storm to go back to our post, and dressed ourselves in our oil suits from head to foot by the time the rain poured down again: Just then a rapid and heavy cannonading began over the water, and we ran up the sand hills to see what it was; but the rain hid everything from our sight. Except the dim outline of two ships— fast and furious the guns replied to each other for a while, and then all was quiet as before; in half an hour the rain had ceased and the fog cleared up a little so that we could see five steamers to-gether, the largest of which seemed to be aground and the others working her off: The supposition is that one of our boats was lost in the fog— was chased by the enemy and captured— and that the large steamer we saw ran aground in the persuit— Since I came back to the fort I find that they had a better view than we had; as it was not raining so much here; the persued vessel fired from her stern guns at those who were chasing her, and they think that she must have been disabled or she would have escaped as she seemed to sail very rapidly— The rain and fog closed in to hide the denouement— who she is, how she was taken we can only imagine— I can testify that many a shot was fired before she gave us the race or the battle— Oh! it is glorious music to hear the heavy throb-throb, of a vigorous cannonade! When will we see our own little fort enveloped in clouds of smoke, underlined with living fire— while she plays the defense of Mobile, on that magnificent organ— whose pipes now lay silent over her walls!— let me finger the keys of a thirty two pounder and I will be a happy man that day![45]

The fog has lifted itself up this morning, and for the first time in a week we have a good view seaward, only three of the enemy are in sight— . . .

What "we few will do" when the enemy comes to attack us is simply this— we'll whip them like *everything*— and I have often told you so before, . . .

                                               Williams

                                               Friday— [Feb. 21, 1862]

We are ordered to Hall's Mill—
leave to night—
or by daylight—

                              Camp Memminger near Hall's Mills.[46]
                                               Feb'y 24th 1862.

Dear Lizzy:

I had a good long letter from you this morning: my dear thoughtful wife! who but you would have taken so much pains to minister to my little comforts, and my little taste for the beautiful, as you have evidenced in the handiwork that lies before me; who but my own dear Lizzie cares enough for this poor soldier to work for hours over such a pair of shirts as these; . . . I could not manage to write to you sooner   I have been very busy making ourselves comfortable in the Bazaar and this evening we pronounced the job *finished*— hoisted the battle flag and the Bazaar ensign and opened house— The Bazaar is now, I think, better fixed than it has ever been; we are living in tents it is true; but have had plenty of timber and we built our floors high,— walled the sides of the tent and pitched it away up so as to give us plenty of room overhead— someday when I feel in the drawing humor I will sketch you the Bazaar as it appears now— I have not time to-night—

It is very difficult to get a furlough now; and when we do get one it will only be for twelve hours, leaving camp about 7 o'clock in the morning, and returning about dark, as soon as I can get even this miserable respite, I will come up to see you, but when I will be so fortunate I can't say. . . .

                                               Williams

                              Camp Memminger, February 26th 1862.

My dear Lizzie:

The topic of our conversation and our letters to-day is all the great tornado which passed over our camp this morning before daylight; it levelled every tent in the regiment to the ground, blew down one of our hospitals which was filled with sick soldiers injuring men by the score and instantly killing two— one of whom was the sentry before the building— the scene at the ruin of the hospital is described as terrible and harrowing in the extreme— men were under the ruins shrieking for help— with their bodies or limbs crushed by the mass or ruin; and what made it seem even more horrible was the fact that these were poor emaciated sick soldiers— I walked through one of the hospitals this evening and saw many of these men, and their poor thin and anxious faces haunt me now: to think that these poor fellows, tottering on the brink of the grave, were plunged headlong amid the ruins of a two-story building, into the drenching rain, and Egyptian darkness— what a picture!—

After such a picture it seems almost shamefull to speak of my little troubles: The Bazaar could not weather the storm; when it began to storm we all got out of our beds and seized the tent poles and tried to brace it up; but it had to go, and down it came over our heads— by the flashes of lightning I gathered my clothes and put them on, crawled out from under the tent— wet as a "drowned rat" and found shelter in a log hut not far off.— We have been drying our clothing all day and begin to feel comfortable again—

Williams

FEB 28. 1862.

My dear little wife:

(Not so *very* little you will say, as you always do when I call you so) This soiled sheet is all that the ravages of the tornado and of the furlough hunting members of the Washington Light infantry have left me; and if you want me to write you any more letters you must manage to send me a quire of paper by the first opportunity— As to the tornado I have told you all that I desire about it; it was too terrible among some of the regiments to dwell upon; and our sufferings which were severe, were too trifling to speak of beside those of the Hospital patients: but, I must, by way of explaining any very long absence from home which may,— and in all probabillity will happen, give you an account of the manner in which furloughs are obtained under the new regime— which has caused the ravages upon my paper before alluded to— I being considered the most skillful hand at preparing all kinds of military documents having nearly all the applications to prepare; Suppose I wanted a furlough for twelve hours, the longest time that is granted— I must write a note to my captain stating my business something after this manner:

CAMP MEMMINGER FEB 28. 1862.

Capt. F. V. Cluis:[47]

I respectfully apply for a furlough to go to Mobile for twelve hours— My business is to procure underclothes and shoes of which I am nearly destitute— I

have not been absent from camp since January the 17*th* at which time I had a
furlough for 48 hours,

Benjamin Home-sick
Private Co A. 21st Regt Ala Vol.

this I carry to Capt Cluis after folding it up so:

Camp Memminger Feb 28
Application for furlough
Private B. Homesick
Co A. 21st Regt
Approved and respectfully referred—
F.V. Cluis Comd Co A.

Approved and respectfully forwarded
A.J. Ingersoll
Lt. Col. Comd 21st Regt.

Approved by order of Gen.
Gladden
W.K. Beard A.A.G.[48]

If the captain believes what I say and is willing to let me go he endorses it as
you see and gives it back; then I must take it to the colonel, and if he too has no
objections he endorses it— he then sends it to the general if *he* has no objections
(but he generally has) he marks it with a "G." at the bottom— (— which means
"granted" I suppose) and the adjutant general puts the last and indispensible
endorsement which appears at the bottom— and then your furlough is complete
and you are at liberty from reveille to tattoo— But if the general does not think
that your "business" is of suffcent importance, his potent pencil marks the
bottom "N.G." (suppose to mean "not granted") the adjutant general then
writes the fatal words which dissapoints poor Benjamin:—

"Not approved
By order of Gen. Gladden"

The applications which I have written out for our boys have generally proved
successful; you know I have a very persuasive way of asking for what I want;
which you never could resist, and it generally tells upon the general.— I am
affraid that I can't get one for myself however, because I can't think of any
business calling me to Mobile for twelve hours which would pass the ordeal at
general headquarters; of course I would not sign my name, and ask my captain to
vouch for a barefaced lie as I see others doing every day.

I have often spoken of the incompetency of Lieut. [Nathaniel] Whiting as an
officer. You will not be surprised that there has been an explosion in the
company on his account— Day before yesterday a very severe note was

circulated, and signed by nearly everybody that was present in camp, reflecting upon him as an officer, and calling upon him to resign his office— I was among the signers of course— Nat. will never forgive me; he seems to look upon me as the Brutus whose friendly hand struck the unkindest cut of all— he says he will resign— but, somehow I don't believe he will—

Williams

The regt. to which Pippen belongs was ordered off suddenly. I did not even see John to say good bye before he left—[49]

II
Fort Pillow, Shiloh, and Corinth:
March 7 – May 18, 1862

On March 3, 1862, General P. G. T. Beauregard, the "hero" of Fort Sumter and First Manassas and temporarily in command of Confederate forces west of the Tennessee River, ordered the Twenty-first, First, and Second Alabama Regiments to Fort Pillow, north of Memphis on the Mississippi River. [1]

MEMPHIS TENN. MAR 7. 1862. FRIDAY EVENING

Dear Lizzy:

We have just arrived here, the trip was slow and tedious beyond anything I ever experienced in R.R. travelling— we take a boat up the [Mississippi] river this evening and when we arrive at our destination I will have time, maybe, to write you a description of the tour; I cant do it now— we have stacked arms at the depot and are waiting a little while for the wagons to carry our baggage to the boat where we will march through town— I am writing on my knee— on the platform—

Mr Conning came to see me when the cars left Mobile— he says that if it was pleasant to you he would like to take you home in a few weeks— and I hope you will go as soon as he intimates that he is ready for you.— I know that you will like all his folk and him too when you are well acquainted and as you will not be so heavy an expense to him as you are now, and besides will be cheerful company for his wife, who is in a delicate situation, you will not feel under so many obligations to him— I am sorry that you will have to leave Mrs. Turner's for she has always been very pleasant and good but you will be better there having her to care for you and protect you, which Mrs Turner cannot do— were she ever so anxious and earnest in the attempt . . . [2]

Good Bye my love
In Haste
Williams

FORT PILLOW TENN. MARCH 9. 1862.
SUNDAY MORNING.

My dear Lizzy:

Last evening we camped within the lines of Fort Pillow— just a week from the time we struck tents at Hall's mill; I wrote you a hurried note from Memphis, day before yesterday, which I hope you have received (direct your letters as I told you in it—) "Co A. 21st Ala Regt. Fort Pillow Tenn")— I have no military news to tell you, even if I were allowed to do so— We are *not in the presence of the*

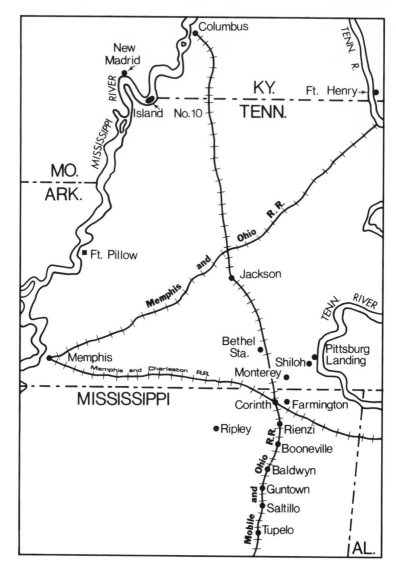

NORTHEASTERN MISSISSIPPI AND WESTERN TENNESSEE

enemy— he has never yet penetrated so far down the river; it is reported that he is between us and the part of our army at New Madrid Mo. and that his guns drive back all our steamboats that attempt to go up there— You must not be alarmed when you hear of fighting on the river it will be in all probability above this post; and even if it comes here the battle will find the 21sters behind formidable entrenchments well sheltered from our enemies fire— I never felt so perfectly safe in Fort Gaines, as I do on this blessed Sabbath morning in Fort Pillow.

Maybe it would be worth my while to go back and give you a short sketch of the trip from Mobile, from the time I kissed you good bye till the time I sat down on a knapsack to write this letter— I looked in vain through the throng around the depot at our departure for the faces of any of our folks— many were there that I know, and I was almost affraid that some of the ladies would seize hold of me and snatch from my lips your last kiss— I was glad that you would not come to see us off, for the crying scene there would have given the blues to you for a week— We came along very slowly owing to some break in the locomotive— sometimes an oxteam would have outstripped us in speed.— The people on the road cheered us at every house— women, children niggers and men waved their

hats and handkerchiefs as we passed— one dear, fat old woman with her dress open in front waved wildly over her head something that might have been a night-gown, and jumped up and down in a sort of Indian dance, in her enthusiasm— we all cheered her in return, and I blew her a bugle blast— In Memphis we met a very different reception— we marched through the city in fine style— every body praised our appearance, and we were acknowledged to be the finest body of men that had ever passed through the city— but (and here's the bad part of the story)— they manifested little or no sympathy with us = not a confederate flag was waved, no cheers greeted us, and the only handkerchiefs that waved us God-speed were in the hands of sweet ladies— Crowds of young men, pale faced, white handed, perfumed, bedressed, and white shirted stood on the walks and stared upon us— oh! how my blood boiled to see the cowards and traitors gaping at us as we filed along the street, with our knapsacks slung, going to meet the enemies of our country and theirs!

—There is no doubt that of the men left in Memphis there is a large proportion who if not Lincolnites at heart, are lukewarm in the southern cause and if the Yankees will protect their cowardly carcases— and save their property, they would give up the Southern cause without striking a blow— I believe that there is now in that cursed town many an United States flag ready made to hoist when the Lincolnites come— If in the fortune of war we should ever have to abandon this position and the city of Memphis, I hope that our general will order the town to be burned to ashes— thus compelling them to make the sacrifice which every true Southerner would make voluntarily— We came up the river with-out any event worth mentioning— and as it was night and I slept I saw nothing—

Nat Whiting's resignation has been sent to general headquarters, I will soon know whether it will be accepted or not—

Williams

(Send me papers— wrap them up and put on a 2 cent stamp)

My dear Lizzy: By the aid of a lively imagination you can see me seated by a big stump on the bluff overlooking the Mississippi— looking down upon the tops of tall trees on the bank below— and beyond over the river to the forests and swamps of the Arkansas side— the scenery— though not quite so utterly dismal as my outline above, is bleak and cheerless = not a single spot of green breaks the uniform dusky brown of forest and banks— the river itself is but a shade lighter of the same color— muddy always but now at flood, it covers the banks and can be seen at spots through the trees far away on the other side— This is the extreme left of Fort Pillow intrenchments— the battery which is to play the deuce with Lincoln's gun-boats is away to the right and not visible from this post of the guard— for that is the cause of my being here, a mile from the cabin which is the Bazaar at present— I am on guard—

—The last time I wrote I mentioned that the mail arrangements for our regiment have not yet been made— nor are they yet— I have written twice since I left home— hope you received them— and so that you may know if you get all that I write I will try to remember to number each one at the bottom, something after the military order style— so if you receive no 3 and no 5 you will know that 4 is missing—

The regiment is under the command of Maj Stewart— Col Crawford we left behind us sick in Mobile— and our favorite Lieut Col. Ingersoll had hoemorrhage of the lungs the day we arrived at this post— we are worried very much about this, and it may be that we will have to elect a colonel before long— don't know who will be the man— Several times I have been almost on the point of writing to you to send me my gray coat and the lady shirt— by some of our men that are left behind— but I am glad I did not do it, as I find that we are liable to be moved any day, and I might have to throw clothes away which I could not carry—

We found it inconvenient to keep up our small mess while travelling and so we joined with the "Battering Ram mess" which contains three of the best kind of fellows— one of which is Dixon— our mess now numbers seven— all "Hail Fellows well met"— as soon as Mr Cocke arrives he will go in with us too—[3]

We hear that Lieut Cluis is too ill to follow us, and we are all *very* sorry— he is beloved by nearly every man of the company—

We hear new rumors every day about our movements; the last is that we are to have the post of honor, and in a few days will be moved three miles outside of the lines as an advance guard or outpost— I don't believe anything untill I am certain that it is true— We hear no news from Mobile, and be sure to send me the papers as I requested— Maybe I did not tell you that we had quite a snow storm on our way to Memphis— it was the first fall of snow I had seen for several years— and lasted long enough to whiten the ground for an hour— the weather has been very pleasant since we left that city, and today the sun shines warm as it did on Dauphin Island— I see Gen Withers coming— the guard turns out to salute him, and I am too far away to "fall in" well I suppose no harm's done . . .

(3) Fort Pillow

Tuesday March 11, 1862

Williams

ON BOARD THE STEAMBOAT "SCOTCHMAN" AT MEMPHIS WHARF
SATURDAY MORNING MAR 15, 62

My *dear Lizzie:*

We are ordered to join the grand army near Corinth and are on our way—[4] . . .

so far, the trip has been far more unpleasant than any we have yet made— we had to carry our tents and most of our baggage from camp to the boat— about a mile— through a drenching rain, and the slippery mud of these clay hills— on the landing particularly the mud was a very loblolly— It is cold and drizzling rain and the balance of our journey promises to equal the first part—

I have come down to the habit of a soldier's life better than I ever expected— last night I lay and slept comfortably on a dirty floor of the boat which was litterally covered with sleeping soldiers, till you could not find footing to walk about— rolled in a blanket with my knapsack for a pillow— and two nights ago when I was on guard I slept equally well on the ground in the open air, though the night was cold— The service has benefitted me greatly, and when I return home, I will be more ruggedly healthy than I ever was—

I have no letters from Mobile, and had just began to look for them; of course I will not receive them now for a long time as they will go on to fort Pillow— you must continue to write however, and after while I will be fortunate enough to receive your letter— if you will notice the telegraph reports you may frequently know better than I could tell you beforehand where to direct them—

You would laugh if you could see the scene that surrounds me as I write this morning— the room is crowded like a fair, and there is a roar of voices— Knapsacks are piled all about and hung overhead— stacks of guns elbow the crowd— men are splattered over with yesterdays mud; some smoking— some drinking coffee from tin cups and making a breakfast of hard crackers and bacon— some rummaging among the baggage for lost canteens and haversacks— some singing— two drummers quarelling by a pile of drums— no one cares for appearances— and you see everything but care and sadness which we banish; a soldier's life is cheerfull and happy always and we never indulge in the blues as you might imagine— I am glad that we have bidden farewell to Fort Pillow— it is a nasty muddy hole— and now that we have left it I must say that it was, by far the most comfortless place we have ever been in— . . .

Good bye my love— keep up your courage— and hope as I do that the day is not far distant, when I may go back to you the happiest man in the Confederacy! and the sweetest wife!

Love to All—
Williams

CORINTH MISS. [TUESDAY] MARCH 18TH 1862.

My dear Lizzie:

Mr Cocke has doubtless told you of our excursion from Fort Pillow from the time my last letter closed, until last night, when he came into our camp to bid us good bye = it was a very severe trial to many of our weaker brethern in arms, and no trifle to any of us— Until last night we did not have a good sleep unless like myself the sleep could be taken in any position and circumstances— Thursday night [March 13] we were roused up at midnight to cook five days rations for the march, Friday night we were crowded into the steerage floor of the boat— Saturday and Sunday nights we passed in miserable freight cars packed as close as we could be stowed in— but last night made up for all— we pitched our tents, threw some rails and pieces of board on the ground to keep us from its dampness and slept the deep refreshing sleep of babes and soldiers— We came here to Corinth— and were ordered up to Bethel [Station] within five or six miles of the enemy— but without leaving the cars were ordered back again to Corinth— how long we will be here I can't tell = we are ordered to hold ourselves in readiness to march at a minute's warning, but I think that it is not likely that we will be moved very far from here for a few days— I saw Lieut. John Pippen yesterday— he looks fine and cheerfull— but says that he has seen some of the roughest times that have yet fallen to his lot since he has been in the service; but something like myself the roughness of the life has a wild charm over him and he rather likes it for a change

Our life at Fort Gaines and Halls Mill was city housekeeping compared to the way we have housed and boarded since we came to Tennessee—

At least half the people of this country are open or secret Unionists—

We don't know yet whose brigade we will be in— I hope that we will not be still under Withers— Will know to-day or tomorrow;[5] . . .

We don't know whether there is to be a fight here or not, but the general impression is that there will be a battle before many days somewhere in the neighborhood.

The two resignations have not been heard from— I think that with their accustomed stupidity our officers have made a blunder and forwarded them without being properly endorsed here, in which case no notice will be taken of them,— Old Nat [Whiting], is very sick of the soldiering that we have up here, and would give anything to be out of the scrape—

Good bye my love— . . .

Williams

CORINTH MISS. MARCH 21ST [1862]

Dear Lizzie—

My last letter was written from our camp on the other side of town— yesterday we moved and are now about a mile and a half north of it— I have not yet any but the one letter from you— there are no mails— you must continue to write however, and I think it will not be many days before they will come in in floods— Up to this time we have been in hourly expectation of a battle with the enemy who was advancing from the Tennessee river = but last evening a rumor came into camp which I am inclined to credit— that the river is falling rapidly, and for fear that it will leave them all aground, they have taken to their boats and retreated down the river again— If this is true we will have no fight for some time: and probably have to march in pursuit before long—

Lieut Whiting's resignation was sent in and accepted last evening I have been unanimously nominated by the company to fill the vacancy and before you receive this I expect to receive my appointment as second Lieut— I will send Mr. Conning for necessary equipments and I want you to send to the store the shirt I left behind— a pair of drawers— and my gray coat— so that they can be packed up and sent to me—

Good bye— I write in haste

Williams

Send me all the white gloves that I left behind— and a silk handkerchief— my sash— and both volumes of Hardees Tactics[6] and a little book called "outpost Duty" which I left behind— that is all that I think of now

6

CAMP OF GEN GLADDEN'S BRIGADE. CORINTH, MISS. MARCH 24, 1862.

Dear Lizzie =

I forgot to mention a number of articles that I want you to send me = My Shawl— a towel— a pair of shoes— 7's— a valise which I can carry in my hand; such as I took with me to Augusta— the battle flag— ask Mr. Taylor to go to

Provost and get some scraps of the blue cloth of which he is making my coat; enough to cover my cap which is faded brown— I can have it done by some tailor in the regiment here— send thread suitable with it— one thing more I would like to have a neat pair of blue pants with a white cord down the seam like the flannel ones I brought with me— for dress parade— light blue cloth is too expensive and it is suggested by a friend to have a pair made of merino, (or what-ever you call that goods of which my red shirt is made)— you would have to line them throughout I suppose— if you can find something of that kind suitable— send it to Provost and he having the measure will cut them out for you = I would rather do without them however than pay an extravagant price as is charged for blue cloth— the color should be as near that of the flannel as you can get— I believe I did not write for a pair of drawers send them.

In the enclosed letter to Mr. Conning I ask him to send me the valise and shoes; if you have not the money you may send it to him and let him buy them for me— It is necessary to have a valise for my baggage of which the government allows me 80 lbs. and my trunks are too large and unwiedly— I do not care for a fine one; the service is rough, and anything which will keep out the weather will do; I have the use of Capt. Jewett's sword which will do for the present, and until I can buy a good one. . . .

There is no prospect for a fight just now, so far as I know = though I believe that the enemy have not retreated to Nashville as was reported. Beauregard, is here and a whole constellation of [generals'] coat collar stars, and before many days something will be done without doubt— The camp is as usual full of rumors but they are not worth retailing, being generally manufactured in the regiment— one of the most current ones, I know, was originated as a joke by our "little Joker" King—

Your letter by Mr. Van Antwerp came yesterday—[7] and is the second that I have had from you— John Pippin is camped beside us but has not received the other letter that you mention— I look for it today— Do not think of coming here as a nurse, it is *no place for a young and inexperienced lady* and I would have no peace of mind if you were in the hospitals— let older women come— *beside,* my own services are all that could be expected from so small a family! = If I should be wounded I promise to send for you— don't think of coming unless I do— Miss "Phoe" must not think of it any more than you; you cannot imagine the labor you would have to undergo, *and how disgusting much of it is.*

My address at present is Corinth, Miss—

Williams

I have not time to write Mr. Conning as I intended— & send him this letter to read—

Mr Taylor will send a gilt bugle with silver 21 in the center for my cap— Simon makes the latter—

CORINTH MISS. SUNDAY MORNING MARCH 30TH 1862.

My *dear Lizzie* =

I have neglected to write to you as often as I should for a few days— and of course I have a good excuse for it— In the first place I was sick = I do not like to acknowledge that I had to go to bed one whole day; but it is the fact— I can't brag so much as I used to do now— the sickness was nothing more than a disordered stomach and diarrhoea— I am well again as ever— Then my increased duties as an officer have ran away with time—

Promotion comes to me soon again; Lieut Mann has resigned and I will be elected to his vacancy, making me senior 2d Lieut— John Cothran will probably be elected junior 2d— Capt. Jewett is running for Lieut. Colonel = his prospects are not good— If he should be elected— Cluis will be captain and I first lieut— Whether he is elected or not I will be second in command of the company; as Cluis is detached from us as regimental commissary—

The last letters I have from you are those of the 19th and 20th The letter which was sent in care of Mr. Pippen must have been one of these— I suppose that as old Provost the tailor is a slow coach my uniform will be still in his hands when you get this— get Mr Taylor to hurry him up— I am affraid that the army may move from here before it comes, and I will have difficulty in getting it, or maybe lose the package altogether— I have forgotten to tell you to send my watch which I need now very much— and a quire of paper and bunch of envelopes— a bottle of ink would enable me to write more legible letters sometimes— I have not half so much time to write now as I used to have when I was a private in the ranks, and you must try to be content with fewer letters— I will continue to write as often as I can— I can give you no war news; the enemy is not far from here in considerable force; we have a formidable army here, and troops continue to pour in every day; we are formed into brigades and divisions and our army organization is pushed forward rapidly— as soon as it is completed something may happen— whether we will advance, or await the attack of the enemy is known only to our generals— Our regiment has not done any picket or out post duty yet— instead of that we have had charge of Corinth as Provost Guard.— Old Major Stewart is determined to run for Lieut Col— of course he will be badly beaten— and I hope that after the election he will resign his present office— in that case will have a major to elect too— Cluis will run for major— John Pippen went with his regiment a few days on a foraging expedition to secure some corn from the enemy   they brought some 75 wagon loads from under their very noses— but did not have the skirmish that they expected.

Good bye
Williams—

Soldiering is no childs play here, we are experiencing hardships that were never thought of before we left Mobile for Tenn— we used to imagine that it was a rough life that we led on Dauphin island but it was lolling at ease compared to service here—

Girardey's artillery company from Augusta is here   you remember it, the dutch Washington Artillery— Lieut [George T.] Barnes and Jacobus are still with it—[8]

CAMP NEAR CORINTH.
APRIL 1. 1862

My dear Lizzy:

Time is tedious here: we see little of what is going on; we are part of a grand army whose tents are pitched on the ridges all about us as far as we can see through the woods: at reveille we hear bands of music in every direction: some so far off as to be almost inaudible; by this we know that our force is considerable, but what its number is, and what it is destined to do, is kept profoundly secret by the generals in command and we can only guess: My opinion is that we are fifty thousand, and that we will very soon advance into Tenn. and Kentucky = if so, we will have some adventures worth relating on our return— Beauregard is here! We rely upon his valor and discretion— where he leads we will follow!— Night before last and yesterday a part of army moved forward; and I would not wonder that you would hear of a skirmish on our front before long—⁹

The Infantry is again in a stew— Capt. Jewett is put out with the regiment for electing Cayce Lieut Col. and with the company for voting for him—¹⁰ Jewett is trying to get out of the regiment, and expects to be appointed on the staff of the Brig. General— Cluis is Commissary and expects to receive his commission in that department soon which will take *him* out of the company— Whiting and Mann are both discharged— and I am the only officer left: if all this comes to pass I will be captain— unless Cluis should resign and come back to the company— And as to myself some of my friends think that *I* will be appointed adjutant of the regiment before many weeks— indeed I will do that anyhow as I have no body to interfere with my drilling it now— it is remarkable how much it has improved already— I put it through some manoeuvres the other day before a crowd of soldiers and as we passed I heard some of them say that it was the best drilled company they ever saw and they wished they had "that fellow" to drill them. . . . This is "all fools day" and we have had a great sport in camp with its practical Jokes— some of the boys early in the morning ran whooping into the bushes in rear of our camp and raised quite a crowd by the pretense that they were after a rabit— that is standing sport with us— if a rabit starts up the whole camp chases it and of course somebody manages to catch it soon— if a squirrel goes up a tree he is sure to be caught for either somebody will climb up after him and chase him down into the crowd below; or they will chop down the tree and catch him before he can get up another; you would laugh heartily if you could see three hundred soldiers after one—

Good Bye my love—
Williams—

I find I can't remember the number of my letters and give it up as impracticable

CORINTH MISS. APRIL 2. 1862

My dearest wife I wrote to you yesterday, but this letter which has just come calls me irresistibly to write you my love again. I write on [the back of] your letter partly because I am out of paper and don't want to borrow— but more to save your letter which I can't do in camp as I have no place to keep it— . . . if it is not too late leave out my shawl and my gray coat   I will get along with my big blanket (which can be strapped on the outside of the valise) and my uniform coat and fatigue jacket— as the cold weather is over this will be sufficient— . . . I expect to leave even that behind when we come to make forced marches, so that the smaller the package the longer it will follow me— . . . Our company is being paid off this morning— I will be glad to send you an ambrotype as you wish as soon as we turn up in some place where a good one can be taken— There has nothing transpired yet in reference to the changes among regimental and company officers, which I spoke of— and I cant tell what is going to happen— . . . I have the honor to be spoken of for major by some of my partial friends—

Williams

. . . Good bye again— don't fret about my things which I have sent for— I am not ashamed to go out on parade in privates dress— I am rather proud thus to show that I came from the ranks!—

CORINTH APRIL 8TH 1862—

Dear Lizzie =

I telegraphed to you to-day that I am well and safely through the two days of battle [at Shiloh]— I have not time nor disposition to attempt a description— when I go home it will take me months to describe what I saw on that terrible field— I commanded the Infantry [Company A] in the whole battle— The wounded are being brought into camp and they claim all my time and attention— [Private John] Emile Herpin was killed early in the action.— King is shot in the mouth and, I fear, mortally wounded   George Dixon, shot in the hip, the ball striking a gold piece ranged upwards and came out of his side; will probably recover if he can be well cared for   My friend (now lieutenant)— Cothran very slightly wounded in the Knee   [Private Henry L.] Plum is badly wounded in the side— may recover— is probably a prisoner   [Private Emanuel] Chevalier slightly wounded   [Private Walter] Gilsinan shot in the arm— [Private Tobias R.] Hays buck shot in the leg   [Private] Jno Keeth wounded in the head— [Private] Wm Keeth slightly wounded in the head— [Private John] Milligan flesh wound in the arm   [Private Martin] Shay shot in the foot— [Private John E.] Werthman badly wounded in the hip— [Private Samuel] Westermeyer dangerously wounded in the hip— [Private Robert R.] White shot in the leg— These are all that we know of now— about 30 are missing and many of these may be yet on the list— I thank Providence for my preservation outside of my own company I may mention that young [Private Edward] Skates was killed— and Mr. [Michael F.] Eldridge slightly wounded   Eldridges wound will not trouble him very long and he will be as well as ever in a few days—[11]

Good Bye— I will tell you all when I see you—

Williams—

I send you as trophies of the field a brass eagle from a Yankees hat— and some of their fancy envelopes &c button off coats gun caps— after the first days battle we slept in their tents—

CORINTH APRIL [9,] 1862

Dearest Lizzie:

I have a chance to send you my love by the Rev Mr Dorman who leaves for Mobile in a few minutes. Nothing new has transpired that I have time to write.

Sergt. George E. Dixon was sent home badly wounded yesterday, he boards at Mrs Willey's 79 Dearborn Street— call there and maybe you can be of some assistance to him— call on him anyhow for he is a dear friend.

Do not have anything sent to me now for a while until I find out what is to be done— we might possibly move from here though I hardly expect it.

I was astonished last night to find that John Pippen has not telegraphed home that he is safe.

Bassett telegraphed to Mr. Conning for me as soon as I got here.

Williams

CORINTH MISS. [THURSDAY] APRIL 10TH. 1862.

Dearest Lizzie:

I need hardly stop to tell you about the wounded and killed, so many reports have already gone on; the final result in our own company is that we have one killed and fourteen wounded, and seven missing including four of our wounded men— The missing ones are Mr Plum wounded in the side— Martin Shay shot in the foot— John Keith shot in the head— and Robert [H.] Ward slightly wounded in the leg— besides these are Corporal Gazzam— [Private] Junius F. Williams, and [Private] E. M. Treat who are not heard from, they were not in the fight but it is likely that they, with some or all of the four wounded men are prisoners to the enemy: Corporal Gazzam and Williams I detailed to gather up the wounded and dead and I think that they were captured Monday [April 7]— Treat showed the white feather at the very commencement of the fight, dropped behind; and he too must have been taken prisoner,[12]

We marched from Corinth last Thursday afternoon towards the enemys lines— That night we lay on the ground in the open air, at daylight we were drenched with a heavy rain— Friday we moved two or three miles further through the mud and water and made another camp of the same kind: we had just begun to make fires and coffee when a very rapid firing on the left made us think that we were attacked and we were drawn up into line of battle. it proved only to be a brisk skirmish, and we were moved a little further on and lay down in the woods; the rain fell in torrents nearly all night, and we suffered greatly. Three o'clock Saturday morning [April 5] we resumed the march and our line advanced by a flank all day with great caution. we were now near enough to hear the enemy's drums and the firing of our cavalry scouts all day long kept up the excitement: we had now reached our position and when night came we lay down on the hill in line, ready to spring to arms at the least alarm; we had no rain that night and I made a bed of little sticks and bushes to keep me from the wet cold ground and slept soundly until daylight: soon after it was light we began to move forward in line of battle. Oh! it was a grand sight to see our brigade making this advance— regiment beside regiment we moved forward over hills, through ravines and bushes—[13] soon we came in range of the artillery which was thundering like mad in front, the enemy fired too high and the shot crashed among the trees overhead— on! on! we marched— now we could catch glimpse of the [Eighteenth Missouri's] white tents through the trees— now the enemy commenced a scattering fire of musketry on us— then the [Fifty-second Tennessee] regiment on our right dropped down on their faces and poured a stream of fire upon the enemy— we then got the word and opened on the battery and camp: here fell Herpin and King. Dixon came down a minute later— then we charged into the camp and carried it and the battery; the horses lay dead in their harness all piled up by their own struggles: Two more of our men fell in the camp— from this time till night we were almost incessantly under fire; and moving forward, sometimes the fire was too hot and our men fell back, but we would rally again and advance to the attack—[14] Night found us in the last camp of the enemy under a galling fire of shells from the gun-boats; at dark this ceased and our regiment was moved back to the first camp we captured where we lay all night in their tents— early in the morning we were again in line.[15]

Maybe I will have time to finish this this afternoon— *Williams*—

CORINTH MISS APRIL 11, 1862.

Dear Lizzie:

I heard from you to day through Bob Wier, some of the ladies of his family had called upon you to know if you had a letter to send to me— and you taking trouble by the forelock said that you did not know if I was living and would not write, I suppose that you must have received Mr Bassett's telegram early on Tuesday which set your mind at ease— after I had sealed my last letter which I sent by Mr Allen I was appointed adjutant of the regiment—[16] Maj Stewart's resignation has been accepted and some of my friends are soliciting me to run for the office when the election comes   I don't think I will consent to run, as Lieut Cluis will probably be a candidate— however I may change my mind— and *If I do run* I will tell you privately that I stand probably as good a chance of success as any man in the regiment— I intended to have given you a short account of the second day's battle but the duties of my new office more than fill up my time, and I have to be assisted; I will defer the story until I return; it will not be lost by time as the terrible scenes of the two days April 6 & 7— The Battle of Shiloh— are indellibly fixed in my memory—[17]

Don't forget to call and cheer up my dear friend George E. Dixon at Mrs Willey's— he is badly wounded— and even if you can be of no service in nursing him it might be cheering to see you— however if he is fevered or very much in danger it may be best not to see him   Give my love to all. Tell Mr Bradford that I saw his son on the field attending to his duty on Sunday Morning— I hope he survived but have not heard—

Williams

HEAD QUARTERS COL WHEELERS[19] COMMAND.
MONTEREY TENN. APRIL 15. [1862]

Dear Lizzie:

A day has passed since I wrote to you and all's well— we are not gobbled up yet: and as the weather is as fine as heart could wish, trees coming out in their Spring Dress, and all nature awaking into life. we really enjoy ourselves— However the duties of officers and men are very arduous, our force having ⅓ of its number constantly on picket duty— I hope that we will soon be relieved by fresh troops better able to endure this fatiguing duty than our poor battle-worn men—

It is hard for me to get no letters from you— that was one of the few luxuries that the war had left to me: and now the privation frets me not a little. . . .

I don't think that another great battle will occur very soon, at least not here = the enemy are entrenching themselves at their former position, and it is likely that both parties will pause to recuperate a little before engaging in the desperate struggle again— How the battle of Shiloh is looked upon by the country I do not know, but I believe it to have been one of the fiercest and most desperately fought conflicts of the whole war— The Yankees fought bravely and only gave way inch by inch, before our advancing lines strewing the ground with their dead and wounded and our own

Yesterday an officer of this regiment solicited me to run for Major to fill the vacancy occasioned by Maj. Stewart's resignation— I believe that if I run I will stand a fair chance of election, but don't know whether I will allow my name to be used or not— as I dislike a struggle for office, and the spiteful feelings that a success would engender in the breasts of envious and disappointed men—

What do you think of a man sleeping on the field in the hottest of the battle with bullets whistling all around? Once while we were all flat on the ground to avoid the storm of missles I saw one of my men fast asleep— worn out with the fatigue and excitement of the three previous days he had fallen asleep— poor fellow— half an hour later he was badly— perhaps mortally wounded—

Good Bye *again love*
Williams

(This is some of the Yankee letter paper)

MONTEREY [TENN.] APRIL 17, 1862—

My *dear Lizzie—*

What a strange exciting life this is!— and how soon custom has made it easy— a year ago and I was a clerk writing in my books and a well fed, clean— peaceful man— Now I live out of doors, sometimes without a tent to shelter me from the weather, a dingy suit of clothes which have not been off longer than to take a bath for a week— my fare is fat bacon and heavy bread— my life is dangerous— and yet I sleep well at night *as* I used to do: and am happy too— A serious feeling has kept brooding over me since the battles I confess— But it is caused by our heavy loss— even in the old Bazaar mess see how we have suffered— George Dixon— Jno Werthman, and King are badly wounded, and Cothran slightly— Myself— Crimmins and Tell are the only original Bazaar men in the fight who entirely escaped—[20]

As I have mentioned before I am astonished when I think of the insensibility to danger that I see in others, and feel myself At midnight a mounted soldier will gallop up and wake us to report some movement of the enemy which may mean mischief— the colonel issues his order to guard against surprise— I carry it to the officers of the guard; and then roll up in my blanket and go to sleep as quickly as if I were safe from a night surprise, at home—

A great many of our men have treated us shamefully— taking advantage of the hurry and confusion among the surgeons since the battle they have gone home on sick leaves, and trifling wounds— leaving men as sick as they, to do all the duty of the regiment— our men are now going on 24 hours watch one day out of every three— which is too hard for fresh men, to say nothing of our poor weary sick soldiers— All of us are suffering from diarrhoea— brought on, doubtless, by the unusual exposure and rough fare that we have had here— and the poor fellows feel it very hard and unjust that they should be still in danger— labor and exposure, while so many of their comrades are swelling about town, and telling great yarns of the battle field— some that I know of did not see *over much of it* — as the fight grew hot they dropped out of the ranks and never turned up till the fight was all over!—

Williams

Corinth Miss.   April 18, 1862

Home again! Hurrah! Don't be jealous of the rights of your genuine, original, only authentic home— for I never forget it; it is the lode star of my life, and I think of it oftener and more lovingly than most Christians do of Heaven— And you know that you are the good angel that awaits me there— But I call this poor camp home, and I hail it with joy again! I marched away from it to the battlefield of Shiloh, and it seemed like home when I came back from that terrible field, weary, wet, and heart-sick— and to-day I'm "home again" from the rough tour of picket duty— Nothing worthy of record occurred during our term; many times we were called on to exercise extra vigilance to guard against surprise, and once were formed in battle array to assist in a little fight about two or three miles north of us; our men (among whom was the celebrated Morgan and his band) whipped the Yanks without our assistance and sent us word not to come.[21]

In the skirmish John Pippens [Twenty-second Alabama] regiment got a shot at the blue coats at long range, but did not kill any of them; We lost one killed and the enemy two or three; The camp is full of rumors of our transfer to Fort Morgan— I don't believe them, and don't expect to see Mobile very soon— could not even go if I were sick— so many have played the shabby trick of pretending to be very sick, and going home on furlough's, that the General, to put a stop to it, has ordered all the sick to go to the Hospitals until they are well—

I did not receive your bottle until this minute, how welcome it is you can not imagine, I have the first drink now since the battle; on the field one of my men gave me a taste of Yankee liquor; I will save it for extraordinary occasions. . . .

Jas. M. Williams

HEAD QUARTERS 21ST REGT ALA VOL.
CORINTH. MISS, APRIL 19. 1862.

Dear Lizzy:

Since daylight the rain has fallen constantly and now at three o'clock P.M. to an interested observer it appears that it will continue for forty days and forty nights, at the very lightest estimate than can be made. A camp will bear a shower very well, and look none the worse for it; but these soaking rains play the deuce with it. The ground is saturated, and our floors get wet; and all around the water lies in pools; blankets and clothing are saturated with the damp air, even in trunks and knapsacks; only one thing more is required to make a soldier, for the time being, utterly miserable, and that is, to lay out in the woods without tents; as we had to do the second night before the battle. For the last two hours Col. Cayce and myself have been trying to extract a little warmth from a wet-wood fire in a skillet or dutch-oven; but, half strangled with smoke, and eyesight in danger of extinction I have abandoned the undertaking; and, after kindling an alcoholic fire inwardly with half a tea-cup-ful of your whiskey; wrapped a blanket round my shoulders and imagined myself warm, while I write a letter to you— to follow fast on the heels of one sent by this morning's mail.

I have always intended to write a letter home [to Iowa] and this morning I dashed off one which I enclose to you— it is not sealed, read it and then put it away until after the war or something occurs to open the way for it to its destination; when you send it you must put in a little note to tell if I am living and well.— I must confess that the thought that I had left no word to the absent friends that I love next to you, my dear wife, smote me on the field of battle; and I there resolved that I would neglect it no longer, and write at once upon my return to camp— Don't imagine because I do it now that I am in a desponding mood, and think that my days are short in the land— for I'm *not*. I only carry out what I propose to do when I left Mobile; and I feel a hundred per cent surer of my life than I did then because the great, and long expected battle has been fought— God only knows when the next one will be and whether I will be in it or not.

The new conscription law[22] is much talked of now: it dont worry me any, for I have always considered myself "in for the war." it will fill up our regiment, and with a fine body of men it will be a pleasure to be a soldier— for though in my letters I take a great delight in commenting on our inconveniences and hardships I enjoy my life very well indeed— You see we soldiers are so jealous lest our friends do not appreciate the sacrifices we make that we must continually keep up a dress parade of them before you.

My salary now is $90 per month and when I get to be a captain it will be better still so you will not be dependent any more, if nothing happens to me— not only that, but you will have something to spare after while, and can take a trip to Georgia for your health; if the money comes I will draw $118 on the first of May— which will pay my mess bill, my uniform &c and leave something over for you, and after that I can send you a large part of my pay— every two months; you will be able to take your trip by midsummer.

I have written myself warm by forgetting the cold rain that still comes down steadily.

Jas. M. Williams

2d Lieut. & Adjutant

that being my full name and military title now

CORINTH MISS. APRIL 20, /62

Dear Lizzie:

The rain which was spoken of yesterday still comes down as though it never intended to stop any more, even after the estimated forty days are accomplished.

John Pippen came to my tent this morning, and was unexpectedly treated to a glass of your mellow whiskey which seemed to do him a deal of good; lighting up the old glow in his noble countenance, and setting free a little of the old sprightly wit, John is a hardy fellow, and a brave soldier; but, like all minkind, is subject to the influences of the weather, and droops on a day like this.

Lieut. Cothran has a letter from home saying that "his uniform will be done this week, and sent on along with Lieut Williams' " that leads me to suppose that mine will be here to-morrow or next day. Since the battle I have regretted that I ever ordered a blue uniform— it is just like that of the enemy and it is feared that in the confusion of battle some of our officers were killed by men of our own side— I will never go into battle with my blue coat on that account but will wear my old gray jacket— I wish I could have a gray officer's fatigue jacket made— but I suppose the material is not to be had now—

Our sick have a hard time in camp— insufficient medical attendance— lack of proper medicines— bad weather— improper food— and hospital tents— are carrying off men whose lives might be saved: two died in our regimental hospital tent last night; and another one will soon follow; if I should get sick I will make them carry me into the hospitals at Corinth, where the state of affairs is a little better.— Our regiment has sustained a great loss in the capture by the enemy of its faithful surgeon Dr Redwood.[23] He used to be very unpopular— so much so that I doubt if he had a friend in the regt. but his untiring care of the sick, and his devotion to the wounded on the battle-field have made him many friends. There is no doubt that he deliberately allowed himself to fall into the enemy's hands, rather than desert our wounded men on the field.

Chester is the same worthless dog he always was; of course he was not near the fight; he is post-master and is too mean and lazy even to mail and receive our letters at the right time— I was in his tent this morning and discovered that a bag of letters for Mobile which should have been sent on this morning's train, he never moved; and there it will hang until Monday morning, because it did not suit his lordship to walk down to town in the rain— The evening before we left Monterey I rode out with another officer a few miles from camp and brought in some horses that had strayed from the battle-field, I am allowed a horse by the regulations, and I selected one that I would like to keep. don't know whether I will succeed or not— as there is a general order out requiring all captured property to be turned over to government—

We are transferred into Jacksons' brigade— you know the general who used to have an office opposite Osborne's [in Augusta, Ga.], "John K. Jackson attorney at law" I intend to revive my acquaintance with him; now that he is my commander.[24] Mr. Cluis stands the wear and tear of Tennessee and Mississippi service as well, or better than I ever expected of him— was not in the battle—

. . . Col. Cayce has tried a pan of coals to-day instead of the smoking fire in the skillet, and a short sojourn in his tent has convinced me that it is a decided improvement— I've had great and exciting times at night with my dreams since the battle; some of them are tragedies and frighten me more than ever the fight did when I was wide awake; I suppose they arise from a disordered state of health; I believe that I have mentioned the fact that I have suffered from a continual diarrhoea since I first came to Corinth from fort Pillow; otherwise I am as well as ever: Oh! what a god-send it would be to go home for a couple of weeks to rest— can't be however— There are many captaincies vacant now, some in our own regiment and if I am lucky I may soon be promoted to one of them.

I saw Bassett yesterday— looks well— says he learns that King will probably never recover his speech— that would be sad indeed; but I have great hope that the conclusion has been arrived at prematurely; and that with the recovery of his wound his sprightly tongue will be let loose again—

Lieut Cothran is about well, his wound being very slight— Poor Bazaar is now among the things that were; it had a bloody end, though thank God none have yet died, and all may recover: when you have an opportunity send up the old "Battle flag and streamer" Bassett wants it, and I have promised to get it for him.

I wrote a little note to the [Mobile] advertiser signed 21st. which touches up our absentees, I suppose it is published in today's paper—

The rumors still float about which say that we are to go to fort Morgan— but there are no official grounds for them, and I am sorry to say that I have not the slightest faith in them.

A banner has been sent to us from Mobile— it bears an inscription on the streamer, "The battle of Shiloh April 6th 1862"— I like the ragged old flag torn with the enemy's shot, that we carried through the fight, better than all the flags in the Confederacy—

No letters yet—

                                        Williams

                                                    CORINTH APRIL 21. 1862.

Dear Lizzie:
    Colder than ever,— windy,— rain and sunshine alternating at intervals of

two minutes and a half: promising to wind up with a cold and furious storm; that's the present state of the weather. Whisky bottle empty; that's bad— Our sick are suffering very much; and it grieves me to think of them; those in the hospital buildings about town do better, I hope— Many have pneumonia, and if the weather does not improve; or the care of the sick be more intelligently and industriously managed, we will soon lose more than we did in battle. Some are sick, but not by any means all who profess to be so: a great epidemic of laziness has raged throughout the regiment for a couple weeks: and the sufferers all pronounce it malevolent disease. When the commissary wants a detail to drive the wagons to town for our provisions it is hard to find half a dozen well men for the duty: but after the provisions return, it would astonish you to see what a ravenous host is here to eat them; and find fault with their quantity and quality. Now as for me I dont acknowledge that I am sick, for I am not really sick, only pulled down with the irregularity of my system that I have before mentioned.

Capt. Jewett is a meddlesome mean man as ever I met. you know that it is long since I have liked him; I have rarely mentioned him in my letters; but throughout this whole campaign he has apparently studdied how to make himself disagreeable to everybody: superiors and inferiors— and I cannot pass him any longer, without writing him down to you as a fool and knave. He has been disappointed in his office seeking as the regiment had too much discern-ment to elect him over them. It wont be long before he is brought up standing by somebody; and if he gets through the latter half of his enlistment without being court-martialed it is more than I expect— I believe that I never have mentioned one of his freaks, which shows how big a fool a grown man may make of himself when puffed up with his own conceit— It was on the occasion of some Mobile ladies paying a visit to the army, and to their husbands, who are officers on the Generals' staff— Jewett, being slightly acquainted with them, when he heard of their arrival at Corinth, sent down a corporal and ten armed men to escort them up to his camp! Who ever heard of such an absurdity! it would make a chapter for Don Quixote— Of course the ladies had too much sense to be made laughing stock of in that manner and respectfully declined to accompany his grand escort— I will finish up with him; I am— thank Fortune out of his company now— and I hope I may never have to return to it while he is in command; When I go back to the Infantry, it will be after he is gone; and then I will be proud of the association with men who followed me so cheerfully and fearlessly into the battle of Shiloh and all through its terrible acts.

The forest trees are coming out in their new green uniform; but, I have no doubt, that, beside the blooming spring that you enjoy, they look bleak and cheerless yet.

Bob Wier is appointed to attend to our mails and I hope that there will be quite an improvement in the management of that little department— I can't account for the fact that I have no letters from home since the battle— [Colonel William A.] Buck's [Twenty-fourth Alabama] regiment is said to be here, but I have not been to see them yet, they will be in our brigade I hear. I wish we could be sent to Fort Morgan as has been reported in camp for some days; we have a dearly bought reputation to maintain; and put the 21st in that fort and I guarantee that they will make a desperate defence, worthy of the importance of the place, and of their own reputation— However as I have said before I don't think that there is much probability of such a move for us at present. . . .

For company I will go over to the 22d's camp and visit John Pippen this afternoon, we are both so busy with our seperate duties that we dont spend much time to-gether, though John's tent is not more than a square's distance from mine— our regiments joining— we will move our camp in a few days a mile and a half from this ground, and as we will then form part of different brigades I may not see so much of him in future, for a while at least.[25]

Write more frequently or I will begin to imagine that you are sick.

Williams

CORINTH MISS. APRIL 22. 1862

Dear Lizzy:

A beautiful day of warm sunshine has dispelled the gloom that had enveloped our camp and our spirits, and charmed away some rheumatic aches from our bones; trees look greener in the light; and all the camp looks like a wash woman's yard, with the blankets and clothing hung out to dry in the sun. Every body is perceptibly better, more cheerful, and satisfied with his lot as a soldier of the confederacy; if it continues many a poor sick man who yesterday was drifting down to the dark "bourne from whence no traveller returns,"[26] will recover yet: and live to meet friends and home again.

Many a poor soldier dies here every day: principally of wounds received in the battle; while I have been writing this letter I have heard two funeral salutes, And they may be heard at all hours of the day. . . .

The vacancies among officers are multiplying; and I am not without hopes that before long I may get a captaincy in this regiment; indeed I look upon it as easily obtained, as soon as our generals give the necessary orders to fill vacancies.— I do not wish to leave my own regiment; indeed, I do not know that I would accept a place in any other; I helped it to win an honorable name, and to leave it would seem like selling my birthright for a mess of pottage. The battle field has bound me with a delicate chain of affection to all— particularly of my own company— who stood by me and our glorious, tattered flag, in the struggle, with a superior force.

Buck's regiment it seems is not here after all, no-body knows why; but rumors of their refusing to come here are rife in camp; I don't believe it; I can't believe that any Alabama regiment could refuse to lend us their aid in driving back the horde of invaders who still threaten us; particularly just as this time when we are just recovering from the shock of April 6 & 7. when we hurled our small force upon them so fiercely, and so successfully. Something else keeps them back— Our horizon is clear yet, for the time there appears to be no prospect of a fight; when it comes it will not find us unprepared. Beauregard is in command and we rely upon his sagacity tho' we tremble for his life on the field.

Col. Cayce is slightly unwell, and Jewett is in command— as senior captain—
Jewett's boy Tom goes to town to-morrow and will carry you this, he says he is
coming back soon— when he does make him call for a letter.

It is amusing to see how some of our soldiers are working for discharges now;
every one who can trump up some bodily defect on which to found an
application sends it in, and discharges from the regiment are granted at about
the rate of two or three per day— I say every one does so who can— that is too
broad an assertion, for I know a few who might anyday obtain discharges who
will not apply— and there is poor Sam Allen, who had to have his forced upon
him, Sam is a brave boy, but entirely unfit for a soldier. He cried when we
marched away to fight the enemy and left him behind. Harry Gazzam was
another that we determined should stay behind, as he was not well, but the
brave little corporal insisted upon it, and we suffered him to accompany us; as he
was unwell we would not let him go into the ranks, but detailed him to follow us
and take care of the wounded; while in discharge of this duty he was captured by
the enemy on the second day—

I must get ready for dress parade. Give my love to the folks, and write me a
letter.

> *Your true husband,*
> *Williams*

HEAD QUARTERS. 21ST REGT ALA VOL.
CORINTH, MISS. APRIL 23D /62

Dear Lizzy:

Mrs. Ackerman goes to town to-morrow and I must needs write a note,
though I sent a letter no longer ago than yesterday:[27] I saw John Pippen last
night, and he says that he has just heard from home, and that you are well, that
is good news for a half uneasy man as I was; but no thanks to you for it! It is a
shame to think that I haven't a word from you since the fight; it is poor
encouragement for a weather worn soldier; and I will vent my spleen upon the
mails until I am sure you are to blame— for I know that you could never let so
long a time pass without sending me a cheerful word. . . . The weather now is
beautiful, we have lifted the curtains of our tents, and are fast forgetting all the
dismal days of last week— Indeed the sunshine is rather oppressive, and we now
keep the shade of our tents for comfort. as we did then for protection from the
cold wind and rain. . . .

I never will write with pencil when I can do better, and as the adjutant is a
grand clerk to the regiment, I have now greater facilities than I ever had; except
in the article of paper which is scarce and poor of quality: We write notes and
orders now on all kinds of scraps and turn envelopes inside out, to make them
do. . . . I have the use of Lieut Cluis' sword, and I go on parade in my old gray
suit, as independent as Gen Jackson— As to the article of shoes, I furnished
myself with a pair of Lincoln's army shoes out of one of his store tents on the
battle field; and get along with them very well for the present— They are big and
coarse, but good. and "Death to blacking"— so, when the uniform comes I will

dress up as gay as anybody and in the mean time I will take a pride in being a good soldier in citizens clothes!

Williams

HEAD QUARTERS 21ST REGT. ALA VOL.
CORINTH MISS. APRIL 24./62

My dear Lizzy:

I wonder if any soldier's wife gets more letters than you do; or more commissions for shopping and needle work? You may console yourself to think that I soon will be "fixed up" to appear in public as an officer should, and will not then trouble you so much. Since I wrote you a very hasty note (enclosing $20) this morning I have been looking at Lieut Cothrans coat and admire its appearance, very much as well as its price— Now if you have not already got my jacket under way, *do not have it made;* but go to Provost and order a coat similar to the one he made for Lieut. Cothran, and send it to me as soon as you get it done— It is a kind of [rusty gray and?] looks neat; is light and suitable for summer, and very cheap; costing I believe only $16— it will do for every day, and battle wear; If I had known, I never would have ordered the blue one; still it is handsome, and I fancy I look quite military in it. I will bring it out on dress parade this evening— The blue pants are much admired, and will do for an occasional grand dress display— The black stripe on the gray ones is right— As to the hat which I left behind and sent for this morning *send it as soon as you can fix it up*— I have nothing of that kind fit to wear— and I think it will be quite handsome— I dont want any gold band on it— am sick of them— turn it up on one side and fasten with a gold star; or better still, a silken loop and tassel. (black of course)— get me a full black feather if you can find it in town— (I think that Conning has some)— trim it to suit your own taste, but to please me have as little gold as possible— none is the best—

John Pippen says he is going to present me his sash as he captured a better one on the field— so I lack but little— First, a tolerably neat pair of shoes (I have a coarse pair for very rough service) that are a *little* narrower than they are long— if they have not been sent try to find me a pair of 6s that will answer the purpose— Second. my sword— Here I am a distinguished man and without a sword of my own!— . . .

I hear that we are to be paid off on the first of next month; and I will send you the bulk of what I draw to settle uniform bills &c— We are now three years men, and it is worth while to equip with all necessary articles— for your sake I am glad that my hours spent over those "old military books" have enabled me to find a position in the army that will assure you an independant maintainance while I live; and that better, and more honorable positions are before me: to be attained by actively and honestly doing the work that "my hands find to do."

Put me up a couple of pairs of socks. if you have no woollen ones let them be cotton.— I lost several pairs and am rather short— I am also short a heavy single blue blanket, and a Yankee canteen covered with reddish gray cloth and a cut on one side, I have an *idea* that they may have gone to town along with Dixon or

Werthman; you might mention it to Dixon if he is not too ill of his wound; and if they are with his things have them sent to me— Do not say anything to him about it unless he is cheerful and strong as it might worry him.— The blanket and canteen I picked up on the battle field. brought them home, and put them into Captain Jewetts tent.— Werthman and Dixon were soon laid in it wounded and it may have gone off with their bedding as I missed it directly after they were sent away. When I inquired for the canteen one of our boys said that he had filled such a one with water and put it on one of their cots— I don't care so much for the canteen as for the blanket, but have use for both.

I am glad to hear from one of our returning boys that King is improving rapidly and will after while recover his speech— you give the same favorable report.

Williams

[CORINTH, APR. 24, 1862]

. . . More than once we have had reports here that Mobile had fallen into the hands of the enemy— I never believed them— but you can imagine how the bare thought of such a thing makes us feel unhappy— I don't know what I should do if that should happen— and I be shut off from all communication with you for— no one knows how long— I hope that Mr Conning will run away with you to the interior before that ever happens— as I have no doubt he will— I don't mind fighting the Yankees— but I would have a heavy heart all the time if you were in Mobile and it in their possession— But they haven't taken Mobile yet— and if I only was there to help to defend it from them when they do try it I would be glad.

The sun is too hot for comfort to day— and has baked me into a head ache— nothing more is the matter with me now, of a serious nature.

Williams

HEAD QUARTERS 21ST ALA REGT.
APRIL—25, 1862.

My dear Lizzy:

Our old friend the weather claims a word this morning: the old drizzling rain and cheerless expanse of mud and water envelopes us dismally.

Military movements again look serious; and we may have active times again right suddenly, I will observe what you say about appearing upon the field in the fatal blue uniform; I have no desire to be killed by my own friends in mistake though many of our officers wear the blue coats all the time.

There are two late and current reports about Lieut. Parker— One— brought in by an escaped Tennesseean— is, that "two doctors and an officer of the 21st Regt. are safe, and prisoners in the hands of the enemy" The two doctors must be Sergeon Redwood and Rev. Mr. Witherspoon— and the officer could be none other than Parker— [28] The other report is that on Monday night after the battle some one approached our pickets, the sentry hailing and receiving no answer fired— the next morning upon examination an officer was found dead:

he was from his uniform taken for a Federal— but his discription tallies fearfully with Lieut Parker— I am rather inclined to believe the first story, and to think that he is a prisoner and unhurt—

I saw John Pippen yesterday and had quite a long talk with him— John and I agreed that our military dreams were now realized; and that we were fully satisfied with our military experience; and if the war were now to come to a close we would joyfully return to our homes again— satisfied to leave war in future to those who have an abiding taste for its glory and its danger— While the invader is upon our soil we have no desire to quit the service; but we pray for the day when it will not be necessary to oppose to his mail clad hosts our bare-devoted breast.

We are ordered to move our camp to new ground to-day— but on account of the weather I hope that we will have a reprieve for a day or two more. . . .

My little complaint sticks to me pertinaciously and I am weak and listless— I have been threatening to report myself sick, and take a few days rest in my tent for some time; but I don't do it; Whenever things begin to look a little less stormy I believe I will do so— indeed I may have to do it anyhow if I don't get better.

Col. Cayce and myself have violated an order of the Com[mandin]g General which may get us into a scrape yet— I have just been thinking of it— we have each of us retained possession of horses that were picked up on the battle-field— and there is an order requiring them to be turned over to the government; it would be a bad case if we were to be cashiered on the score wouldn't it!— Say nothing about it down there or somebody may report me from town.— I believe that I will turn mine over, and put myself out of danger— but I confess that I don't fancy the parting with my horse.

Lieut Cluis is well; and we are now in the same mess— though occupying different tents— Col Cayce still sick— Capt Jewett in command of the regiment— Sergt Campbell will get into a scrape with his "8 or ten days longer" the General Orders [state that] all "officers and men who stay seven days over their time to be reported as deserters, and dropped from the rolls"— and there will be quite a little settlement of accounts soon with some of them, . . .

Williams

CORINTH MISS. APRIL 27, 1862.

Dear Lizzy:

A beautiful day of sun and gentle breezes has dropped in among the rush of bad weather— like a canary bird in a pig pen— or a flower in a mud puddle— a beautiful lady in a Tennessee camp— or any other beautiful and delicate thing among rough and uncouth surroundings.

We bask in the sunshine and enjoy the sweet breath of spring while we may— nothing new worthy of mention has occurred in camp since I wrote: we are daily in expectation of some more "fun" as some of the boys call it with the Fed's. but whether or not we will be disappointed time will tell— certain it is that we have lived in greater expectation of a battle than we do now, without having it to come upon us; and we may not fight again for a long time— When the fight comes off it will be a big one— The burning sun to-day makes me glad that I sent you a note to send me my hat; and I look for it now most any day: You must tell me if the note came to hand which enclosed you $20— I will draw my pay in a few days and will send you the most of it— I mention the same thing generally two or three times in different letters because I don't think you receive near all that I write . . .

Good bye—
Williams

NEW CAMP IN THE WOODS NEAR CORINTH APRIL 28 /62

My dear Lizzie:

Sometimes it is very bad to be an adjutant; this is one of them. A detail of twenty men is called for to escort prisoners to Mobile; they might detail every man in the regiment one after another; poor me would have no turn! However, though I can't go myself, it is a pleasure to send others, and I carried around my notifications almost as well pleased as if I were going myself— Nothing to write about: I only did so because you like to receive letters often— and I never let an opportunity of sending one slip me. Also I like to receive one occasionally— remember that.

Military promotions keep us in a stew all the time; the talk now is that we are to have no election, that our officers will be appointed— Capt. [Charles S.] Stewart, it is thought, will be appointed Major, if he is that will spoil my chance for a captaincy in the Infantry—[29] unless Jewett should resign— which I think probably— and his resignation be accepted— improbable—

I have— as I have perhaps told you before— a rush of work to do; and— barring the honor of the position— I am persuaded that the post of adjutant is not one greatly to be desired— if it did not free me from all guard picket, and fatigue duty I would not have it.

I get along very well, considering that everybody who might assist me is gone away— Col. Lieut Col. and Sergt Major are all gone and even the cook has gone out this evening for permission to go to Mobile for a week— I have (beside my own work) to do much of the duty of all these officers and am almost affraid that some of the cook's work will be added to the burden yet!

Speaking of Cooks reminds me that I have not of late grumbled much at my fare— I am used to it, as the Irish-man's eels were to being skinned and don't mind it now: but it is bad and not improving— Salt Beef of very tough quality which our boys always call "mule meet"— Bacon— Beans and hard bread or such indifferent rifle ball stuff as soldiers make out of their flour— that will make a dinner for a man once in a while and be called good too— but when it comes to living on it all the time— no vegetables— or fruit— it is tiresome and tasteless—

We have just moved our camp about a mile from the ground we have occupied (when at home) for a month back— it is in the thick woods— bugs and ticks were abundant— water scarce and of a quality that would unnerve a fastidious person entirely— it is horrid— we shut our eyes to drink it— generally make it into coffee or tea if we can— and avoid seeing the holes from which it is obtained—

Whether we have any reason for it or not, I dont know: but we do not look for a fight so soon as we did a week ago: I believe it is coming before long however— And I have confidence that the men who whipped them in their own camp can, thrash them again if they venture to come here— unless indeed, they have been greatly re-inforced and fall upon us with overpowering numbers— to crush us out—

John Pippen is well— I saw him last evening— I am affraid that I will be delayed in getting my pay— the Paymaster is sick and goes to Mobile tomorrow— I suppose we will have to wait till he comes back again— I don't like it. for I need the money—

Buck's regiment has just arrived— I have not seen them, but I hear that they look fine— clean— and city like— wait till they have seen the service that we have and they will be rough as the 21sters— I have never had a chance to show my fine blue pants off— and never *will* until I have some other tips for the bottom than an immense pair of Yankee army shoes— it would be the sublime and the ridiculous!

Williams

APRIL 29 TH 1862. HEAD QUARTERS 21ST REGT
ALA VOL. NEAR CORINTH,

My dear Lizzy:

A letter and the battle flag came this morning: date 23d— I am delighted to hear from you again, and that you are well and thriving so in my absence; you will be as plump as Miss Rennison by the time I return; and I will love you more, even, than ever I did that young lady— As to any "compliments" that I could make you, you know that I can't do that too much— I never can find words to tell you, or my mother, how deeply I love you; and how good, gentle and loving you have always been to me; when I am again a free man my life shall be wholly devoted to you— even more than it ever has been— My absence of half a year has opened my eyes to the "vanities and vexation of spirit" that await a man struggling, even successfully, in the mad persuit of fame and position— and I will return to you convinced that by your side, and there only can I be truly a happy man: If fortune smiles upon us we will know how to enjoy it; and even in a cabin I can be happy still; and in contrast with my rough life here it will be comfort and luxury—

A log cabin is a palace to a tent in the woods, or a bivouac by a camp-fire— and the company of my sweet wife— better than a company— or the whole regiment of brave soldiers around me now!

Heavy cannonading was heard, just before I began to write this letter, in the direction of our out-posts: it was probably another skirmish between our forces there and the enemy: They are of daily occurrence, only this was cannonading instead of small arms which makes it attract our notice. The firing has ceased and we do not know what it meant. The Clinch Rifles are there some place now—[30]

News from Mobile of the fall of New Orleans [on April 25] has depressed our spirits very much: we fear that Mobile may follow soon, and I hope that Mr. Conning will remain there; not because I have any great fears that you will be molested; but, I cant bear the thought of being cut off by them from all communication for an indefinite period: It would take away all my heart, and I would be constantly under the dominion of blue-devils— Don't let the Yankees get you; but if Mr Conning should not leave Mobile I would rather have you remain under his protection than have you alone a fugitive and myself a captive in the army unable to see you cared for and protected— However I don't suppose that Mr Conning would keep his family there in such an event— Send my letter home, if you ever have an opportunity, and when you do so put the date in it and mention whether I am safe and well or not: but I believe I have already told you to do so.

Some of my friends were laughing at me because you directed your letter to Mr. Williams— my army title is Lieut. J. M. and the Mr. everybody but you dropped as long ago as the date of my commission.

The flag I will send to Bassett, as he requested it; and it was for him I wanted it.— I dont like to part with it either as it is a souvenir of all the happy days gone by; the Bazaar alas! Expired in the battle of Shiloh, and the Infantry now has no mess by that name— its members suffered more casualties than any other mess of the company— I am delighted to hear such favorable reports from King and Dixon— two of the best fellows that ever lived.

As to the Ambrotype I fear that you will have to wait awhile for that— as I don't know how or where I could have it taken— even if there is any one to do it in Corinth I have no time to go there, it is two and a half miles from this camp. . . .

I presume that you are not in the delicate situation that you imagined some time back, as you make no allusions to it. That is not what I had forgotten, but often think of it—

The firing was a little fight at Monterey—the enemy hold it now I hear—[31]

Good bye,
Williams

CAMP. NEAR CORINTH
APRIL 30TH/62

Dearest Lizzie:

I can't keep from writing to you, even more than is necessary: I think of you constantly; and after twenty four hours, it seems a long time since I have written to you, and I must go at it again = I have plenty of opportunities of sending you letters, and that too makes me think of writing— if I know that some one goes to town (Mobile of course is the only place we call "town") I feel that it is a shame to let him go without carrying you a letter; so at it I go. They make so much fun of me for writing so often to you, that I sometimes do it almost on the sly: taking time when Col. Cayce is absent, or spreading out some report before me, that I might appear to be copying— Every time Col Cayce sees me writing he tells every body that I am writing to my wife.

He is sick, and going to Mobile I believe; I am not a little unwell myself to-day— (a nausea that probably will cause a little explosion before long) but I am determined not to get sick— until after the fight anyhow; and maybe then I will someway obtain a furlough for a few days. I believe that we will not fail to give the enemy a sound thrashing should they venture to attack us here— I hope so at least—

We are being mustered for pay to-day— and nothing happening to prevent will likely draw our money very soon; I am wistfully looking for my hat, as it will be quite a comfort in the baking sunshine that we begin to have: I am sick and tired of caps for a while. I often get homesick, and the blue devils annoy me exceedingly, and the worst of it is, that I will always be sure to write in the midst of such a state of mind as they produce; so I fear that my letters are not even so cheerful as my life— and the average run of my thoughts. So if you think that they are too sombre, remember that they are about three shades darker than the facts would justify— [Sergeant] Chester has failed to obtain his discharge—

I might have a captaincy I presume easily but I intend to wait a little while in the hope that the Infantry may fall to me yet—

Good bye—

Williams

I find the adjutant's duties fully up to my expectations in the way of work— and I can hardly eat a comfortable undisturbed meal— Boom! goes a cannon away off in the distance— another— and another!— Nobody knows what's up and all are now so used to daily excitement that they don't pay any attention to it— When the fight comes it will be time enough to worry!—

NEAR CORINTH MISS.
MAY 1 /62

"May Day" Lizzie!

What a flood of delightful memories have rushed over me for an hour, while I lay in a reverie! Pleasant thoughts of past happiness— mingled with dreams of future joy have carried me captive; I have thought of the dear ones far away at home— [in Iowa] and I forgot *all* the time, and distance and the horrid cloud of War that seperates us— and with them I saw in imagination you my sweet wife— When will it come to pass? when will I see to-gether all that I love so devotedly— unclouded by care or the dread shadow that now overspreads our country and ourselves? God speed the day!

I sent my last letter by Col. Cayce   he asked for your address, and promised to call on you himself when he arrives in town. . . .

Don't worry yourself about the coat if you can't find the braid, . . . I wont mind the coat so much when I get the hat— I saw no Yankees in anything of that kind.

Can't tell anything about the expected fight; it may come tomorrow— or to-day or next week— or never— You will hear of it probably within an hour or two after it begins; do not worry yourself— you may not hear from me for several days after, as it is not likely that I will be able to get a dispatch over the lines, overcrowded with important matter. I will send word to you as soon and as often as I can—

It is not likely that the 21st Regt. will again suffer so severely as it did. So rest easy as possible till you know that "all's well" again

Cannonading is again going on in the distance; that is a daily occurence; sometimes it is skirmishing— sometimes practice— sometimes it is one side or the other throwing shells into some suspected place for a "Masked battery" or ambush.

Again I urge you not to be frightened when you know that the battle has opened; before we charged their camps in a perfect hail of shot: this time we will await their approach behind the secure shelter of breast works made of earth and logs; which will save us from the terrible fire, that cut us down before so fearfully.

Williams

CORINTH CAMP. MAY 2D 1861. [1862]

Dear Lizzy:

Capt Stewart of the [Mobile] Cadets [Company K] has been appointed Major. I am pleased. He is a good officer; and proved himself a good and brave man on the field of Shiloh— among the changes that suddenly came over me on the 6th of April, was my opinion of Capt Stewart; I there suddenly dropped a little prejudice that I had always felt towards him; and am glad to respect him as a gallant officer and gentleman— I like to see him standing up to the cause without the least attempt to shirking the danger of the position, now in the darkest hour of our adversity— Scores of our officers and men seem suddenly to have discovered like Hudibrass:

"— The perils that environ"
"The man that meddles with cold iron"[32]

and are making all kinds of pleas to get out of service— While we had fine times at Hall's Mill and Fort Gaines, our officers stuck to us like leeches and we could not get rid of even the most imcompetent of them— but *now* when we are in an active campaign, that calls for all to endure unusual hardships— and some bodily danger— they "fall as the leaves do fall" in Autumn. In such a state of things it is pleasant to see a man as Stewart— the *man* and the *soldier*— so, hurrah for Major Stewart!— I hope that he will be appointed colonel—

I have not had a chance to send my yesterday's letter yet— Some of our folks

begin to think that the fight is not coming off for some time.
                                                         Williams
the Hat, Sword and letters have just come— the hat is very much admired—
and I am delighted—beyond measure

                                              CORINTH MISS. MAY 3. 1862
Dear Lizzie:
    I had finished my letter yesterday when Campbell brought yours of 29th &
30th   I only opened it to barely acknowledge the receipt of them and the very
acceptable accompaniments of sword— socks and hat— As I told you the hat is
very much admired by everybody— The design is new— and the "fixings" are
simple and exquisitely tasteful— every body says— I am delighted beyond all my
expectations— I cant see a feather in the whole army so gracefully set in, and
pinned— like "nights sable curtain"— with a "star." Indeed I am almost
ashamed to cap my phiz with such a piece of work!— my wife cant be excelled
for taste every body agrees now— The great beauty of the thing itself is
enhanced by the fact that there is not another like it in the whole army— (there
will be soon I'll venture)— Maybe you think that I make too much of a trifle? It
cant be— I love you and every work of your hands that reminds me of you—
though it is only a pincussion— So if I write of the hat all day, it will not be silly
or childish!— The socks are good and comfortable— and made by my wife; the
sword is handsome, and enables me to return the one I had borrowed from Lieut
Cluis— When I get my grey coat I intend to sell the blue one and be done with
everything that looks in the least Yankee-ish— I have not drawn pay yet— will
send you some money soon as I do— what with your heavy star business— and
my good and probably increasing pay as an officer, you will soon be able to visit
Augusta if you choose   I hope that you will not fail to escape from Mobile with
Mr. Conning's folks, before the Yankees occupy it— which calamity I fear is
inevitable— . . . There is quite a little Caucus goin on for *Colonel* (how the
printed word came in that time!) and Jewett is again a candidate! he is
unterrified by former defeats, and maybe will succeed yet— if he *does* it will be a
miracle of perseverance and effrontry!— I dont care much whether he succeeds
or not though it would give me the Captaincy of the Infantry which I covet so
much![33]
    Glad to hear from King and Dixon and that they are improving so rapidly
They are two of my best friends in the whole company—
                                                         Good Bye—
                                                         Williams

                                              [SUNDAY] MAY 4. 2 P.M. = [1862]
Dear Lizzie:
    We are awaiting the attack quietly— last night the 21st lay in the trenches—
Wrapped in a blanket I slept soundly and had no dreams of the future or the past
to mar my rest. The morning broke beautifully and quietly: and before dinner

time we were relieved temporarily from duty and returned to camp again; which is about the fourth of a mile from the embankments. We are to assemble again at a moments notice— and as a steady rain has fallen all afternoon I hope we will not have to go back to them to-night. It may be that the fight will not begin before Teusday: the present rain, if it continues, may even defer it longer. Our troops are cheerfull, and hopeful; and I trust that you will hear glorious news from Corinth, by the time that you receive this letter. As for myself I feel that I will again be protected by Him who guides every little unseen missile; and though I do not expect to telegraph to you, I will write as soon as possible of my safety— I am more fearful of falling prisoner than anything else— as I can't help staying sometimes after nearly every-body else has left.— and came within an ace of being captured in that way once in the other battle— And if I were so unfortunate I could not send word to for a long time— However I will stick close to the Regiment and you will be sure to hear from me and it at the same time I hope—

The Clinch Rifles are posted within stone throw of us, in the line of battle. I stopped among them for a few minutes and recognized many friends and familliar faces. Mr. Whiting—[34] who used to stay at Clarks Jewelry Store, mentioned that he had passed you on the street in Mobile, and he is doubtless the young man that you alluded to in a late letter. After while when we get a chance to visit a little I will go over to their camp.

The shoes suit me in every way— cheap,— good and comfortable— a little too big but that is a very good fault— Thank you for the envelopes— I mean to send them back to you as fast as possible

I will lay down and take an afternoon nap, which will enable me to stand up in the rain all night if it becomes necessary— I am taking light doses of your medicine and I think I already experience beneficial effects.

Williams

May 5. (Monday) 9 o'clock A.M.

We lay again all the night in the trenches— rain fell the whole night— and continues yet— it will doubtless keep off the battle for a day or two—

CAMP NEAR CORINTH MISS— MAY 6. 1862.

Dear Lizzy:

All quiet yet— The very heavy rains have probably delayed operations for a few days— last night our regiment was permitted to sleep in camp, and all feel better able to stand up against the shock of battle than we did yesterday morning, after the night's drenching.

I have just received the accompanying [pro-Southern] documents from Mr. Osborne— he has rushed into print again, he cant help it— he must print or die I believe!— lay it by for me— I wish to keep it as a souvenir— Henry's regiment is expected here shortly— it may be here now— I have a curiosity to see Capt(!) Osborne—[35] The old gentleman really seems to have quite an interest in me yet, and it gratifies me a little to see it. No more letters from you yet— I am so busy now that I do not write as often as I have done; you must be content with what I can send until after the battle— I'll write as often as I can—

Jewett will resign as soon as the fight is over and I expect to be captain of the Infantry then— I saw John Pippen last evening— his regiment has gone out on advance guard duty for three or four days— unless the Yanks drive them in sooner— I am sorry that I can't send you the ambrotype you desire, in full uniform and armed cap a pie— I have heard that there is a so called "artist" in Corinth— but it might as well be in Mobile— for in these exciting times I could not get permission to go so far from my camp. Never mind, I'll come myself soon as possible— . . .

Williams

[WEDNESDAY] CORINTH MAY 7. 1862.

Col. Cayce would have laughed, Lizzie, had he seen the formidable envelope that Mr Welsh carried to you this morning;[36] but, as the letter it contained was not long; and I am again in the humor for writing, this one will soon follow.

When I go home from the wars I want to have Mr. Osborne's pamphlet substantially bound, so that it will be preserved as long as I live; as a picture of the man it is to me better than a thousand photographs. I see him in every line— Besides it is the only trophy or relic that I have of the war against the tribes of Northern Goths and Vandals, and "mock auction Peter Funks,"[37] and "itinerant Cheats", and "perambulatory venders of bogus watches" and so on through the whole vocabulary which I have by heart. [In Augusta] I used to copy circulars and newspaper articles until I would regret that I ever learned to write— and then go down to Mr. Calvin's and grumble to you!— What worried me then amuses me now— . . . The battle does not seem so imminent as it did a few days ago, and may not come off for some time yet— everything has been quiet since Friday's heavy skirmish, which sounded almost like a battle the cannonading was so rapid and heavy—

John Pippen is out with his regiment on advance guard duty for four days— The weather is fine again.— Some think that the enemy has fallen back towards his former position, and will not make the attack at present— I don't know nor care, I would not trouble myself to find out if I could, I expect to fight him if he comes, if he don't it is all right until the General says that I must go out after him and I am ready for that— I have seen his blue coats beaten off their own ground— by our inferior numbers— and I know that when we have a "fair showing" as we have here we ought to whip them easily— I don't fear the result— and if the enemy will only come on I think if you do not hear of a great victory of the Confederate army it will be strange.

Williams

CORINTH MAY 9, 1862.

Dear Lizzy:

There was skirmishing on our front last evening— we were up nearly all night— a battle appears to be imminent— I am elected Captain of the Infantry and will take command in a few days— all the votes are not counted yet but I think that Geo Dixon is 2d Lieut.[38]

I am in great haste to get this line off in the mail—

Williams

CAMP IN THE BRUSH STATE OF M
CAMP NEAR CORINTH MISS.
MAY 9TH 1862

Dear Friend

It is with the greatest pleasure that I now seat myself to the pleasant task of writing you a few lines to let you know that we are yet alive and doing well with plenty of hard bread and spoiled meat and nothing in

As our unknown friend was suddenly routed out of his "camp in the brush" on the "9th of May" this delectable draft of a letter was cut short— and the "pleasant task" remains in this unfinished state—

Williams

CORINTH MISS. MAY 10TH 1862.

My dear Lizzie:

The telegraph has of course long since informed you that we have had another engagement to-day, and that all of the 21st are safe but one man. Providence has favored us to day, and although we have manovurred all day, and advanced upon the enemy some six miles, he gradually fell back without making any stubborn resistance on the part of the line which we occupied— We did not fire a gun— and were very little under fire ourselves— We had a magnificent view of some parts of the battle, which was in a more open and cultivated country than Shiloh—[39]

It is bed time— I am very tired for, I only was in bed last night from ten minutes past twelve till two— not quite two hours— and have endured the excitement and fatigue of the battle all day— so I write but little, and hastily.

I wrote you yesterday that I am elected captain of the Infantry: and will take command as soon as I receive my certificate of election which will be in a few days doubtless

Coat has not come yet—

Williams

CORINTH MAY 10TH [1862]

Dear Lizzy:

More at leisure, and refreshed with a good night's rest I write again this morning!

From the papers you will receive accounts of our splendid sortie, and the masterly manner in which we threw forward our forces driving before us the advancing column of the enemy; I will not attempt a description in which I would be excelled by the first news-paper correspondent. The 21st. lost but one man who at first was supposed to have been accidentally killed by his own gun; but that was found to be a mistake— We were not in any of the hot places yesterday the enemy not disputing the ground over which we passed: there was some hard fighting in other parts of the line however.

We found that the enemy had put up a line of telegraph wire which they used to convey information and orders from their front to the rear— one of my men climbed up the pole and broke the wire— I send you a piece of it, and a ball which I picked up at my feet, that is bruised by striking something— this paper and the Yankee envelopes with the high-falutin letter were taken from a Yankee's Knapsack— which were found all over the ground, where they had cast them off in their retreat—[40]

My coat came this morning and pleases me greatly— I am now "fixed up" and will not worry you so much as I have done with my supplies—

What effect our move yesterday will have on the great battle that is to come, I can't imagine— it may sting the enemy into a retaliatory advance and thus precipitate it— or on the other hand, our driving in his advance & our manifest willingness to fight him out side our intrenchments, may deter him for a time from battle— It has done much to encourage our men, and give them perfect confidence in themselves and their Generals— I am so glad that I have now a complete gray uniform and am in no danger of being mistaken for a Yankee by our own side. . . .

Williams

The excitements and alarms of the past week have interrupted everything— and we are not yet paid off—

SUNDAY MORNING MAY 11— [1862]

My dear Lizzie:

A brass band at Gen. Jackson's head quarters, not far from here is playing that sweet old negro air "Oh! dearest Mae!" and the effect here in the beautiful spring woods is charming; all is quiet and apparently peaceful; we have heard no firing outside and one might imagine that there was no enemy within a day's march— But here around me lie the armies of the South— the hope of our country— and the object of its prayers on this Sabbath day— awaiting with a stern determination the advance of the hated invaders of our homes— And there— in that dense forrest to the eastward, are the hosts of the United States, with whom we must soon close in the fierce and terrible encounters of war. I have every confidence in th result; we can, and we *will* beat them and drive them in confusion to their gun-boats again— What a proud day that will be for us all— and it is not far distant.

I have sent you another little package of trifles from the scene of our exploit on the 9*th.*

You mention Beauregard's battle address; how it affected you at home I do not know. But you should have seen its reception by the 21st.— It was about sun down and we were all in the trenches and confidently expected the battle to open early the next morning. A courier galloped up with the address and waited till it was read to the regiment— I mounted the embankment in front and read the stirring appeal to the men who were perfectly silent and evidently touched with its soldierly feeling— It was a scene that a painter could never reproduce and I always will remember it vividly— That mass of resolute, sun-burned men, leaning on their muskets, with earnest faces turned up listening in profound silence to every word and then as I closed suddenly bursting into cheer after cheer— three times three— for the noble, fearless cheiftain in whom we trust!

It was a glorious sight— John Pippen is well and safe— was not in the late fight—

Williams

EVENING— MAY 12 TH [CORINTH 1862]

My *dear Lizzy:*

The question is solved! We are not to wait the motions of the enemy— but under the lead of the gallant Beauregard go out again to give him battle— Hurrah for Beauregard! and Southern Independence!

I am delighted with this dashing and splendid move; and I feel that it must be successful—

Good bye— Good bye—

Youll hear from me soon. Be of good heart—

Williams

All the weight is off my mind now that the day of action has come and I never was more bouyant in spirits than I am to-night—

I will send word to you as soon as possible— but I may not be able to do so at once on account of the rush of business in the telegraph office—

Be a good girl, and wait cheerfully the result of this great— and I hope final conflict— The God who shielded me before, yet watches over us all—

Williams

NOON— CORINTH, TUESDAY MAY 13, 1862

Dear *Lizzy:*

When I wrote last night I thought that by this time I would be paying urgent attentions to the enemy— and hallooing through the woods like any indian; but for some reason we have been delayed six or eight hours; and marching orders are not here yet. They may come any minute We are ready. Five days rations are prepared. Blankets are rolled up. Cartridge boxes filled with their 40 anti-Lincoln pills each, and everything ready for the roll of the drum to "fall in" and the command *"Forward 21st."* That is the word that will save us yet "Forward!" Forward!— Forward 21st Forward Beauregard! Forward army of the South! Till the last accursed foe is driven out of the land— Every able bodied man who leaves us now on a trumped-up plea of sickness is a coward and a traitor— Every such man who fails to come to our aid, when he can, is no better.

Will our country remember those who now stand by her cause undaunted? I fear not! I fear that it can never discriminate between the sheep and the goats— But whether it does or not, they have the approval of their own concience and that of their brave comrades.

As for myself the good opinion of these two, and yours— my dear wife— is all the reward and remembrance that I care for.

The camp is full of rumors on all kinds of subjects, but probably are mostly of home manufacture— Tennessee river falling rapidly, which will probably make the Yankee's move— 80 of their transports have come up, and consequently they must be preparing to fall back— Gun-boats hardly able to float now. Our men successfully attacking them in the rear— through Tenn and Kentucky— &c &c. I hope that they are all true: but camp rumors on the average are not worth a snap of a thumb.

If any-thing "turns up" before I can send this I'll add a line or two—
Williams

Sun down—

All quiet yet and the expected orders not come— we sleep in the trenches to-night— Jewett is gone and I expect to receive a certificate as captain very soon—

CORINTH— MAY 17— 1862

Dear Lizzy:

I have not written to you for several days, being slightly unwell: I have been threatened with a billious attack: but have pretty well worried through it, and feel quite well this morning, only a little weak— in a day or two I will be as well as ever again— I have eaten so little that I think I starved out the demon of disease that seemed to have fastened on me—

Believe me that I am almost well, and that you have not the slightest cause to be uneasy about me— If I were sick seriously I would send for you to come and nurse me.

Williams

. . . I have not yet been examined for the Captaincy— expect to be soon— I am in command of the company however— The enemy is very close to our lines—

Pickets are constantly shooting at each other—

Their firing wakes me up every morning about daylight or before

SUNDAY AFTERNOON CORINTH MAY 18— 1862

Dearest Lizzie:

I thought that I would have been up and well enough to do duty by this day but great weakness keeps me still in bed— I know however that I have got over the bad part of my sickness and that as soon as I get back a little appetite, I will recover my strength. I have eaten not much more than a canary birds allowance since I was taken ill—

I received a letter from Dixon just now— which I will answer when I feel better— He speaks of seeing you—

I write in haste for the mail—

Williams

CORINTH MISS
MAY 18TH 1862

Mrs. Jas. M. Williams

You will pleas pardon the liberty I have taken in addressing you this note but Capt Williams has just handed me a note to mail to you and I only wish to say that he is improving and in a few days I hope to see him quite restored to health again— I did not know that he was unwell till this evening and as I have just recd a box from Mobile I hope to be able to give him something that he will relish and with a bottle or two of Porter to strengthen & give him an appetite I expect to have him all right in a day or two— So dont give yourself any uneasiness for he shall receive every attention (save those little ones that ONLY a WIFE can give) that is possible to have— Allow me to subscribe myself

Your Sincer friend
Geo. W. Bassett

III
Tupelo
June 1 – July 22, 1862

Williams's illness forced him to take a medical furlough to Mobile.

GUN-TOWN MISS SUNDAY JUNE 1, 1862

Dearest Lizzie:

Here is Sunday and I have not yet been able to join my regiment— I have lived in the cars ever since I left you on Thursday evening— [May 29] Let me give you an account of my experiences in that time—

The train left Mobile at 4 o clock— I had the vegetables in charge which were left at your house, and about as many more were at the depot— the train was crowded, but I squeezed into the ladies car, with the expectation that as the ladies would not go on to Corinth I would soon have plenty of room— I was not disappointed— by night the most of them had got out and I had a whole seat to myself and got a good night's sleep— as, we neared Corinth the following day we began to hear rumors of its evacuation; and when we got to this station we heard that an enterprising body of the Yankee cavalry had come round to our rear and burned a train and tore up the track at Boonevile—[1] I determined to put off my baggage here for fear I would not get it back if I carried it further and I left my black boy Bill in charge of it— I went on with the train but at Baldwin, five miles above here it came to a halt and would go no further— I slept in the cars that night, and as there was abundance of room I took three seats and made a fine comfortable bed as heart could wish— the next morning the train went up to Rienzi for sick, and all passengers were put out— for fear that they would spoil on my hands I gave about half my stock of vegetables to the superintendant of a hospital— and took up my abode in the Express car and determined to go back with it to this station— it did not come back all day yesterday and last night I slept in the car on a large box— this morning early it was run down the road and I came off here where I found my darkey waiting— I have been invited to share the tent of Major White who has command of this post and I will remain here untill our army has fallen back to its new position where ever that may be, as soon as I can learn where our regiment is I will join it, but while they are on the march it would be a useless labor to attempt to join them— If I had known the state of affairs were such as I find them I would not have left home so soon by several days   I might as well have rested myself until Monday at least— I am well, and have a good appetite— but I find that I am weak and debilitated— I am sorry that I did not take your advice and stay with you longer, If I had not left Mobile till tomorrow I have no doubt I would have reached my regiment just as soon as I will now—

That feat of the enemy's cavalry was worthy of [John H.] Morgan, they came around our forces and destroyed a train, and a large quantity of ammunition on it's way down the road from Corinth—

I hear that Bassett has gone down the road but I did not see him— I dont think that he has gone as far as Mobile—

I hear nothing from the regiment further than that they are retreating with the rest of the army— They did not lose any men in the skirmishes last week.

I dont believe that there will be any battle here for some time, our retreat will embarrass Halleck greatly, and he will be very cautious how he follows us so far away from his gunboats— We will doubtless take a strong position when water is better and more of it, and I hope that this retreat, discouraging as it is may do us good—²

Williams

BALDWIN STATION MISS. MONDAY JUNE 2D 1862.
Vanity and vexation of Spirit— All is vanity saith the preacher— Lizzie. Of all the humbugging that ever I went through, my last three or four days experience has beat all— Hearing that our army had called a halt at this place I determined to come up on the first train; told my darkie to be ready and when the train came along jumped aboard— toot! toot! and we are off— no darkie! I shouted to him to come up on the first train—

Now for "the situation." It has rained all afternoon and promises to continue all night— I have stopped at the R.R. Depot to wait for the boy— it is now 2 o'clock and the train is not due until 5½— the room is filled with sick soldiers out of the hospitals waiting to be moved down the road— all are miserable looking and some are moaning and talking in a wandering way— One poor fellow is asking every-body that comes near him to take a dirty ink-bottle that he has picked up somewhere and have it filled with pepper tea— He might as well ask for Jove's nectar for in this place over-crowded as it is it is almost impossible to obtain a coarse meal let alone any little fixings for a sick man— Our regiment is camped about six miles from here over a muddy road and it is likely that I will be compelled to lie in a car! or on the platform of the depot— to night. What a pleasant thing it is to be a soldier! Rain, mud— want— sickness exposure— danger— death— and oblivion— are his portion! *And Glory*— I forgot that— Glory! yes it is a glorious thing to be a soldier of the Confederacy— fighting and suffering all that I have named for the cause of liberty— What if he dies unknown and forgotten! is he not the more surely recorded above in the Glorious Book of Noble Patriots!

No! he is not forgotten by Him whose eye is on all his movements, and readeth the motives of his heart!

When you see some one coming to the regt I wish you would send me a cake of chocolate if you can find it: it would make a pleasant variation to rye coffee occasionally— I suppose you will be asked about seven prices for it— And do not send it in case you judge it too expensive for a poor soldier— for I have on

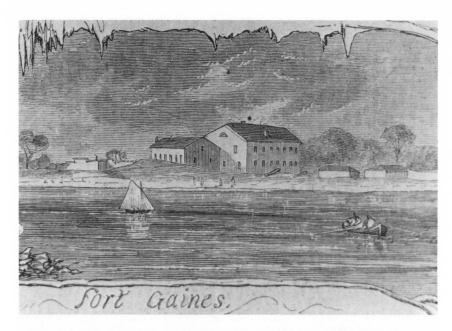

Fort Gaines.

MOBILE ALA.

Fort Morgan.

MOBILE'S LOWER BAY DEFENSES (*HARPER'S WEEKLY*, MAY 31, 1862)

one of my poverty spells now and feel as poor as Timothy Titmouse in his early days— . . .

I was utterly unable to get my fine load of vegetables to the company— but distributed them where they will do good to sick soldiers.

I will be with my regiment to-morrow I hope The road is literally jammed with the sick and cowardly pretenders of sickness— Sick men who were unable to go to the trenches— or a mile or two outside to fight the Yankees, have performed prodigious feats of pedestrianism in marching to the rear— thirty miles a day is nothing to some of them! I *hate a coward* with a feeling like that I look upon a snake, and I feel suspicious of one half the men who are going off on the sick trains—

I can hear nothing reliable of the movements of the enemy— I believe that our retreat has foiled him greatly and that he will not follow very soon— however his cavalry makes dashes occasionally at points of our line   on occasion lively little skirmishes—

> *Good Bye*
> *Williams*

BIVOUAC IN THE WOODS 7 MILES FROM
BALDWIN STATION THURSDAY JUNE 5 [1862]

Dear Lizzy =

I wrote you from Baldwin while I was waiting for the negro— he came up by the next train and Badger with him—[3] we started for the camp of Infantry and came on some two or three miles— a heavy rain was coming up, and feeling very weak and sick I determined to obtain lodging in some farm house—

This I soon found was difficult— every house was filled with sick and stragglers, and they were such hard customers and imposed so much upon the country-people that they were shy of every-body in uniform; however, after making several unsuccessful applications I finaly succeeded in my project as to obtain permission for us three to sleep on the porch of a farm house— we were to feed ourselves as the old lady could not cook for us— I professed to be perfectly satisfied with this arrangement— but at the same time I secretly determined that I would have a warm supper and breakfast and a good bed— So I went to work to ingratiate myself with the old lady = she was very talkative and I listened to her for some time, and then went in to see her husband who was very sick in bed, and entertained him for half an hour; gave the old lady a few butter crackers, and some whiskey to make him a toddy: and then I went out on the porch— sat down by Badger and told him that the thing was accomplished, that we would have a good supper and a good bed if there were such article in the house—

So it proved— when the old lady's supper was ready we were invited in and had a good cup of coffee— and while we were spreading our blankets on the floor for our bed, we were called into another room and given a nice soft country bed— it rested me greatly— and the next morning I arose fresh, and feeling as well as ever— A trick was played me here that I would not have believed any white man capable of— while we were making our bed on the floor I heard a soldier say to his companions that he had no blanket and would have to sleep on the floor just as he was— When the lady offered us a bed, I went to him and told him that I would lend him my shawl for his cover that night— when I got up the next morning the villian had gone, and carried my shawl off with him— I will want in consequence of this my shawl from home— but I do not wish you to send it just yet. I have as much as I wish to carry at present— when we once more settle down a little I will send for it.

At nine o'clock yesterday morning we found the regiment. Each company had two tent flies— and on the average about one or two cooking utensils— and very little to eat— they have suffered great hardships in the retreat— and are now living in the woods— with nothing but their arms and empty haversacks—

At twelve o'clock orders came to march— and we fell into line and marched about two miles on the road towards Corinth   we brought— no wagons— no tents— no cooking utensils— and only such provisions as the men had in their haversacks which amount to very little— some having none, some one meal, some few maybe two— We halted in the woods and sent out a party to find something to eat— they returned with one chicken for each company— and four sheep— I had the chicken cooked this morning and *distributed* (!) it among the men— it amounted to about a smell to each man— the sheep are being killed now, and we will have mutton for dinner without any bread or salt— Last evening we saw that it would rain and the men, having no tents, made shelters of oak limbs which I believe kept the rain off them during the night very well— Cothran and I made a little tent out of a blanket and one of our oil-cloths— and oak leaves piled up at the side Kept the rain from beating in upon us— We may move on today four or five miles further— we are acting as an advance guard— [I] may not be able to mail this letter for some time as [it] will have to be sent to Baldwin—

Williams

— Direct your letters to Baldwin Station Miss—

BIVOUAC— A MILE AND ONE HALF WEST OF TUPELO
STATION— MONDAY JUNE 9— 1862

Lizzie: When you write again send me the two pieces of gold lace which you ripped from my collar, they will do for Cothran— I wrote you I believe last Thursday and dated it Friday by mistake. I had gone wrong in my calculations and did not find out that yesterday was Sunday until it was almost night— Let me begin where I left off, with the darkies frightened by the sound of a little skirmish in front— out of bread sent one of the men back to camp to bake bread and biscuits, he cooked all night and came back in the morning with enough to make us breakfast and dinner— skirmishing continues in front.— though not quite so lively as it was the other day— A very large force of enemy's cavalry is making occasional attacks upon our cavalry and the infantry pickets— Glorious news from Virginia cheers us all up—[4] cotton is being burned all around; so that it may not fall into Yankee hands when we fall back from this position— I walked to the smoking ruins of a planters gin-house, he had burned three hundred bales and the gin: it made me melancholy to see such wholesale loss— Negroes were working corn as if there was no war, and no Yankees to carry them off in a few days as "contrabands"—[5] [First] Lieut [George] Muths of the French guards [Company H], whose comical figure looks like it had walked out of Punch or the comic almanac; came up and visited me in my "leafy bower" he can't speak good English but makes up by signs, and contortions of his lager-beer face = he was speaking of the superior bodily formation of the French over us, and instanced himself as an example— oh! how blind is vanity! The red breeches which he wears set off his figure so that it excites mirth whenever he appears among strangers— and if he would only walk over the stage of a theatre as he appears here, the house would come down with applause.

Saturday was a pleasant morning— I have not missed a cold sweat at night since I have been here out of provisions— some flour sent to us— nothing to cook it in; go off to a cabin half a mile to the left of our position and obtained permission to use a couple of dutch-ovens— boys built a fire and went to work— Cabin belonged to a widow she has four sons and four daughters— the four sons are away in the army, and the daughters are working in the fields, making a crop for their support— some heartless villian has stolen her pony which was her main dependance, as the girls could drive him in the plow— some soldier (I have no doubt,) maybe a deserter making his way into the enemy's lines— A sick Lieutenant of one of the Alabama regiments is quartered upon her and she feels unable to keep him, though she has treated him very kindly— I went in to see him, and found him too ill to walk but able to ride in a wagon— too late, all the wagons are gone and we are ordered to march in three hours— I left him, and I suppose that by night he was a prisoner in the hands of the Yanks— When I returned to camp I found that a beef had been killed and distributed to the men— we had but a short time, and nothing but one camp kettle to cook it in— so we boiled our nice steaks, and distributed a hot lump to each man, and a piece of the doughy bread baked at the widows, and were barely ready when the word came "fall in"— the troops which had been out beyond us came in, and we were about to march away when Gen. Jackson galloped up and ordered our colonel to take his regiment back and drive back some of the enemy's cavalry that were following us and coming across a large field— we went back and were very anxious to gobble up the blue coats, but they had retired, and but two were visible, they out of reach— in half an hour the Gen. sent for us and we commenced the march [south] to the rear, it was two o'clock in the afternoon, the sun beaming hot— road dusty— we marched rapidly sixteen miles— the most severe march I have ever made, thousands of troops had pulverized the dust to the finest powder, and it rose among our ranks until we half suffocated— stragglers from the army surrounded every well and soon it would be dry— the country is not watered   we would pass a "creek" every six or seven miles only— and then the water would be muddy like a hog wallow and sometimes not running but lying in pools in the bed of the stream— I was several times compelled to moisten my hot and dusty throat with the disgusting stuff— men gave up and dropped to the rear by the score, although there were most stringent orders against straggling— nothing but the strong determination that I formed kept me up; and at last— at ten o'clock that night we were halted in a wheat field and lay down— I never awoke till morning, and had no chilly night sweat for once— though it has not failed me since. At half past four in the morning we were aroused and ordered to be ready to march at five My toes were all skinned on top, and I patched them up with court plaster (By the way send me a sheet of it in your next letter) so they did not trouble me much in the day's march— but I find that my little spell of sickness has left me weak and unable to endure what I used to delight in— and again I kept up with the army with great difficulty— about an hour before sundown we arrived at the ground selected for our camp and lay down on the ground. we were out of provisions but the men who came with the wagons had cooked some more dyspeptic biscuits, which were served hot— and a modicum of molasses given each man in his tin cup gave it a relish— also some more boiled beef steaks— water here is but two degrees better than on the road— and until wells are dug we will suffer more than at Corinth— In this retreat which has carried us below Guntown, I have been very uneasy on account of my valise which I left there, so this morning I went down to Tupelo, and determined to send up to Guntown for it by some of the railroad men— but was agreably surprised to see it in the office when I entered— the obliging agent at Guntown must have sent it down for me— to my dismay I found one bottle cracked and all leaked out— and another— that had half slipped away through the cork— found the hospital wagon which brought it up to camp, and a dram out of the half played out bottle reduced its spirits and elevated mine—

Good Bye—
Williams

CAMP NEAR TUPELO, JUNE 11TH 1862
WEDNESDAY— NOON—

We have now gone into dull camp life, which however grateful it is to our wearied sore-footed men, would offer few points to interest you in the narration— we have fallen back far enough from the enemy to be out of his sight and reach for a few days anyway— whether he will push forward and give us battle, we do not yet know; if he does we'll whip him soundly and he will regret that he ever ventured so far away from his gunboat shelter— we suffer greatly for good water, can scarcely get enough to cook and drink, and as for washing it is almost entirely out of the question— our army has come down to the principles of price and Van Dorn—[6] when we move all baggage is dispensed with so I mean to pack a knapsack and send my valise home or throw it away—

Do not send my shawl, it is too heavy to carry and I have determined instead to carry an oil cloth which when it rains and I have no tent I can stretch to small trees or stakes for a shelter— Badger will carry another, and the two together will make quite a good little tent—

Great numbers of our regiment went off to Mobile before the evacuation of Corinth on the pretense of sickness: and Major Stewart went down yesterday to hunt them up and bring the sneaking villains back to their duty: and to share with us the labors of the regiment— Two companies are to be discharged from the service entirely— the Spanish and French Guards [Companies G and K]— I am glad of it— they are more trouble than all the rest of the regiment put to-gether, and not worth a continental shin-plaster for any duty or a fight— In the battle of Shiloh they discharged their pieces away up into the trees— with perfect safety to the Yankees—[7]

I have been living off the too scanty rations of the men since I rejoined my company— it has been impossible for the officers to buy anything from the Commissary department— last evening with great difficulty I succeeded in buying a little ham— but could get neither flour or meal— it has vexed me greatly and I have promised to raise Cain with the brigade commissary if he don't provide for us— I have urged Col. Anderson[8] to hurry up and have us examined so that I may draw my money again if I pass— or in case I don't be put out of my misery—

By the papers I see that Conning has been robbed— I told him when I first went there that he was not safe with the second story windows unsecured as they were— and this misfortune proves it—

I hope that you can succeed in making out my pencilled letters, for I cant get ink and pens; or a desk better than the back of a knapsack to write on—

They use this regiment up here just as they please, the last imposition is a company of sharp-shooters which is being formed from the brigade— and which will take sixteen men from the 21st— Some pet of the general wants a command— so they get up a company of sharp-shooters for him— and we have to furnish the men out of our companies—

Camp rumors are hardly worth mentioning for they are manufactured for fun by the boys here— and invariably turn out all humbug— one that is going around this morning is that the 21st is to be disbanded and thrown into the 22d to fill it up— of course it is only a lie, like the rest— . . .

Williams

If you can get another of those little cheeses and have the money to spare you may buy it, and I will send for it by the first opportunity— our mess has pitched into the one I brought with me and it is almost gone already—

CAMP NEAR TUPELO MISS. JUNE 13TH 1862

And a very dusty, hut, smoky camp it is becoming; at first it was a beautiful little grassy field, but the whole brigade was crowded into it as close as possible and the result is that the dust rises through the fast disappearing grass until it is almost unbearable; filling all our clothes, and making the inside of our tent look like the place under a barn where hogs sleep, and hens scratch, and hide away their nests; then the smoke, oh! my eyes! how dense and pungent it is, about meal times particularly, when a hundred fires are in full blast, in this little seven by nine field; The sensation is like strong ley soap in your eyes, and the only refuge is to shut them up and half smother by rolling head and ears in a blanket— But enough of grumbling   the bright side of the picture is that we have obtained a weeks rest from harrassing duty; and the continual strain of mind in anticipation of a great battle which all of us had felt for a long time before leaving Corinth

What we are to do now, no one can conjecture; but we rely upon the skill of our generals and government— certain it is to my mind that we will not long remain idle or inactive—

I am on duty to-day— busy— and no time to write more— I have not yet heard from you since I left home— why is it— *Lizzie*
                                                    Williams

CAMP NEAR TUPELO. JUNE 17, 62

Preach as I may, about the little difference it should make to you or me if once in a while one of my letters should get lost entirely in the labyrinths of the post office department; yet I confess it vexes me to think that while I have written to you about every other day, sometimes every day for several days in succession; you can't receive a letter once in a week— Dixon says that is the case— while if any-body were to doubt it, I could prove by the whole Washington Light Infantry present in camp— viz. three officers— three non-commissioned officers and twenty three men— that I have written as often as I say above—

Dixon came yesterday— of course he should not have come so soon, and I have persuaded him to go back to Mobile again, which he will do as soon as he can get his papers through the circumlocution office. He will tell you how we live— only so far as eating goes he knows nothing— as he brought so many good things with him— (your sack of vegetables being no inconsiderable part) that we have improved our bill of fare, till it is past all recognition.

I will not be able to send you any money this month, as I can't draw any for several reasons— one of which is that our paymaster is out of funds— I will write to Mr Conning to advance you what you need until I *am* paid—
                                                    Williams

CAMP NEAR TUPELO MISS. JUNE 18TH/62

Dear Lizzie:

Our bill of fare has improved vastly since George came: but I remember now I have in a former letter told you of the good things that he brought us; besides he

brought our favorite black boy Charlie— the same whose coffee-pot the Yanks shot off his back at Shiloh— Charlie is going to stay with us— and he is smart enough to improve our bill of fare a little—

Our officers have been ordered on duty and Dixon and Badger yesterday came out on parade for the first time

I am called off   it is not likely I'll get another chance at this so good
bye— . . .

Williams

CAMP NEAR TUPELO, JUNE 18, 1862—

Dear Lizzie:

George Dixon has suddenly obtained his leave of absence and will go on such
short notice that I haven't time to write—

He will give you all the news—

Williams—

CAMP NEAR TUPELO. JUNE 22. 1862—

Dear Lizzy:

I believe that I was born to be a soldier, grumble as I may— and home-sick as I
do be often— even to the extreme— I like the soldier's life,

Now what do you suppose worries me most, next to my absence from you, and
the indiferent character of my rations? it is *inaction*— I have had a taste of danger
and uncertainty, and now I long for its excitement; as the tobacco chewer does
for the nauseous leaf which custom has made sweet to the taste.— I want to be
moving.— to be doing— it would be music to hear the rapid rattle of musketry
or the sharp report of the picket man's rifle again; and then to listen to the
startling alarm of the bugle— which calls every man who can fire a gun, sick or

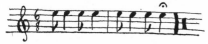

well, to the alarm post.— When I came here I was weak and tired, and was
overjoyed to rest— now I am refreshed and well— and I long to be off to the
wars again— I am more than hopeful for our cause, I feel that they never can
conquer us if the people are true to themselves— and how can they be
otherwise? I can't believe that Southern born men will ever submit to the
degrading yoke of a hated abolition master—

Here's a fragment of a letter that was broken off short the other day— you
make anything out of it you can—

So Hurrah for Mobile or Huntsville or Chattanooga—or where-ever they
want *us for a big fight*

CAMP NEAR TUPELO MISS. JUNE 23/62

I have again to write a very short letter— Lizzie for the want of time— Mr.
Stirling a corporal of my company received a permit for a furlough of five days—
last evening— the cars leave early this morning, and he will start for the station
at 6 o'clock. Mr. Wainwright last evening gave me your letter, and the nice
little cheese— the first cheese is not quite gone yet, though we all like it very
much and have patronized it well. George Dixon's box of good things still holds
out, and Capt. Sossaman[9] of the [Chamberlain Mobile] Rifles [Company E] who

has joined our mess temporarily brought with him some nice butter, so we still live tolerably well— George left his valuable box with us without saying a word as to cost, or leaving us a chance to ask how much it was; but after he left we took an inventory of it and have credited it to him on the mess account— When ever you send anything in the way of eatables mention the cost; so that I may do the same with my own contributions— . . .

I was officer of the brigade guard yesterday and up all night— with the exception of a little nap that I found by chance about eleven o'clock it kept me fast until broad day-light—
Good bye— . . .

CAMP NEAR TUPELO MISS. JUNE 25 1862.
My dear Lizzie:
What a bad humor you was in on the 21st of June, when you wrote the letter that has just come to me: you find fault with me because I don't write, and then when I do, you are not pleased because the poor letter was delayed on the road— I did tell you that the cake was very good and the blackberry cordial delicious— and now that they are both gone I am like Oliver Twist longing for more.

As to my looking so fine— that, (begging Dixon's pardon) is something I really was not aware of— I certainly *feel* very well, but I have no opportunity of judging of my appearance; I did see the reflection of a dirty dust begrimmed face once or twice in a glass since I have been here, and with the recolection of that fresh in my mind I did not imagine that I appeared to such great advantage—
. . .

The examination is at last coming off— and I will take my turn today or to-morrow— as soon as it's over and I receive my appointment from Gen Bragg I'll send you some money
Williams
I dont believe that we are going to Mobile— But we are soon going somewhere—

CAMP NEAR TUPELO MISS. JUNE 26. 1862
My dearest wife:
I wrote you a letter, or part of one yesterday. Many a letter that I begin comes to an untimely end, cut off in mid career by one of the peremptory demands upon my time and attention, which are as frequent as unexpected in these days of captaincy.

When I commence writing there is no certainty that the letter will ever be finished: if I am called off I do not throw down my M.S. for the delectation of the first loafer that enters my tent; but, if it has grown to half a page or so and I have time I fold it up and let it go as it is; if not it is torn to shreds— Such letters of course are short, unsatisfactory and curt and you think I'm cross, as two sticks or bloody bones   My very much over-petted Lizzie must be content with such letters as the rough soldier can send her, and when they appear gruff she must think that he is always cultivating that peculiar style of conversation and prides himself in brevity and, the imperative mood— and not be surprised to see it creeping even into affectionate composition— unknown to him—

I often allude to the routine of camp duties; and as it is a little varied at different times I'll outline it, as it is now.

Reveille and roll call at 5 oclock in the morning— Police duty (that is the cleaning up of all trash &c about the camp) half past five— Company drill 6 to 7— Breakfast 7— to 8— Guard mounting 8— Non-commisioned officer's drill at 9 to 10 (I drill them)— school (in which the sergeants and corporals recite lessons from the books of tactics) at 10 to 11— From 11 to 4 in the afternoon it is too hot to do anything but sleep in the shade— 4 to 5, drill— 6 evening parade— 7 supper That is the *regular* duties of officers and men— besides that every day we have— fatigue parties to dig wells— cut down trees— repair roads— &c &c, and camp and Brigade guard duty— . . . I expect to pass my examination to-day— I mean to pass a very satisfactory one too if they will only give me a chance by asking questions enough for me to show them what I know   Young Barrett of Augusta is one of the board— Col's Anderson and Strawbridge the others—[10] a new uniform for the entire regiment has arrived in town. (Tupelo)— I have not seen it   it is doubtless some home-made cotton stuff, but in this rough service that is just what we want . . .

Williams

This letter met with but little interruption but it is too hot in my tent here to write or even think—

CAMP NEAR TUPELO, SATURDAY JUNE 28/62

Dear Lizzie:

Nothing occupies us now but the old fashioned routine of camp life; cramped up for want of sufficient ground for our brigade, in this little and long to be remembered field, we drove along through drill and police guard duty until all are wearied out with inaction; the *soldiers* among us are anxious to pay their warm respects to the old familiar blue coated Yanks: and the babies in beards are contriving how they may get out of the service by pleading exemption on account of over age or under age, or a pretence of physically inability. Shame confound their cowardly souls! Healthy able bodied young men leaving the army and their country's sacred and imperrilled cause, just because they *can* do so! Good Heaven! where is patriotism? where is shame? The enemy in Alabama and Mississippi— and Alabamians and Mississippians laying down their arms, and returning to their homes! If it were not for the brave and determined men who are left behind, I would pray that the war might speedily end in our utter ruin;— They deserve all that Lincolns fanatical rule could bring upon them— *let* him make abolition laws for them; *let* him give them a master from New England, and make their wifes and sisters town-women, as they have threatened in New Orleans![11] Let them lick the hand that smites them. A coward should never be a freeman— But there are those left behind who will yet save the country.

"Victory or Death" is to them no idle word, but is written in the very purpose of their life. They move on to the end undaunted; *one* is killed in a skirmish to-day, *two* to-morrow— *one* here, half a dozen there; and then when a great "clash" comes a *thousand* lay down their noble lives, and *all* are forgotten— But the war is over; our independence is achieved— and through a score of years from now the coward who left us on the 16th day of July 1862 will be feasted as an "old soldier of the war of our independence".[12] There is a record in the hearts of his comrades and another one I believe *above*, that brands him as a slave and cowardly traitor.

Yesterday the long expected examination came off— I know that it must have been highly satisfactory; I was examined less than half the time that was given to any other officer and in about five minutes convinced the board (as I think) that I was entirely at home in the tactics and competent to command the best company in the regiment; which mine is undoubtedly—

The board will make their report in a few days when they are through with the new officers— and then I will receive my appointment as a captain in the army— The path to military distinction is then open, and by faithfully and fearlessly discharging my duty I will rise in rank; and serve my country better, while I gratify the ambition; without which no man can be a good soldier. I am proud to think that I owe my position neither to money or influential friends— I entered the army unknown and unfriended. I have won my way from the ranks and I mean to win a higher place yet, if fortune favors me. Action! Action! let us have it! it is the way to live— and at the worst it is there I would die. In active service incompetency falls from high places, too weak to maintain itself in the rush of accidents and events; and there the young and friendless soldier can win a place and a name.

It is hard to be away so far from you and a quiet home and I pray that the war may soon end that I may return, but that cant be now and I must fasten my affections on the service without— as you jealously hint sometimes— forgetting my darling at home or loving her the less— I glory in the war, and I know that you would rather have me now under the sod of Shiloh, than clasp me to your bosom a living coward— for you have told me so— . . .

Williams

CAMP NEAR TUPELO MISS. JUNE 30TH 1862

"Dearest girl in the world" Mrs Traddles not excepted— though you do scold once in a while like a little Tartaress— (I wonder what you'll find to scold about in this letter?)— here I am writing to you when I should be working away at a couple of unfinished pay rolls which though lost to sight (in my valise) and not over-dear to memory, are not forgotten; writing to you, neglecting my work, roasting my brains in this hot tent, all for a little vixen who will be cross if the mail should not put this into her hands two days before the fourth of July! what a crabbed little wife for a soldier to bother his head so much about, day and night, awake and asleep!— I have found that nothing makes me forget you but a big fight; probably if some one were to ask me on the field whether or not I was married I would have to stop to think a while! (Here came in the inevitable interruption; and I have been off the whole afternoon seeing my men fitted to a new coarse uniform which has been obtained for the regiment) The air has cooled off with the decline of day; but the hour for evening parade is so near that I will soon be cut short. Glorious news from Virginia came to us last night:[13] I hope that as we gather the truth in time it will not be less favorable to our cause— The dispatches which came to Gen Bragg were read to all the troops at evening parade, and every ones heart beat the lighter at the news— but a shade of sadness could be seen over the faces of the soldiers as they listened, for they know by terrible experience what such a victory costs, They have seen the field strewn with the dead wounded and dying and witnessed all the horrible forms of mutilation that gunshot and shell can produce— They have listened to the poor dying soldier tell of his home far away and of the dear ones left to mourn his untimely fate— They can feel the glories of victory swelling in their breasts, but oh! the horrid picture that cannot ever be seperated from it in the minds of all who have fought a great battle.

Drums are beating— companies are forming under the first sergeants— I must don uniform sash and sword and go on parade

Williams—

CAMP NEAR TUPELO JULY 1, 1862

. . . It was not many minutes after I had closed my letter last evening, Lizzy; when, as if in answer to the wish contained in its last clause the orders came to "be ready to march in the morning at five o'clock with two days cooked rations and ten days raw". Here was a new excitement; and all hands were soon at work making biscuits, and fussing over fires— cartridge boxes examined and filled up with 40 rounds when any were missing— Knapsacks packed; and all the camp alive with a thousand little preparations— an hour, and again the word came down the line of our tents that "the order is countermanded"— so, I to-day am not trudging over the dusty roads in quest of a battle or a skirmish as I thought I would be. I did confidently look for a letter from you to-day— but am disappointed; you dont write as often as you might, no stars to make any more— you might at least let me hear from you every three or four days. Don't you think so too? Pass a law that when you are writing no one must disturb you, on pain of your severe displeasure; and then write away; scold as much as you please, for your crossness is the clothing in which you vainly attempt to hide your over-fondness; it don't hide it for the garment is altogether too scanty and transparent.

I have X X X X X X X X

(was interrupted here and forget now what I was about to say when called out about a fatigue detail— Confound the soldiers they are as hard to manage as a lot of children, and I often compare myself to an old woman with a large family— say, "nine small children and one at the breast" making ten as I believe— X X X X X X X X X X X X X X X X X

Called off again to correct an error made by the first sergeant on the 19th of last

March in his morning reports, which has come up again to play the deuce with calculations and returns that are being made out by the adjutant— but to return to my soldiers— the detail case was one which in spite of all my lectures occurs daily— that is— that when a detail is made for a working party one or two will say that they are sick, or sore-footed, or something of the sort, and must be excused, and as there is generally no doubt but that they really are so— of course they must get out of it— The fault is that they do not report themselves in the morning to the surgeon and be regularly excused— The troublesome fellows don't report sick in the morning— thinking that they will have very little to do in the day— and then when the sergeant puts them to work, the captain has to be sent for to get them out of the scrape— I am determined to lay down the law to them this evening after parade, and tell them that if they are sick when they hear the surgeon's call sounded and fail to report they will be made to do "*well-man's*" duty all day. . . .

Good bye—
Williams

CAMP NEAR TUPELO. JULY 2. 1862

Dear Lizzy:

I must thank you for two letters this morning— . . .

The cocoa was good, coffee is better but is too expensive   you must not be so extravagant in providing for your husband— I wish you to take any extra funds that I may have to send you for *yourself*— take a buggy ride when you want it, and then a hundred and fifty or two hundred dollars can be laid out in the manner that I wish and mentioned to you— so don't be too lavish in your expenditures for coffee— Ill try to get along without— (or with a corn or rye substitute); and when I go down home I'll use plenty of *tea* which don't cost so much and is really far better and more palatable— What do you think of my plan? isnt it good?—

Rap-atap-tap goes the drum for dinner— and the darkie wants the board that I write on for his dishes— so good bye my Lizzie—

Williams

CAMP NEAR TUPELO MISS JULY 2, 1862

Hurrah for "old Bragg" Lizzie— he is now our commander in chief— He is a fighting man; and promises in an order issued this evening to fling his banner to the breeze and lead us on to meet the insolent Yanks— Hurrah for Bragg. You will soon hear news from us of an exciting character— in his words "a few more days for reorganization and then" we'll emulate the deeds of our brethren in Virginia; and our own little exploits at Shiloh—[14]

Williams

CAMP NEAR TUPELO, JULY 3, 1862.

Capt Johnson's boy is going to town this afternoon and will carry you a letter;[15] I have not much to write nor much time to write it in   we are cleaning our decks for action by moving away all sick and disabled soldiers; and at the rate things are moving about us I should not be surprised at any moment to receive marching orders; that will stick by us long enough to get us away from this dull cramped up little camp— and into closer and more interesting proximity to the Yanks— confound their uniform!

Dont be alarmed if you should not hear from me, that is a pretty good sign that I am safe— nothing can happen to a captain, but it will be known at home right off— it is very likely that on the march my opportunities will not be frequent for sending letters home.

James M Williams

CAMP NEAR TUPELO MISS. JULY 4. 1862

Dear Lizzy:

    . . . I have just come in from our drill ground where I have been giving some theoretical instructions to my class of non-commissioned officers— we marched past the colonels tent— where he lies sick— and he has just been complimenting me for their marked improvement in marching and appearance— We were (I mean we who were reelected— and elected to office on the reorganization of the regiment) appointed in orders yesterday, and now I am *legally* entitled to the rank of captain which I have held for nearly two months— all the officers of my company passed satisfactory examinations and I am sorry that Dixon was not here to have gone in with us—

Col. Anderson is very sick and I fear that we will have to march away without him— he is a fine officer— formerly of the U.S. regular army— and it will be a great misfortune to us if we cannot be lead by him when the next fight comes off—

There are now two captains who rank above me in the regiment only— and three of the same rank— when our rank is determined therefore I will be either— third fourth or fifth.— I would rather be third of course as if I am so fortunate. my company will have the custody of the color— if the Infantry carries the colors I mean to see that they are borne steadily and bravely all the time; the [Chamberlain] "Rifles" [Company E] stood nobly by them at Shiloh as their heavy loss shows—

Williams

CAMP NEAR TUPELO. JULY 5, 1862

Dear Lizzy:

Our regiment is so reduced by our loss at Shiloh— by discharges— by the number of men that are on detached service, and the few who are absent without leave that it turns out on dress parade only a little over one hundred men— (one full company and no more—) . . . if conscripts do not come speedily— we will be thrown into other regiments— or others merged in this— and the officers discharged from service— I don't want to quit and in the event of such an end coming to the 21st, I will try my best to be transferred to a command some where in the army— and will apply for it immediately after I receive the first intimation that such a thing is about to happen— rather than go home before the war is settled I would accept a second lieutenancy again—

All this is conjecture of course— and it may be that such an unfortunate thing may never happen— and I hope not— one thing is certain— we will before long be filled up or disbanded—[16]

By Mr Crimmins I send home a pair of shoes which I have bought out of army stores— Keep them and send them to me when I need them—

Good Bye
Williams

CAMP NEAR TUPELO, JULY 5, 1862.

Dear Lizzy:

If ever I could be guilty of writing you a "cross" letter; this is a time that I would be sure to do it = under the inspiration of an aching tooth, there is no telling at what angles even the best natured man will approach his dearest friend— I am conscious of having snapped at several little things to-day which ordinarily would not have ruffled the even flow of my feelings: and unless some way can be found to exorcise the little dental demon that possesses me I am in a fair way to lose the little reputation I have acquired as a good natured man. I have been troubled by it for a week or more every day, but a few whifs of a short pipe, would always give immediate relief— last evening this remedy failed and I have passed an uneasy night, and an uncomfortable day— so soon as the pipe would not sicken me any more and I had become accustomed to it its charm was gone for the tooth— but it had still a charm for me that has almost taught me the filthy habit of smoking— on the very first opportunity I will try the effect of cold steel upon the offender.

So much for that,— considering that I run to you with complaints of all my little troubles— from a weeks illness down to a sore finger you will give me due credit for not mentioning my little tormentor for about a week at least after his first attack— This whole country is as dry as Sahara— it is said that there is now but one running stream between us and Corinth— and even the disgusting pools out of which we drank on the last march are drying up— some say that we will not move until rain comes— and others again keep alive rumors of immediate movement   there is one now current that we will have to move to-morrow morning at Daylight for Saltillo ten miles up the R.R.—

Have not heard from you for some days— The Quartermaster has no money yet and I cannot draw my pay— he will soon be in funds I think—

I have no patience to write any more my tooth claiming too much of my mind

Good Bye
Williams

John Cothran has gone down the road to Lauderdale Hospital—[17] he may go on to Mobile before he returns here— Col. Anderson has gone to Mobile sick— a bad thing for us if there is to be any fighting—

BIVOUAC NEAR SALTILLO MISS. [TUESDAY] JULY 8TH 1862

Dear Lizzy =

Any description of the hot march we made yesterday which I might make
would fail to give you an adequate conception of its fatigue. we received orders
the day before [Sunday] to march at four o'clock in the morning—[18] reveille beat
before 3— and we all were ready but from the fault of the general in command
we did not get off until long after sun-rise— the road was dry, and the dust
kicked up by thousands of feet was thick enough to strangle— on we moved and
the hot sun beamed down on our heads with all the concentrated fervor of
Mid-summer— it was horrible— [the?] orders for the march read that— any one
firing a gun on the march should be shot— and all straggling from the ranks was
prohibited all commanding officers to be held responsible that these orders are
executed— with great labor I kept my company to-gether until about ten
o'clock— I had provided myself with a small flask of liquor, and when I saw one
of the men becoming faint— I would give him a sup to keep him up— and
sometimes carry one's gun or knapsack for a while to relieve him a little— in this
way I kept them together as I said until about ten o'clock— the heat was like
that of an oven, and as we passed a fine little running stream with only a ten
minute's halt— (instead of stopping there until the cool of the evening as they
should have done) I determined— (secretly d——ing the commanding officer
for his criminal folly in thus forcing the men) to say no more to the men and
whenever they wished to leave the ranks let them go— the result was that in an
hour more I was alone— every man in the company and lieut Badger had
dropped out one after another— I kept myself out of pure bravado to show that I
could do it to myself and every body else— and so we got into camp about 4
o'clock PM worn out— brains cooking in our skulls— to judge by the way mine
felt— about twenty were all of the 21sters that kept up to the last— and most of
them were officers who not being so heavily loaded, could stand it better— it is
reported— how truly I dont know— that five or six hundred men lay down
overpowered by the heat— and five of these died on the road— the officer who
conducted such a wickedly foolish march should be court-martialed and turned
out of the service— for he is not fit even to drive an ox-cart.

By my own endurance in this case you will discover that I am strong again as
ever I was— and that I am still tough and wiry as I used to be—

I saw one very amusing scene on the road as we passed a camp of cavalry— a
darky had just come in and he imagined that we we[re] all Yankees— he had run
away from his master to join the enemy and thought that he was all right— The
crowd humored his delusion and asked him all kinds of questions about the
"rebels" and he answered them as much to our discredit as he could— He knew
where there were plenty of "rebels" and offered to lead us where we could get
them!— some of the questions asked him were very ludicrous and the unsuspect-
ing answers he gave made it one of the richest things I ever saw— up to the time
I left he was still un-deceived, and fully believed that we were the Yankees and
that he was a free nigger— We will probably stay here some little time— have
not seen any Blue Coats yet—

Dear little wife:

Once— let me record it for the delectation of our little posterity, which you say is to read in my preserved letters the history of my campaign in Mississippi and Tennesse— once, we have made a camp where we have abundance of cold water— pure and living it gushes out from under one of these dry barren hills, in an immense stream that would I believe supply our army— I never saw a finer spring— or tasted better water— If we had had the use of it since we first came to Corinth, our army would have been more vigorous— and more numerous by thousands— many a poor fellow who has gone home or to the hospitals sick (X X X X X X X an intermission of two hours occupied in making out two reports— ordnance and list of detached men absent— and in blowing up our acting adjutant for abusing unjustly my first sergt-at guard mounting X X X X X X X X X X) or now lies buried in our old camps would have been well and able to serve his country in the active campaign which lies before us— So Gen. Bragg says—

I began with the intention of writing you a long letter for once, but my time has all been taken away by calls alluded to above— and Mr Cartright who will carry this for me will leave in a few minutes—[19]

I will endeavor to obtain a few days leave of absence when Cothran returns to have this tooth extracted and some two or three others filled—

Au Revoir
James M Williams

Lizzy dear:

. . . I am again on the watch, more hopefully than ever, for Cothran, Anderson, and the Quartermaster's strong box; and if they answer my expectations my begging note [for a leave of absence] may yet be before Gen. Hardee this week.

I must mention a very remarkable fact; we had a good rain last night, and it brought wind enough with it to upset some of the officers tents and more of the soldier's flies.— my men had a good ducking— I went out in the rain, in shirt-tail costume, and brought several of them to my tent; where they packed down on the floor heads and tails like candles in a box, or a litter of pigs on a frosty morning— No-body is any the worse for it this morning, except a little loss of sleep— which is being made up manfully now by all those off duty— A little more rain like this and it is likely Gen. Bragg will put us in motion again— and then away goes all my pet plan for a long time! The clouds portend more rain. I hope it may come for it will take much to moisten the parched ground, and fill the beds of the streams.

I was going over to the 22d this morning to see John Pippen, but am told that he is still in Mobile or somewhere else—

I meant to have written you a long letter but am called off "all the Captain's being wanted immediately at the Colonel's tent"

Williams

Strange to say George Dixon's application is not back yet, and a paper asking a furlough for Mr Cartright's son— if they enquire of you the news you may tell them so—

I have a better baby story than your or rather "Mr Reynold's"—[20] Day before yesterday while our brigade was was out drilling there came up a smart little shower— Dr Payne the surgeon of our regiment ran to a little house for a shelter and arrived in the very nick of time to deliver the lady of the house— by the time the cloud had passed over the Surgeon came out on the parade ground again—The child was born and both it and the mother as well as could be expected—[21]

NEAR SALTILLO JULY 20TH 1862

This will be the shortest letter you ever saw Lizzy. I have very many to write this morning and am not very well either— the diet of the army here will be the death of me yet, I believe— and when I "peg out" you must inscribe on my tombstone "died of salt-bacon— old pickled beef (better known in camp as "mule-meat") and clammy biscuits"— I did very well on this fare for a long time— but constant dropping wears away the stone and so the hard fare begins to tell upon me seriously— But to business,— for I'm determined to make this a brief business letter— . . .

No news— no money— not much sick only a little out of order— wrote to Cothran not to hurry— think he will be back about the 25th, will immediately make my application, and if successful will be with you about the 29th; so be ready for me if I come— which I more than suspect is doubtful— if I don't you must wait more patiently than I do, for I am all impatience—

Williams

[NEAR SALTILLO, MISS.]

Lizzie, dear

This is my sorrowful anniversary, the 22nd of July [1862], and a host of painful recollections oppress me even admidst the rush of business from which I snatch time to write to you: last night I childishly gave way to my feelings, and sat til after midnight before my tent— in a melancholy reverie. I felt like one watching the dead— how vividly the parting scene came with my family came up before me as it was four years ago— The tearful group of brothers and sisters— my mother's last convulsive embrace— poor little Beckie her slight form emanciated and bent by disease— trembling in deep grief. a tear in my father's eye— and his parting words "My son, if you will go— God Bless you!"— I have never written these words before, but they ring in my ears yet— God grant that this war which separates me from you and all that is dear to me may speedily close.

I have to go off with my company this afternoon on picket duty— no Yanks there to shoot at us however— I will have beside[s] my own men the "Montgomery Guards." [Company B] the same who stood [heroically?] by my side in the battle of Shiloh.

No letters lately
Williams—

IV
Fort Morgan, Choctaw Bluff, and Oven Bluff:
August 13, 1862 – November 27, 1863

When Bragg began the rail movement of Hardee's Army of the Mississippi via Mobile into Tennessee for the ill-fated invasion of Kentucky, the depleted Twenty-first Alabama was detached, on July 26, "to duty as a part of the garrison of Mobile." It was initially assigned to Fort Morgan as a replacement for Lt. Col. Robert C. Forsyth's First Battalion Alabama Artillery. [1]

FORT MORGAN— AUG 18TH 1862

Dear Lizzy:

The "Crescent" has stopped at our wharf for a few minutes on her way to town I am well—

Williams

FORT MORGAN ALA. AUGUST. 18TH 1862.

Dear Pa;

I have just learned that the steamer Yorktown will attempt to run the blockade to-night, and hasten to write a line in the hope that it may reach you.

I heard from you last in January through Mr. Proctor and the Fortress Monroe [Virginia] flag of truce.

Knowing the views I entertained of the political questions which culminated in the present war you will not be surprised to learn that I am in the army.— I entered the service last October as first sergt. of the "Washinton Light Infantry" an old Mobile company: we were stationed at Fort Gaines— one of the defences of Mobile until March when we went to Fort Pillow Tenn— after a fortnight we were removed to Corinth, where I was elected 2d Lieut to fill a vacancy in the company— In the absence of the two senior officers I commanded my company ("A" 21st Ala Regt) in the bloody battle of Shiloh— or Pitsburg as you call it— I was specially mentioned in the colonel's official report for my services— and though out of 550 men we counted 217 in the list of killed, wounded and missing I was untouched— After the battle I was appointed adjutant; and soon after that Captain of my old company in which position I remain.

Lizzy my dear wife is in Mobile, She is indeed my good angel. I feel that I posess in her that inestimable treasure a good wife. Her disposition is cheerful and always hopeful— not the slightest jar has ever occurred to mar, even for a moment, our happiness; and the first angry or fretful word is yet to be spoken. She is a good soldier and bears my absence, and all the uncertainties that surround me bravely, and with a cheerful confidence that few women can command. I have no more children. Mr Conning is still my friend and has continued my salary: of course I only drew on him for what I needed while my pay was small. Mr. Osborne corresponds with me, I have a long letter from him before me which contains many expressions of love and respect for you.

My health is remarkably good— as it was when I was in the West, I find that the life out-of-doors improves me: with the exception of a two-weeks illness (billious attack) last May my health has been unimpaired.

Write to me occasionally, addressing the letters to Havana, and I think that I will sometimes be able to get them here.

My whole soul is in the sucess of our struggle for independence; which *sooner or later we will win*— If I should not survive the war to see you again be assured that I feel that my life has been devoted to a good cause: Love to Ma and the children— grandpa and all friends.—

James—

I hope that John's adventurous spirit has not led him to join in the Crusade against us—[2]

FORT MORGAN AUGUST. 19TH 1862.

Dear Lizzy:

. . . I am on duty to day as "officer of the day" and have not time to write as much as I would,— . . .

Last evening we had an interesting target firing by the forts guns and those of the gunboat lying near the wharf— I suppose that as the wind was favorable it is possible that you could have heard us in Mobile. . . .

I wish that you would make me a pair of pants of that blue blanket which I left at home— make them full in the leg, and large at the foot. with a black or dark blue cloth stripe on the seam so   wide— that is an inch and a quarter— if you cant get the material for the stripe put in a white cord, but I much prefer the stripe as it is according to regulation. if you think that the blanket is *very much* better, a sample of which I enclose I will send it to you— still I would rather use the other one which is already cut—

— Capt Dorgan[3] has a pair of blanket pants and they do very well for every day service and really look well, though they are rough—

Good bye. write by every boat: send down the pair of shoes I sent to you from Tupelo—

Williams

FORT MORGAN AUG 23D 1862.

Dear Lizzy:

Send me by the next boat my letter file— and if you can find it my old pocket memorandum book: at the request of my colonel I have undertaken to collect the materials for a history of the 21st Regt which will be written by an able man, and included in a work devoted to the Alabama troops in this war— and the letters written to you will assist me some in my task— There is nothing new here except that we are about to elect a major to the regiment, dont know who it will be yet as the subject is not discussed and excites very little interest yet— I wish you could have been to-day at our dinner table to discuss with us the merits of a fine red-fish the first available fruits of my fishing tackle   it was a fine fellow of some 15 or 20 pounds— and made a superb dinner. I have written a letter home which is aboard the Yorktown, and she is waiting to run the blockade.

> *Good bye*
> *Williams*

FORT MORGAN. AUG 25. 1862.

Dear Lizzy:

Your letter came by the Saturday boat, and with it the shoes, which I wanted for one of the men who was badly afflicted with bare feet—

I am so occupied with my duties, drill, writing, and the time that I must devote to the study of artillery practice and theory; that you must not be surprised or vexed if my letters are not so long or so frequent as they were; indeed I feel so near home that it seems useless to write so often; if I were at home of course I would not write at all and the further I am away the oftener will I do it— dont you see? my little jealous wife!— We are to have another target firing this afternoon and before many minutes I will have to hasten off to witness it, with my company, in answer to the "long roll"

I have been assigned a battery of four 24 [pounder] and one 42 [pounder] rifled guns and when the fight comes hope to be able to make my respects in a very elegant manner to my old enemies the Yanks— It seems to me that if their vessels should try to run the gauntlet I could bore them with all ease— But time will tell—

I have procured a pass for you which with a pass from the provost Marshall will let you come down when you like, come any time and often— I want you to see my battery and how and where we live, and maybe I'll be able to go home with you tho I dont *much* rely upon that. Come along then, the sooner the better, I want to see you often as possible and the only way to succeed is for you to come here—

Now for a *secret*— I believe that you can keep one— though you are a woman (a dear one and pretty too) Col. Stewart asked me to walk down to the boat with him on his way to town and told me, quite to my surprise that Col. Anderson was determined to hold an election for the office of Major and that I had the preference at head quarters and that when the question comes up they will throw into the scale all their influence to have me elected— if they do, and the election does come off, I will certainly be called to that post: still as the thing is uncertain, the election not yet ordered: and the possibility that it may be delayed for three or four weeks; I dont want to say any thing about it, or even to let any-body know that I will be a candidate— if I obtain the office a regular promotion two grades higher will make me colonel of a regiment before another year— See what a field is open for my ambition, what a glorious field for a man who loves the art and practice of war for its own sake as I do— Those "old military books" that you used to dislike so heartily may yet give me an opportunity to win a more honorable and conspicuous place in the history of my country— If this opening should fail me I stand a very poor chance for promotion for a long time   I will be sixth captain only, and regular promotion will not raise me for many months if ever during the war. I have lively hopes that this will turn up to my advantage.[4]

My company is recruiting slowly, I have now forty two men at the fort. two of whom are sick— we are crowded into the closest kind of quarters; but are promised more room by the first of the month. I suppose that Miss Phoe will be down to-morrow and if she comes I can send this letter by her. . . .

Col. Anderson has brought his wife and children down here and lives at home as comfortably as though there was no war, or danger of one— I wish to Heaven that I were a[s] well off in that particular— How happy I will be when I am again permitted to be with you— to enjoy your sweet and cheerful company day after day— without counting the days of my leave-of-absence— and fearing no courts martial or the reprimands of superior officers for overstaying them! Those will be happy days to me— when they come; and I mean to leave my record on the bloody pages of this war's history, so that I will have a consciousness of duty well done, and an honorable name to bear away to my peaceful retreat— Then my darling Lizzy will come to be petted every day as of yore— wont you? . . .

FORT MORGAN AUG 26TH. 1862.

Dear Lizzy:

The smoke of the boat is visible in the north. How it brings back to my mind the old Fort Gaines days when it was the signal for me to take my pen and write you your regular letter; I feel the old influence now, and the warning cloud sends me to my desk, forgetful almost of the fact that your letter was written yesterday and is ready for the mail.

The Yorktown went out last night; I stood upon the glacis of the fort and watched for half an hour, but the fleet showed no rockets, nor fired a gun, and I know that she got through safely— I hope that she will not be picked up on the way, and will be equally successful in entering the port of Havanna. My letter will then undoubtedly reach my fathers house safely, and what a relief it will be to hear from me again after so many months of uncertainty and fear: I tell them to write to me occasionally at Havana and I will endeavor to get the letters from thence by some of the boats that are dodging the blockaders— What would I not give to hear from the dear ones again— and I know that my letter will be equally welcome.[5]

I expect to send you some money soon   the pay-master is absent, but will certainly be here in a few days. and when he comes will have the money I hope—

The officers raised something more than a hundred dollars and sent up to town for a seine, we look for it down on to-day's boat, and will have abundance of fish, and more fun in catching them— we now and then catch a magnificent redfish with the hook and line, sometimes a shark

FORT MORGAN. AUG 27. 1862.

Dear Lizzy:

I certainly expect to meet you on the boat to-morrow and to place this letter in your hands: but I will not do as you have so often done me, by relying upon your arrival so much as to neglect to write— If our positions were changed, and you were here in command of my glorious old company (A), and I at home, my only chance would be to come down for you would in expectation of my visit delay writing for weeks— Maybe that is the reason I never try to tell you when I'm coming home or expect to make the effort? what do you think— I have saved up your present which came with such a sour message; and if I can keep Cothran and Dixon from stealing it, will return it too you. If the message *was* sour I forgive you, by sending it by such a sweet messenger you made it rather pleasant than otherwise to take.— Next time you have something crabbed to say to me dont put it into such a pretty mouth as that of Miss Bond— I love her like— everything! What do you think of that? I sent you a letter and the fragment of another by her— Dixon has something to tell you he says so you had better come down and see about it at once. I won't come home for a long time. have plenty to do now with all kinds of work on hands from commanding my hot shot-battery in drill to drawing the seine— neck deep. I'll be officer of the day to-morrow and if you come will have to watch that you dont run away with me as the Miss Smith's did— upon a time— I hope you will come and that the boat will make a long stay= At last we have a prospect for more room, two companies will be moved from this post which will enable us to expand comfortably. I will then only be obliged to share a room with the officers of one company (other than my own) instead of four— as it is now.

The imbroglio of the offices are not yet fixed up. And as I hinted it will be a month before they are: my hopes are lively, but there is no knowing what may turn up to my advantage, or the contrary, in that time.

It is five minutes of five P.M. and the drum will beat for drill at five— X X X and so it did only five minutes earlier, and I had to drop my pen and march my men into the fort, an hour's drill has driven out of mind what it was I was hastening to say in the beginning of the sentence. A party has just been made up to draw the seine to-night after dark, and of course I'm one,— we will appear in a fancy costume of shirt and drawers.

A sail-boat load of ladies has just arrived and I suppose that they have come to see the dress parade: they are Navy Coveites and I hope they are pretty as I think they are viewing them from a distance.[6]

Williams

10 o'clock P.M.— have had a glorious time fishing caught fish enough for the whole regiment— just got back.—

Send me an old pair of pants to wear in the water and a pair of old shoes and hat if you can find 'em— be particular about the old shoes for I never go in the water without fearing for my feet: what with cat-fish— and "stinger-ees" and oyster-shells on the banks feet are in danger.

Thursday morning is a hot day and if you come you will be well baked before
you get off from us—

— Dixon and the fishermen are off again— and the fun goes on without me—
It is not often that I mention the quality of my pens, but the one that I have used
for this letter demands a notice for once, and has been anathematized at every
line—

Williams

FORT MORGAN SEPT. 6, 1862.

Dear Lizzie:

Great sport we had last night fishing— two large sacks full of scaly characters
rewarded our toil— or, more correctly speaking our frolic— Abundance for all
concerned, and half the regiment besides. I wish you could have seen the party
as it appeared by moonlight in fishing costume, consisting of superannuated
clothes hats and shoes; Some of the scenes were extremely ludicrous, One would
cry out "What is that man doing? why dont you haul in on that lead line? Who
is that fellow any-how?"— "Only me!" and the voice tells that the soldier has
been ordering some captain or other superior officer about like a deck-hand—
Then follows a laugh at the expense of the two— Speaking of scenes however I
must mention the glorious one of the day before yesterday— We were out on
parade— when the heavy sound of a gun at sea, followed in quick succession by
others until it sounded like a naval battle arrested our attention— and orders
came from Col. Powell to dismiss the parade and man the batteries—[7] The
troops were marched into the fort in double quick time; and after seeing all the
company of my regiment properly stationed at their guns I mounted the parapet
and witnessed a most exciting and magnificent scene— a long low steamer was
coming through the Yankee fleet amid a perfect storm of shot and shell— she
steamed on for life and gradually emerged from her enemies, out-running them,
and entered the ship channel; the shells following her with that wild cry, which
could be heard here distinctly, and bursting all around and above her.— she
exhibited the signal of a friend, and coming opposite to the fort came to, in
answer to its friendly gun— It was a bold thing that she attempted, and nobly
executed— Imagine the vexation of the Yankees to see her run the gauntlet so
fearlessly and so successfully— Bringing them all to shame . . .

Show the $20 note I gave you to some one that is a judge and see if it is
genuine the $100 that I got with it was counterfeit— in the genuine twenties the
two hearts between the **X X** in the lower right hand corner do not touch $\Diamond$ $\lhd$
in the spurious they do thus: $\lhd\!\!\times\!\!\rhd$ —If it is not good send it to Mr Conning and
tell him that I got it of[f] Paymaster Vass along with the $100 that I sent him
Thursday—[8] I suppose that the $20 is all right— Buy me some white gloves if
you can find them— if you can't get white get buff— and if *neither*, any color
that you *can* find—

Williams—

Send down my old worsted sash for Cothran—

FORT MORGAN TUESDAY
SEPT. 16, 1862

Dear Lizzy =

The stormy winds again, in real old last-winter- Fort Gaines-style have blown upon us from all points of the compas, for the past two days— And still rush round our house and through several broken panes of glass furiously as if they were in league with Lincoln and assaulting us in our very beds—

The storm has for a while put a stop to the manoeuvres of the fleet— and the desultory skirmishing with big guns, and ten-inch bombs that resulted—

Some of those who were inclined to believe that the Yanks contemplate an attack, are now proclaiming that they evidently are but waiting for the equinoxial gale to blow before commencing operations

The same persons often remark that if the enemy come and make the attack they will come prepared to succeed without doubt— I believe that they *will* come prepared— so they did at Vicksburg— so they did at Richmond and the two Mannasses![9]

I hope and believe that in the attack upon us a like fate will overwhelm them! at any rate we can suffer some in order to punish them for their temerity—

I send the basket of clothes to-day— and hereafter it will go up regularly on Tuesday—

Maybe I'll come up as soon as I hear from Stockley and Scott that my uniform is finished— it should be done about the last of this week

The next time you have anything to send to me, I want you to put your ambrotype in the package— I forgot to bring it with me when I was home— and I have a longing for it every time that I feel homesick or lonesome— . . .

FORT MORGAN. FRIDAY EVENING
SEPT. 19. 1862,

Well! it is not necessary to say that the hope in which I wrote a line to you yesterday was vain— you know that as well as I; may be you have listened for my step and watched from the window all day— Yet I believe that I am the more disappointed of the two— I was so anxious to see my sweet Lizzie again— and so penitent in the matter of the farewell kiss which you say I omitted (Speaking of the kiss— don't you think that it was ungrateful in you to remind me of one lost, when for two days you had received them gratis by the hundred? you might in consideration of the many, have forgiven that one; which was in the presence of company too?— and you know that, to me, that robs them of half their sweets?) I was doubly anxious to go. But the Crescent didn't go so I couldn't— She did make a flying trip to town last night but as I had made one such excursion not long ago I did not care to see the Mobile wharves again by starlight without the privilege of seeking you.—

I sat up last night till past midnight to watch the [steamer] Cuba— she made a faux-pas which hapily was not fatal, got aground a short distance from the fort, and for a while we thought we would not get her off before morning—

In that case the Crescent (which had just returned from town) was ready—
and I would have gone out to the vessell with two companies to astonish the
Yankees if they had attempted to board her from their launches— But as I said
she succeeded in moving back again— and prevented our possible adventure—
it would have been an exciting little fight if it had happened— I hope she will be
able to slip out to-night without a mis-hap— X X X X X X X X X X Quite a little
breeze is blowing this Saturday morning [September 20]— and if you are now on
the boat you are probably a little sea-sick— The morning is beautiful— and
barring the sickness you have a fine day for your visit— I have made arrangements for my washing here— and will not send it up in future— Capt. Cluis will
deliver this— unless you come and receive it with your own hand from mine—
                                                              Williams

*Williams apparently received a two-week furlough, or the letters are missing between
September 19 and October 2, 1862.*

                                                       FORT MORGAN OCT 2, 1862.
Dear Lizzy:
    A move is on the tapis again— part if not all of our regiment will be sent to
man some batteries up the Alabama river— The *probable* division will be— four
companies to remain here under Lt. Col Stewart— and the other four under
Col. Anderson and myself to take the river batteries. I don't care how they
manage it much; but if I could get charge of the detachment I would be glad to
make the change: I dont like the prospect of remaining here after part of the
regiment is ordered off—
    It is likely that we will know all about it when the boat comes—
    "A Kingdom for a horse!" This move will demand of me the long expected
horse, and I must have it. A dismounted major would never do outside of a fort.
    I will add a line when the boat comes, if it brings any news.
    Give my love to those I love
                                                              Williams
Boat's here— nothing certain known— will move probably in the course of a
week.
    Send you a brush which I find in my trunk the ink on it will do no harm—

*On Oct. 6, 1862, the first Battalion (Companies A, B, C and F), Anderson
commanding, was ordered by Special Order No. 236 up to Choctaw Bluff (Fort
Stonewall Jackson) and Oven Bluff (Fort Sidney Johnston) on the Alabama and
Tombigbee Rivers, respectively. The Second Battalion (Companies D, E, I, and K:
194 enlisted men and officers), Stewart commanding, remained at Fort Morgan.*[10]

                                                       CHOCTAW BLUFF. OCT 7. [1862]
Dear Lizzy:
    In a few minutes I will move over to my post "Oven Bluff " and as soon as

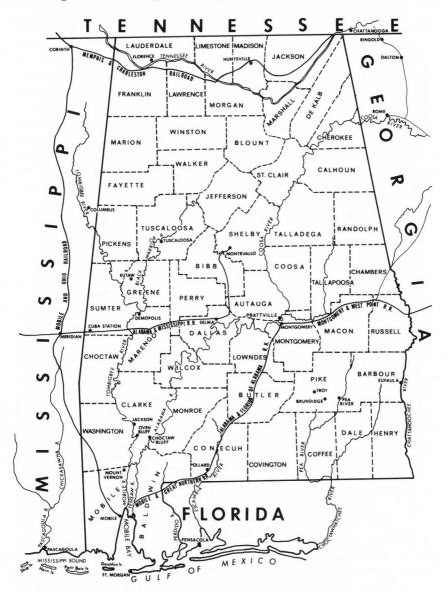

MAP OF ALABAMA

possible will write to you= I am determined to bring you up here if you are willing, and if I cant find a house, will build a cabin— are you willing to live in a cabin; as Mrs Anderson expects to live in tents for a while you will not be singular— I will have command of the post— if I have to build a cabin I presume you can have such articles of furniture as we will require in Mobile— and a good negro girl would complete the Establishment   I would not like to purchase much; for there is no certainty that I will be here for a long time— I would therefore rent what we need and buy as little as possible—

When you come you will be out of danger when Mobile is attacked.

All we will want is a set of bed room furniture and some cooking and table utensils— If you know where you can hire them write to me— if not I think that I may get Mr Conning to let me have what I want—

Write to Choctaw Bluff and have your letters put on board the *Alabama River* boats which leave every evening at 4 o'clock.

Williams

Lizzy, pregnant for the second time, lived with James at Oven Bluff from October 1862 until May 1863, when she returned to Mobile to have her baby.

CHOCTAW BLUFF MAY 6, 63[11]

Dear Lizzy:

I have been ordered to the command of this post— Col. Anderson having left for Mobile last evening— If I remain here and you desire it you may come and keep house for me when you are well— the Colonel's house is large and pleasantly situated about a mile and a half from the Bluff— There is a good Kitchen and poultry house— by the way speaking of poultry reminds me to report that your hen has now a lively brood of seventeen chickens all of which were alive and doing well when I left Oven Bluff this morning   As soon as the Colonel moves his family I will take posession of the quarters and gather up your chickens and pig and all the properties ready for a grand reception when you come— It will be a glorious place for you— ever so many square yards of planed floors which you can have scrubbed to your hearts content!—

I received your letter this morning and the papers and was so glad to hear from you; short as the time is since we parted I have felt very lonely and deserted and I pray that we may be again together very soon— Col. Anderson will apply for my promotion in Mobile and it is probable that I may be ordered down for examination in a few days—[12] Capt Cothrans Co [A] and Smiths [C] went up the river to Selma this morning— Dixon is with them but will return in a few days unless there is a chance for a fight—[13] He says he had not been to see you yet— King has been very sick— for some hours dangerously even— but is better— His face is swelling rapidly and I fear that before long he will be wishing for you to make poultices again

Write often to Choctaw Bluff

Williams

CHOCTAW BLUFF MAY 8, 63

Lizzie dear, you take my very breath away with surprise and pleasure— It is well that I have some control of my very restive and excitable nerves or they might have led me into extravagancies, this morning, that would ill accord with the dignity of the post commander— My first impulse was to go home in all the eagerness of a boy when "school's out"— and though I can not deny that I feel the same desire lingering in my breast yet, I have made up my mind to wait patiently for an order to report to Mobile for examination— which I think will come in a few days— I am reading it now and try hard to keep my mind on my work— but my wife and the black haired baby charge into my thoughts— break my lines of battle— harass my columns and demolish my squares in four ranks in a manner unknown before to military art— Sometimes I am almost tempted to disband my battalions, and appoint a rendesvous before the board of Examiners— and even when I marshall them *there*, a similar charge may put them all to flight again incontinently

King is delighted and has notified me that now there is no necessity for him to marry as "the boy" (So he calls him) will be the heir to all his property! I have written enough to tire you in the reading— So good bye till the next boat—

This letter will go down to-morrow morning— Until you can write yourself I must beg Mrs Turner Phe— or Mrs Parrot to drop me a line every day—

Williams

CHOCTAW BLUFF MAY 9, 63

Dear Lizzie:

My expectations of a letter to-day were disappointed— I did have the one which Mrs Turner sent to Oven Bluff, but it seems to have been written about the Same time as the first— If I don't receive orders in the mean time I will try to come down by the last of next week; for I am burning to see my darling wife and her babe— Now don't look for me too certainly for it may be that I can't come; but I will *try*— I am so glad that you are with those who can care for you so much better than would have been possible for me to do here— even if I knew how to do it as well as they— The boat is coming now, for which my yesterdays letter has been waiting so long

Goodbye
Williams

CHOCTAW BLUFF MAY 11. 1863

Lizzie dear, You thought I was long about writing to you— did you not? But I was not to blame— the boats have been behind time, and some of them, I hear, detained at Selma to transport troops. Tell Mrs Turner she does not satisfy me entirely by reporting you "bright as a button" on the seventh of May, and then leaving me to the cultivation of a fertile imagination. I cannot hear from you and the babe too often, and until I come down I would be so gratefull for a single line every day, that the trouble it would put her too would be nothing in comparison to the load of obligation which I would cheerfully shoulder—

Dr. Key has returned— and though I have not seen him I learn from Col Sherron that he brags on the baby very much— I envy him for having seen you before I could—

Mrs. Anderson will not move down to Fort Morgan for some ten days or two weeks I think— When she does I expect to occupy her house, and establish the pig, chickens and turkey-hen at once in new quarters— and then wait patiently as possible for you to come and take command of me and the rest of the poultry—

Williams

CHOCTAW BLUFF— MAY 12, 1863—

Dear Lizzy:

Still I have no orders to Mobile— I have made up my mind to go on a flying visit, whether they come or not, about the last of this week. So if nothing unusual occurs you will see me, or what is more and better I will see you very soon. To-morrow I will go with several of the officers here to spend the day at Mrs. Davis'— we expect a good dinner and a good time.

Have not heard from the two Companies that were ordered to Selma, and Dixon has not returned as he said he would "if there was no chance for a fight"— still I believe that they are at Selma with a very microscopic specimen of the Chance in question.

I am not pleased with the exchange of the little old house on the hill— the fine shade trees and constant breeze of Oven Bluff— for this level— uninteresting— hot and dusty place— but when I get the Col's house, it will be a great change for the better and you will like the location almost as well as the other— and the house much better— Indeed you will be delighted with the house and the surrounding grounds   a fine gallery on the shady side of the house and a broad open Hall through the centre makes it very pleasant.

Williams

CHOCTAW BLUFF MAY 23 [1863]

Dear Lizzy:

Col Anderson came up on the boat with me with orders to take command of Choctaw Bluff—[14] for the present I will return to Oven Bluff but I think there is no doubt but I will soon be ordered to Fort Morgan— I am affraid that our little plans are sadly interrupted by this new arrangement but will see in a few days

I will pack up my bed this morning and move over to Oven at once—

Good bye
Williams

OVEN BLUFF MAY 23D 1863

Dear Lizzie:

I am as you see at the old place— Col. Anderson was ordered back to Choctaw; and came up on the boat with me. I will remain here until I receive orders, there is but little doubt but I will be sent to Fort Morgan in a few days

King I am glad to see is nearly well— though he has been sick— He is delighted with the accounts of baby George[15] and is well pleased, to judge from appearances as if Mrs. Turner's suggestion had been carried out

If I should be here three weeks and have a prospect of remaining longer you can come up if you like— but I think there is [little] prospect of that— Mrs Turner had better write to Mrs. Ainsworth that you will not want her servant— I wrote to you from Choctaw this morning but you will probably receive this letter first

Williams

Oven Bluff May 30. 63

Dear Lizzie:

I have a letter from you and Mrs. Turner's note— Could not get her a bale of [corn] "shucks" for this boat, but will try if possible to find it for her by the next trip— all the plantation hands are so busy that I may not be able to induce Mac to put it up for me— have not seen him since my arrival—

The pig is large and fat and I have a notion to send it down to Mrs. Turner next week—

If you can spare me $50 enclose it in a letter and give it to Taylor   Sergt. Burke who goes down to-night will call at Conning's for it.[16]

I have not heard from my promotion— nor anything to indicate that I am not forgotten entirely here at Oven Bluff— it is quite a disappointment of my Fort Morgan expectations— I am not anxious to remain here, for even if I did I would not like to bring you up while there is so much evidence every day of the sickliness of the place— many of the soldiers are sick of billious fever and chills & fever— I still hope to be sent down to the Fort— and if I should go before your money letter comes I will direct King to open it and apply the proceeds to the payment of the few debts that are still unpaid here— So that he may know it from your other letters, mark it "$50" on the outside—

I hope that you have had no serious trouble with your breast and that the baby is still able to whip you at pleasure—

Good bye
Williams

My homespun coat will be "done" in a few days all— ready for a pair or two of stars.

Oven Bluff. May 31. '63

Dear Lizzie:

Your letter of yesterday, with a newspaper, caught me in bed this morning early. . . .

Capt. Johnston and his wife are both sick— not very seriously, however.

I saw Mrs Scott on the Clipper last night as it went down, and delivered to her two children in good order— She had much to say about the baby and you which the short stop of the boat did not give me time to hear

I have a letter from "Henry J" [Osborne] which expresses much interest in you and I; very kindly— Mrs. Osborne is particularly anxious to hear from me, and does me the honor to call me still a member of the family— I wonder (but it is an ungracious thought) if she should have so maintained the cousinship if I had remained a private soldier? I dare say she would after all, for I really believe she had considerable regard for me, which she was willing enough to acknowledge and exhibit when it would not interfere with her ambitious struggle for position— Aside from her ambition she is a fine woman, with many excellent qualities of heart and head.— Henry [Jr.] was at Vicksburg when last heard from; and I have no doubt has had a taste of his quality within the last few days, in the fights there—[17]

Mc'Cabe has completed my coat and made a very good fit— I will have him to make up the other uniform at once; and I wish you would ask Mrs Turner to buy any trimmings that are necessary— you will have to purchase lining if all my old coats are played out— I can buy the buttons when I come down— I wish it to be made here because it will not cost near so much as at Stockly's—[18]

The clucking of an old hen at the door reminds me to say that I believe I wont send any chickens down for some time, a number of them are setting and I'll put them in charge of King— if she wants the pig she can have it as a present when the Clipper goes down next week—

Good bye
Williams

OVEN BFF JUNE 6 1863

Dear Lizzie = I am well— received your note with $50— Send the pig down to Mrs Turner as a present— Col Anderson has written to Mobile, to have me sent to Fort Morgan and if the order is not granted I will go down on leave sometime next week

Williams

James was ordered to command the Second Battalion at Fort Morgan and received a furlough to visit Lizzy and his newborn son in Mobile.

FORT MORGAN JULY 2 63

Dear Lizzie:

It seems like old times to be writing you from Fort M. and thinking of the time to the next trip of the boat, and the little letter in the white envelope that is so confidently expected— In those old times (— not so very old either) there was no thinking of the dear little black headed Dixon at home, who so often tries your patience and your strength— I am better every day— the breeze is delightful, and soothes me to easy and refreshing sleep, which is only broken by raids of fleas who muster in great strength here— Think I'll have no more night sweats.

I don't know when I shall come up   Capt Cluis is not here, will be down to-morrow— I will not make any permanent mess arrangement until I see him— unless it is necessary I will not be up for some time— I find that my duties are very light— the old brigade officer of the day has been abolished: and my hardest work will be to drill the Battalion every other day . . .

FORT MORGAN JULY 4, 1863

Dear Lizzy:

I have not heard from you since I came down— I regret among other things that I have not the letters belonging to persons here, which were left at home— I have been pretty well until yesterday, when I had a violent head-ache and nasuea which kept me in bed all day— I feel quite fresh this morning—

I am messing with Capt Cluis and the [Mobile] Cadet [Company K] Officers: and as they have plenty of mess furniture I will not require any of my stock at present—

There being no particular business for me in Mobile, I will not ask for leave of absence for some time, unless you should want me or something unusual turn's up—

Mosquitos and fleas are rampant here— the bar protects me from the first but the fleas worry me not a little

I look for a letter from you to day

Williams

FORT MORGAN [TUESDAY] JULY 7, 63

Dear Lizzy:

I have nothing important to write— all feel very sorely the loss of Vicksburg [on July 4] which we learn by telegraph.— but are not discouraged, it is the fortune of war, our cause is not fallen; brave hearts and strong arms are left to our Country, and will save it yet—

I may possibly go to the city next Thursday but cant tell yet— I have really very little to call me there and should save up my application for some urgent occasion— It seems strange that I have never received a package from you. pillow cases, white pants &c— I hope that you have not sent them for in that case they are lost— your letter says nothing on the subject— I look for a letter and an explanation by the boat to-day   Col. Powell's house was struck by lightning last night— no-body hurt

Your letter and package came—

Goodbye
Williams

FORT MORGAN [WEDNESDAY] JULY 8. '63

Dear Lizzie:

I was pleased to hear from King and his good opinion of George— although that was a foregone conclusion: He could not help thinking him a perfect miracle of a baby if he tried ever so stoutly. I hope the young angel/chap/devil gives you less trouble by day and sleeps as well by night as when I saw him last— a week ago!

Good bye
Williams

FORT MORGAN JULY 13, 1863

Dear Lizzy:

All's quiet as usual— two or three blockade running steamers are out and as many blockaders are absent from the fleet: whether they are in chase or only cruising on suspicion we don't know— I am interested in one for there's a letter on it for my mother— I hope the Yank's won't get her— I mean the steamboat not Mother.

I am quite well and strong— no sweat last night— the result is I'll be able to go on drill for the first time this evening— thanks to the doctor or the trip home— or both— or a good constitution— I don't know where to place the credit you see

A new difficulty besets the visitors to the Forts   they are not permitted to enter and ramble about at pleasure, unless they have permits from the Commander of the Post to obtain which they must be well vouched for by officers here.— I am not sorry for too good opportunities were given to spies to be lost upon that dangerous and I fear numerous class— Yes we *do* all regret one thing, and that is the tri-weekly exhibition of pretty ankles— not to mention legs— which the dear ladies furnished us in climbing up and down the steep steps to the ramparts.

Williams

FORT MORGAN JULY 18, 1863

Dear Lizzy:

In a few minutes the boat will be here, and I will make this brief

I am almost as well as ever I have been, and for two nights have had no night-sweats— Day-ones I have plentifully— the weather is squally and between the blows we have a calm that is almost suffocating— it is strange weather for this place and will soon be over I hope—

Two more of our steamers went out last night, and were discovered by the Yankees, for there was a terrible excitement among them and whole broadsides fired— I presume that they chased them but it may be that our boats have escaped in the dark[19]

Williams

FORT MORGAN [MONDAY] JULY 20, 1863

Dear Lizzy:

You know how I detest a fool, how I fume and fret and make use of forbidden language— under the breath— when I am forced to undure their society and conversation for many minutes at a time— A board partition is all that seperates me from four or five of the most contemptible sort; I am forced to listen to every word of their delectable conversation and have no relief to my feelings but a half smothered anathema when they are more than usually noisy and silly. After all, I should blame nothing but the fortune which gave me a board partition instead of a thick wall of seperation = for according to my theory which you have often heard, a large class of our fellow citizens are born fools and can't help it— Consequently are not to blame.

Without altogether disclaiming the connection of ideas, I mention that I have just read "Beulah" and of all the muddy— "flat stale and unprofitable" works that I have lately worried through I think it bears off the palm[20]

After the boat left Saturday a letter from you was received dated the 15th it had been in Mobile Post Office and was advertised, it told me to look out for some clothes on Tuesday's boat which I will do; So many things are stolen from the boat that I am almost affraid to risk anything valuable on it in future—

I wish you could have some of the fine fish which we get here; right fresh out of the water— for instance at dinner today we had— baked red fish— pompin— blue fish and trout— a flounder for breakfast— all of them the very finest fish that swim the bay— and all but two or three hours out of the water, and cleaned while "kicking"— It is well that we can get fish and crabs (for we had them too and I forgot to mention it) for without them it would be sorry fare for us; many a meal that is now good enough, would be as bare as though it came from the larder of good old "Mother Hubbard" of the nursery rhyme.

I am very anxious to go home again and maybe I will on Saturday or Saturday week. You spoiled me last winter by coming to keep house for me; and now I want to be running back all the time to see you— If I were a believer in religion I would pray on my knees every day for the end of the war to come quickly, that I might go to my wife and babe, where my duty and inclination call me— it will come I hope soon even without my formal prayers—

It is most likely that I will not go up until the Saturday at the end of the month so that I can draw my pay while in town. If you can get some one to wait on the baby for you, you might come down on that day, the ride will be pleasant and then I can go home with you—

Tuesday, July 21

The shirts came to-day I have written by every boat—

Williams received another brief furlough to visit Lizzy.

FORT MORGAN AUG 7, 1863.

Dear Lizzy:

All females except laundresses are ordered away from the fort, and we are clearing the decks for action: I begin to feel more of the old spirit, and could hail the booming of the enemy's cannon and the bursting of shells— The grand martial music!— with some delight— I believe Admiral Farragut will find Ft Morgan a refractory nut to crack when he has a mind to try it—[21] I want to fight for a victory just now to stop the bragging of the Yankees who are really persuading themselves that the rebellion is crushed— I don't believe that they have commenced the crushing process yet but I would like to see their confidence clipped— Shiloh was the dawn that followed darkness deeper than that which overshadows us now Let Fort Morgan and Mobile follow a victory at Charleston and dispel the cloud of to-day!

I have heard that the Sub-marine is off for Charleston, I suppose that Dixon went with it.—[22] with favorable circumstances it will succeed, and I hope to hear a report of its success before this month is out; still there are so many things which may ruin the enterprise that I am not so sanguine of its triumph as Dixon. May-be I'll add a line when the boat comes to-morrow— Good bye—
Williams

FORT MORGAN AUG 10, '63[23]

Lizzie Dear

Whenever I go to write to you I am always so overcome by my thoughts of you and baby, and by a half childish impatience to run away to see you, that I am almost unable to compose myself to the task— and never did they ruin a letter more than they promise to do for this one: I began by staring at the sheet for a quarter of an hour in a brown study dipping my pen in the ink at intervals, but my mind busy with pictures of Master George asleep and awake, in bed and perched like a bird on his mothers arm— and in-all kinds of temper, from violence of baby passion down to the good nature that lies on the bed and crows by the hour.— Whatever you may think, I assert that the train of ideas was *not* suggested by the stain on the sheet above.

The sun is low and before long the drum will call me off to dress parade— what an every day hum-drum life it is we lead— drill twice a day for an hour— dinner you can wager five to one roast beef (you know how I like that) and fish— with a dessert of bread and molasses— watermelons no more— What a glorious awakening of all our faculties it would be if the Yanks were to come in and batter away at us— In five minutes we would all be different men and some of us would not regret the change— I want to see an artillery fight betwen the fort and navy— without it I will never look back upon my experiences in the war as complete—

r - r - r - rat - tat - tat the drum calls— may be I may take up my pen in the morning again— cant write any more to-day   after parade comes supper, after supper dark and I couldnt burn a candle if I had it without closing the windows and putting myself in a stew—

Co D's laundress presented us with a child of the regiment but the poor little thing could not conquer the difficulties of Fort Morgan life and was burried to-day

Williams

FORT MORGAN AUG 12, 1863

The weather, Lizzy, that unfailing subject for conversation, demands a "mere-mention" to-day, as having attained to the sixth degree of comparison— for some time it has progressed steadily through the other five— hot hotter hottest Hottentot Hottentotter— but yesterday it arrived at the stage which can only be described as the very hotten-tottest, that is compatible with existence to any one but a Salamander or the Fire King, who went into the oven with his hands full of poultry, shut the door— and brought them out roasted to a turn—

Which feat I shall always think was nearly equal to that performed by you in roasting the big turkey, of happy memory before the fire— Not a breath of air is stirring— away up the bay the thunder is rumbling to call our attention to the dark rain cloud which don't offer to come any nearer, and which promises us no more relief than Lazarus in Abraham's bosom did to Dives in torment— Officers are lounging about in their under-clothes— soldiers who have a big job on hand, of unloading the wood-boat are slipping away from work to shady places in the hold of the boat— in the wheelhouses under the wharf— anywhere so that it is out of sight and out of the sun— and the very dogs have abandoned their usual occupation of hunting for cats, and are panting under the houses with tongues extended to the utmost— As for myself it is hardly necessary to say that I am in that state of fusion, that but few ever arrive at, it is a comfort for me to think of the plunge into the bay that I will take to-night— how I'll revel in the salt water— I wish I was over head and ears in it now!

The little Yankee steamer Buckner came in last night, in what is called the Swash Channel, quite near to the fort— a shot was fired which by an accident came quite close to her, the shell exploding at the water's edge— when the smoke cleared away she was discovered making off with all speed: if Admiral Buchannan would give us a small armed steamer we could keep such impertinent visitors at a more respectfull distance[24]

Quite an amusing incident occured on the occasion that we have been laughing at to-day— it was after midnight when the gun was fired— thinking it was some blockade runner coming in I jumped up and went into the fort, and met one of our captains on the way— we were just coming to the top of the steps near the gun, when we heard some one call out "Don't shoot   there's somebody in front of the gun"   looking up sure enough the gun was aimed right over our heads and the man was on the point of pulling the lanyard   the captain retreated to take shelter behind a traverse while I hastened to place myself by the gunners— The piece was elevated so that the shell would have passed high above our heads, and it is likely that we would not have felt what is called the blast, still we were not anxious to stand before the formidable columbiad— and became "demoralized" very suddenly— . . .

Williams

FORT MORGAN AUG 16, 63

Dear Lizzy:

It is Sunday morning, the rain is pouring down aslant in torrents, A soldier who has managed to be caught in it, somebody is always caught, is rushing for the quarters as if he expected to save his clothes from a wetting, but a plunge in the bay wouldnt wet him more than he is now. . . .

TUESDAY MORNING 18TH [AUG 1863]

I believe that I will go up to town next Saturday if Maj Gee returns before that time.[25] I can't prevail on myself to wait until next month: so you may half expect me then.

The [steamers] Vivian and Lizzy Davis got out safely this week— The first may make the trip, but it seems to me the height of absurdity to send out such a snail as the Davis to run the blockade— If she goes through safely we may well say the race is not to the swift[26]

—*Williams*

FORT MORGAN AUG 19. '63

Dear Lizzy:

I hope that I will not be more than a day behind this letter in presenting myself at home, but as many disappointments await soldiers in these days I am preparing myself to view from the wharf the departure of the boat on Saturday. Truly it will be a sad sight— a view to which I fear Distance will lend nothing but vexation of spirit, and if it should happen such a day as this it will be dismal indeed— (I have devoted so much attention to the weather lately that I'll omit the description of the cheerless rain to-day— which looks as if it never would be over if not for a special providence.) Drills are out of the question for several days, except at the guns, for the parade is a pond, if there were plenty of [waterfowl] on it I might find occupation for the idle hours of a rainy day.

I am sorry to hear that King is so sick but hope that the change to the air of Mobile will bring him up rapidly I think that Col Robinson [Robertson] will give him employment as soon as he is well; Robinson is constructing a fine battery now at Grant's Pass which will not be completed for some time.[27]

I have just been ordered to send a company to Grants island.[28] The 21st will not be consolidated as a regiment again until Col Anderson has ambition enough to get them in the field— as long as he is satisfied with the easy (and inglorious I had almost said) service we are doing in detachments we will be divided and subdivided indefinitely— an ambitious officer would carry us into the field and with his advantages easily win honor for the command, and a Brigade for himself.

Williams received another brief furlough.

FORT MORGAN [THURSDAY] AUG 27 '63

Lizzie, I was too lazy to write while I had time, and now I must be brief and hurried, and subject to interruptions— You have probably heard all about the Yankees having shelled our boys at Grants Pass on Monday— They "threarted" us there to 69 shells of which some 6 or 8 only took effect on the island— some narrow escapes are reported, the greatest of which were those of Lieut Savage of our regiment and his gun squad (the gunners were members of the first Ala Artillery Battalion) The gun they were serving burst, but only one man was wounded slightly by the explosion— It was the only long range gun they had and

Lt. Col. James M. Williams, Mobile, August 24, 1863

after that accident they had to stand and take it untill the Yanks were tired of the sport— We sent over a fine gun yesterday and I suppose that by this time they are ready for another visit   No one was injured by the Yankee fire[29]

Since my return I have been temporarily in command of the post— but I look for the return of Col Forsyth to-day

Good Bye
Williams

FORT MORGAN AUG 28 '63
. . . I sent my horse to Col. Anderson [at Point Clear, by the] last boat— He is in fine order and a beauty— if I were disposed to sell him I could easily make a couple of hundred by the operation— but not knowing when I will need a horse I am determined to keep him— . . .

Williams

FORT MORGAN. [WEDNESDAY] SEPT. 9. 63.
Dear Lizzy:
All is quiet, but the dark nights are upon us and we are constantly looking for blockade runners to enter: and even the Yankees might try a sharp trick upon us if we relaxed our vigilance, though we are so accustomed to the sight of them off the bar that they look as harmless as doves—

Williams

Williams received another furlough to Mobile.

FORT MORGAN SEPT 19 63
Dear Lizzy:
We have experienced the delights of a furious north wind since I returned— and it has made a winter for us—

Last night I was quite ill, and slept none with violent cholic pains— better this morning and can attend to my business very well, only cramped with pain semi-occasionally—

Owing to the storm I have been unable to get Mrs. Parrot her bundle of palmetto. But I will not forget it.

I have a letter from Mr Osborne— Henry [Jr.] returned from Vicksburg sick, and died of ulceration of the bowels— They are in great grief

Williams

FORT MORGAN SEPT 24 1863
Dear Lizzy =
. . . I am glad to hear that the Submarine is up again, and hope that it will yet do something to hasten the discomfiture of the Yankees before Charleston. . . .[30]

I am well enough now— with the exception of a slight diarrhoea which followed my night of cholic.

Williams

Fort Morgan Sept 29 '63

Dear Lizzy:

. . . I have not moved into the fort yet and have concluded to wait until the next cold snap comes. I dislike to give up my airy room so long as there is prospect of hot days and nights—

Rumors are plenty that we are to be sent into the field again and our place supplied by some of Gen Johnston's troops.[31] I hope that there is some truth in the report— it is time that I was striking a blow for the cause and a step nearer my goal— the command of a Brigade. Is it not— I want to make a name that master George will be proud of when he says "he was my father"

Good bye

James Williams

I came near adding by force of habit

Lt. Col. Comdg Post[32]

Williams took a brief leave to visit Lizzy.

Fort Morgan Oct 17, 1863

Dear Lizzy:

By the boat I will send a barrell of oysters and some palmetto marked in your name care of Mrs Turner

If I can find a good man— I will also send you a bottle of fine brandy which is part of a lot presented to me by the captain of the "blockade" steamer Isabella— dont get drunk with Mrs Parrot and Mrs Turner now or I will never give you a sample of the next lot I am fortunate enough to receive—

Williams

Head Quarters Ft Morgan
Oct 20. 63

Dear Lizzy:

. . . Everything remains quiet and uninteresting enough The [C.S.S.] Gunnison has not yet gone out and I begin to doubt whether she will get out before the dark nights are over[33]

I have heard of the loss of the Submarine— I telegraphed to know if Dixon is safe and hear that he was not with it—[34]

Williams

Fort Morgan Oct. 22 63

Dear Lizzy:

. . . I am exceedingly busy   among other things I have been hunting up conscripts have succeeded in finding about half a dozen

I have been brigade commander for two days and my honors will hold good for about two more— don't tell any body—

Williams

FORT MORGAN [TUESDAY] OCT 27. 63

There has been no boat since Thursday; the five days seem like a month— We were greatly disappointed that the storm prevented President Davis from visiting us on Sunday as he intended to do: we were prepared to give him a very neat military reception, and are sorry not only because we could not see him but because he couldnt see us—[35]

I would like to go home on Saturday but can not unless an inspecting officer comes from Mobile to do the work which usually falls to me at the last of the month.

Col Smith returned last evening to Ft. Gaines and has relieved me of the command of the brigade[36]

I conscripted nearly all our oystermen last week and I fear we will not have the luscious bivalves in plenty again unless we can make some new arrangements

I confidently look for a letter to-day— I am going up soon

Williams

FORT MORGAN [THURSDAY] OCT 29 63

Dear Lizzy:

Col Anderson's battalion will be here to-day—[37]

I received your letter after I had mailed mine by last boat   I believe that I can find board for you at Navy Cove, and if you desire I think I can go up for you about next Tuesday—

I was pleased with the appearance of the place, and if the terms are living I will try it for a while—

Good bye
Williams

Lizzy and young George did move down to Navy Cove.

CAMP— NOV 27 [1863]

Dear Lizzy:

Business before pleasure— I will not be able to visit you on Sunday as I intended unless something turns up that I don't expect— I have not yet gone up to Camp Powell (which is a longer journey by the way than to Fort Morgan and not half so enticing either) I have been advised by the surgeon not to venture on so long a ride while suffering as I have been from dysentery— I am better now— will probably go to Camp Powell soon and then visit you—[38] if I should get worse I will go to Fort Morgan for treatment

Good Bye James M Williams

CAMP ANDERSON JAN 7, 1863 [1864][39]

Dear Lizzy:

I promised you to be ready to go to the city this time, but find that it will be impossible for me to leave camp for some days to come— The bad weather has kept me back in my work, and of all that I intended to complete before this date much is not yet begun.

It will be at least a week before I can go the cove.

I have purchased a stove for my tent, it is about the size of your hat box and keeps my tent as warm as toast in the rain and cold— The only trouble it occasions me is the loafers it draws in.

Williams

V
Fort Powell, Mobile Defenses, Spanish Fort, Cuba Station: January 24, 1864 – May 10, 1865

Dear Lizzy =

You have heard of my sudden move— but you have not heard how I was disappointed to find that I must pass so near without seeing you—

I am fixing myself up here for a seige— am delighted with my situation, with the single exception that it is too far from my wife and master George—

You must pay me a visit whenever Mr Norville and his excellent lady feel like taking a holiday— with a good breeze it will be a nice little sail

Whenever I can take a day's leave of absence I will go to you— write to me often— I will be attentive and you will hear from me often—

Williams

Navy Cove

Williams was ill for about two weeks.

Fort Powell Feby 18. 64

Dear Lizzy =

I can find now but few opportunities to send you letters— I will write as often as possible— I am getting better every day and expect to be entirely well in a day or two— I am never too sick to fight the Yanks, and if they will come in just a little closer I think I can administer a quietus to some of their gunboats or those confounded little mortar boats[2]

The Norther has prevented them from renewing the fight the last two days.

I have been longing for such a fight as I now have on my hands for a long time, and expect to have an interesting time of it

Your mess bill should be settled at the end of the month, if I do not come over please get Mr Norville to attend to it

Williams

Fort Powell Feby 20. 1864

Dear Lizzy:

It is ten o'clock AM. the tide is very low and the Yanks have not yet come in to fighting distance

BOMBARDMENT OF FORT POWELL BY ADMIRAL FARRAGUT'S FLEET, FEBRUARY 24, 1864
(SKETCHED DURING THE ENGAGEMENT, HARPER'S WEEKLY, APRIL 2, 1864)

The storm which has prevailed for several days has prevented them from renewing the bombardment— Dont' be alarmed when you hear the big guns: They are harmless to us so far, and though I may lose a man occasionally I do not think the casualties will be so numerous as to occasion you any uneasiness—[3]

I see that the paper [the Mobile *Advertiser and Register*] of the 17th gave Col Smith the credit of commanding this fort during the fight— it is not true— Col Smith ordered my flag staff to be taken down and put up in another place— Maybe the papers will give *me* the *dis*-credit of that— I would not have done it for any consideration!

Write to me when you can send your letters to the fort and they will be forwarded to me

                                                    Williams

                                                    FORT POWELL FEBY 23, 1864
Dear Lizzy:
Your letter was handed to me this morning on the bomb-proof just after the Yankees had opened fire   I was quite amused at your ideas on the subject of torn coats.

The account of my accident was very much exaggerated in the newspapers— A shell exploded about two or three yards behind me and a piece struck me on the right side and breast bruising it slightly in a spot about half the size of this sheet of paper— I was knocked down, and stunned for an instant, my coat was torn until you could put Master George through the hole— and my vest was torn but not so much— my side was very sore for several days and is still of a bright yellow color— but beyond that I suffered no injury— I vomitted that night frequently and perhaps that gave rise to the report that I was injured internally— but that you discover was only my old complaint back again— I did not tell you about it for I did not expect it would get into print, and thought it might make you uneasy for me hereafter.

I am truly glad that you are not in Mobile— I do not think that you will have any difficulty in purchasing your rations at the Fort—

As you have seen the Yankees have bombarded me again all day no body hurt— and little or no damage done to the Fort— they keep a long way out and I take it easy and crack away at them very slowly just to let them know that I am still here— I am satisfied that I struck them more than once to-day   They fired today 304 shells— 18 fell on the island— I shot 35 times— I like the fun finely so far . . .[4]

                                                    Williams
If you wish for the latest news from Fort Powell you can always get it by enquiring of Major Gee at Fort Morgan— I signal to Fort Morgan every night— any person from the Cove can bring you word when they go to the Fort—

FORT POWELL FEBY 27 [1864]

Dear Lizzy:

We have had quite a fog which has concealed the enemy from us two days— some of my command thought yesterday that the fleet had gone off, and to dispel such an impression which might be injurous I went out in a small boat and soon found them about 2½ miles from the fort—

I wrote to you on the 25th but believe I did not mention the lively time we had about 10 o'clock that morning— A gun boat came in on my left quite close, and endeavored to dismount my guns by an enfilade fire, (An enfilade— is a fire which comes on the side of a line, so that if one gun is missed another by the side of it may-be struck)— I opened on the bold rascal with all my guns, and both sides had a warm time of it for half an hour— at the end of that time he drew off having been hit more than once— The firing was furious[5]

I am still greatly troubled with my ugly malady— and on quiet peacable days I am so weak and sick that I stay in bed most of the time As soon as our little scrape is over here I will get a sick leave and try to recruit my health again—

There is so much trouble about the Currency now that I will not draw any pay this month if you can get along   by the first of March I can draw my money for two months and not lose anything on it.

I wish that I could go over to see you— I will do so the first day that I can look out in the Sound and see no Yankees

You may rest easy when you hear the big guns— the enemy wont take Fort Powell very soon *that way*— I am taking every precaution to punish them if they try to assault me in the night[6]

Williams

FORT POWELL MAR 3 1864

Dear Lizzy:

I am ordered to report to Mobile for duty— Gen Maury writes me a letter which gives me great credit for my conduct of the defence and states that I am only relieved to give me relaxation

I hope to be able to prevail on him to let me come back again— I feel that this is my fight and that I should be permitted to see it out—

I will go to Mobile in a day or two— You had better remain where you are until I learn more definitely what I will do

I have received a letter from Mrs Turner— she has sent off her boarders and invites us to her house

I will get leave of absence to visit you as soon as possible

Williams

While on duty in Mobile Williams moved Lizzy and young George from Navy Cove to Mrs. Turner's boarding house in Mobile.

In March, he was detached to Camp Anderson again. Then, in mid-April, the regiment was brigaded with the Seventeenth and Twenty-ninth Alabama Regiments,

Cantey commanding, and ordered to Rome, Georgia, to join Gen. Joseph H. Johnston's Army of Tennessee. However, when the regiment reached Pollard, Alabama, according to Pvt. Kierman (Company K), "we had brigade drills . . . but from some controversy, as to the senior colonel of the Brigade, we were ordered back to Mobile." On April 17, the Twenty-first Alabama was ordered from Pollard to Ft. Morgan in Brigadier General Richard L. Page's Brigade. The regiment left Mobile on the steamer Dick Keys April 18.[7]

FORT POWELL THURSDAY MAY 12 64

Dear Lizzy;

You are Keeper of the Keys now I suppose in Mrs Turner's household— and tired enough of the loneliness if not dignities of your position— Thanks to Gen Maury I am Keeper of the Keys of Mobile again in my little pet fort— by the way did you see the honorable mention of our defence of it in the Presidents message?[8]

The fort is much improved since I was in charge before but my opinion is that when we come to fight [in] it again some of the improvements will be found to be rather inconvenient in service— though they look pretty enough[9]

However it is better than it was and I wish the mortar fleet were within range at this minute— or rather as soon as I am done writing— a Yankee small boat came within two and a half miles on Tuesday last looking for torpedoes— for fear that they would not find one I sent them a shell which fell near enough to

satisfy their curiosity and they left incontinently. Coming here I escaped the sand flies and mosquitos but ran into the mouths of a legion of fleas which infests the fort— they robbed me of three nights rest and an indeffinite quantity of blood— and paid not the least attention to curses loud and deep— thank fortune the writ of habeas-corpus don't protect them or any other skulkers and I exercise the "right of search" every day with remarkable success and increasing skill.

I have received another letter from my sister but it is a duplicate of the one you saw—

I am very homesick now a-days, and in proportion as the war seems to be drawing to a close my impatience to be at home again beside my darling wife and boy becomes every day more felt

It will be a glorious day for me when I can hang up my sword for a souvenir for George and go to work by your side again— the excitement and glory of war is a shadow— I have been its willing slave— but oh! the pleasure of a happy home and a lovely wife and child— is a *reality* and not ignoble either— . . .

Williams

FORT GAINES MAY 14, 64

Dear Lizzy:

I haven't time to write you much of a letter to-day— Col Anderson lost his youngest child the other day and has gone to town— I have had to change places with the advantage of an armistice with the fleas for a few days— I will return to Fort Powell to-day if Col Anderson returns.

I have not heard from you— I have a trick working which if it succeeds will place me on duty in the city for a week or two. but I am by no means certain that I will be fortunate enough— There is no thought of moving any of our troops, and we firmly located and iron-clad—

Williams

91 Conception St.

Williams must have "worked a trick." Shortly after, Lizzy accompanied Mrs. Turner on a visit "up the Railroad" to a country farm.

FORT POWELL [SUNDAY] JULY 3, 1864

Dear Lizzy:

The first of July is here and I have no chance to go for you. No leaves are granted for more than two-days— and even then they are very hard to obtain by hook and crook— I begin to fear that the alarm will not blow over very soon: but it may. I am unable to draw my pay— but Mr King— (who is here on a visit) will go back to the city about the last of the week, and I will get him to raise me some money and send to you. I have not heard from you for some time and cannot help feeling a little anxious about Georgie— as he was not very well when you last wrote— I feel quite bad to think you are needing money so badly while I have been unable to send it, but it could not be avoided and I hope that soon after you receive this letter you will be supplied

I wrote to Mr Osborne [in Augusta] for funds some time ago but have not yet heard from him

For two days back Fort Morgan has been keeping the Yanks away from a vessel which in coming in was beached about half a mile above the fort— the firing has been steady but not rapid— last night my sentinels heard firing at Morgan and it may be the enemy tried to destroy it with their launches— I have not heard from Morgan this morning— [10] I spent last Sunday Monday and Tuesday in the city— you can't imagine how lonely it seemed to wander about the deserted house and miss you and Master George from your accustomed places— I cannot help wishing that you may be home the next time I have to go up, but it is a selfish thought: for so long as you are passing your time so pleasantly I should be glad to give you up. . . . How I wish that I could luxuriate for a few days on Country good things— milk— berries— melons and the nice fresh vegetables every day which you can hardly appreciate I dare say

You are keeping George away from me so long that he will forget me— the little darling was just beginning to look at me as though he thought I was his father and now I fear he will have it all to learn over again— I am quite jealous— However I am sure of one thing that he will love me as well as his mother when this "cruel war is over" and I can be home every day as I long to be now— Oh! how impatiently!

The oysters are very fine now and I have sent samples to town frequently— when you return I will be able to send you as many as you want— the boats now make daily trips, and hardly ever miss this fort— If they did not leave the city at the prepostorous hour of half past four in the morning I would ask you to make me a flying visit when you return to the city   I would like to see your dear face again even for a moment, it seems a year since we met.

I write while suffering under a fit of blue devils of the darkest hue— produced doubtless by my old enemy the diarrhoea which for two or three days has prostrated me greatly—

Kiss Georgie and your own sweet face (in a mirror) for me
                                        Williams

                                        FORT POWELL JULY 16, 64
Dear Lizzy: • • • •
Half an hour ago I began this letter and was going to say something that is now forgotten by way of preface to • • • well that is forgotten too— none of it was very important except as the medium of loving thoughts and feelings which continually go out to my darlings at home, and seek expression— sometimes serious sometimes trivial, but always true and heartfelt. But to return I was interrupted by the shouts of the men, and going out to see what was the cause of the excitement I discovered three or four of them sailing toy boats like so many school boys— two of the tiny sloops were racing and the excitement was great, and many bets were taken in pieces of tobacco— I was boy enough myself to watch them for half an hour, an interested spectator not so much of the boating as of the boatmen— Poor fellows they have a dreary enough time of it, and I like to see them able and willing to make the best of everything and amuse themselves— The men I have are cheerful and obedient— I could not be more pleasantly situated. It is not often that I have to punish though "occasional occasions" require it.

I have made the acquaintance of Madame Le Vert[11] since I saw you, she patronises me extensively and I am pledjed to visit her when I go to the city— She is very interesting, yet some-how I cannot talk to her without an odd undefinable feeling of pity— She talks loyally enough— though from all accounts she has not always been sound in her devotion to our cause and for all I know may not be now. Poor old woman! There it is like a flash! I know now why I pity her— Because she *is old*— she should be young and handsome and rich and then how firmly she would grasp the sceptre which is slipping away from her hands every day— she would then be the royal woman— now it is hard to believe she is anything but an old quack pretender.
                              X X X X X

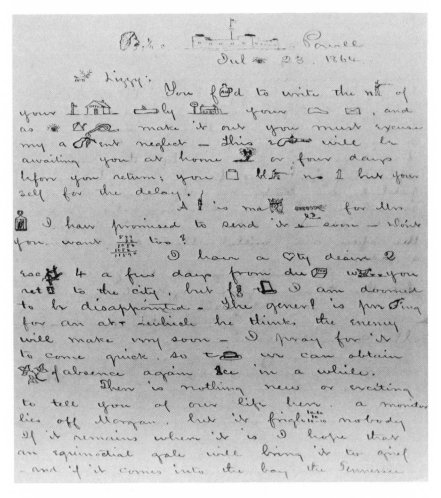

LETTER FROM WILLIAMS, JULY 23, 1864

Here I was interrupted to receive the present of a melon— I have had several sent to me from Ft Gaines and the main land— at different times
Williams

I confidently believe that I can whip anything and everything that can get at me— at any rate I mean to try it. I have not in the least relaxed my vigilance and sleeping as we do, every man at his station I defy them to surprise me— I experience no bad effects from sleeping out though sometimes it is not very pleasant to be roused from sound slumbers by the rain splashing in my face— I have pitched a tent on the Bomb-proof in which I take shelter when it rains— but at all other times I prefer the open air with the sand for a bed.

I will write to you again by the time you get back home
Williams

FORT POWELL JULY 27. 64
Dear Lizzy:
I have just returned from a fine sail in my little boat— had a fine breeze, and got wet from head to foot— the two indispensible accompaniments to a good sail-boat ride

I wrote some days ago to know if you want some palmetto plait— if you do I can get it for you any time— Let me know how many yards you want . . .
Williams

FORT POWELL JULY 31, 64
Dear Lizzy:
I wish that you were sharing with me the delightful sea breeze that makes my room to-day the most comfortable in the state— as I believe it is— The sea is rippling gently under the house, and continually invites me to plunge in for a bath— an invitation that is accepted two or three times a day. Crab-lines hang out of windows and from the "back-gallery" and are occasionally drawn in, for the benefit of our dinner table— A foot-tub is full of the ugly things, who are tumbling about, pinching and clawing each other viciously— and reaching up to grab each unfortunate that is added to their number— Speaking of crabs reminds me of an amusing trick that was played off upon some of the officers the other night— We keep our smoking tobacco in a 100 pound Brooke-shell-box: a crab was put in the box, of course when any one went in the dark to fill his pipe the crab would try to catch his hand— one after another fell into the trap but would say nothing about it and watch for some one else to go there—

It is quite a comfort to me to have clean clothes once more— a luxury that I had not enjoyed while my washing was done here— In future I will draw my soap rations myself, and send them up with my soiled linen to the city.

We will have a fine crab gumbo to-day— wouldn't you like to help eat it?

I have ordered some palmetto braid for you which will be ready next week— I *had* some for you but a letter from Mrs Turner came asking me to get her some, and as I did not know whether you wanted any or not, I took the liberty of

sending her yours— don't scold now and say I think more of Mrs Turner than I
do of you! . . .

Williams

FORT POWELL AUG 1. 64

Dear Lizzy:

I believe now that I will not see you again until after our big fight— The
Yankees are preparing a formidable fleet—

Twenty six vessels three of which are iron clads are in the offing   how many
more are coming no one knows— the last iron clad came up about two hours
ago—[14] the more the merrier— we will have a fine time— Don't get uneasy or
frightened   I'll take good care of myself, and make you proud too—

I only regret that I could not see you again before the opera begins—

I send you my pay account to the end of July transferred in blank— any one
can insert his name and collect the money for you, in case I am shut off from the
city when the paymaster has funds—

I am delighted that I have command of my pet fort for another fight and am
fixed up to make a good one this time. . . . I will continue to write often as long
as my communication with the city remains open— and when that is closed
listen for the sound of my guns, and rejoice in the news they bring you

Every thing has been put in fighting condition for some time back but I never
fully believed the fight was imminent until yesterday when monitor No 2 [the
Winnebago] came up from the westward—

Give my love to all friends— and take care of George until I see you— I hope
we will be able to bring this expedition to grief suddenly, and then I'll apply for
two weeks leave, and stay at home all the time with you and nurse the baby. I
won't go to King's more than once a day nor make long visits at that— and I'll
have no business what ever "down-town"!

Williams

FORT POWELL AUG 3 64

Dear Lizzy:

Mahomet went to the mountain when it would'nt come to him— can't you
make a trip to see me? the sooner the better— say the next day after you receive
this

I'd give anything in reason for a sight of George and have to kiss your pretty
face!

Bassett or King will get the "papers" and doubtless come with you— They will
at least escort you to the boat

It won't cost you much trouble besides what arises from the very early hour at
which the boat leaves the city.

Don't stop to think about it: if you delay it may be too late.

Maj. Johnston's moving his wife to the old camp of the 21st near Cedar
Point— my opinion is that he had better send her to the city than leave her
liable to outrage from the straggling Yankees that will soon infest that country if
they succeed in establishing their fleet in the bay— Col. Anderson will send his

family to the same place— Mrs. A. is up the country— I wouldnt have you at Alabama Port for the worlds—

Williams

Major General Gordon Granger's 1500-man division landed, on August 3, on the western tip of Dauphin Island, and by the evening of August 4, was prepared to attack Fort Gaines. A flotilla of light-draft gunboats covered the operation in the Mississippi Sound. As August 5 dawned, the Battle of Mobile Bay began.[15]

When the Union fleet was discovered to be in the lower bay, Williams prepared for an attack on the eastern face of the fort. His subsequent report to Maury is self-explanatory.

MOBILE, AUGUST 7, 1864

During the morning the fort was shelled from . . . the sound at long range. The fort was hit five times. . . . About 2:30 p.m. one of the enemy's monitors[16] came up within 700 yards of the fort, firing rapidly with shell and grape [twenty-five times.] I replied from the 7-inch Brooke gun on the southern angle. I succeeded in firing but three shots from it while the iron-clad was in range, because there was no platform in the rear and a sponge head pulled off in the gun. The elevating machine of the 10-inch columbiad was broken by a fragment of a shell. The shells exploding in the face of the work displaced the sand so rapidly that I was convinced unless the iron-clad was driven off it would explode my magazine and make the bomb-proof untenable. I telegraphed Col. Anderson that I would be compelled to surrender within forty-eight hours. His reply was, 'Save your garrison when your fort is no longer tenable.' I decided promptly that it would be better to save my command and destroy the fort than to allow both to fall into the hands of the enemy. The tide being low I marched my command to Cedar Point without discovery. The fort was blown up at 10.30 p.m.

The next day, August 8, Maury wrote on Williams's report that "Colonel Williams should have fought his guns. Fort Powell should not have been surrendered." Williams was relieved from command pending an investigation.[17] *He immediately sent Lizzy and George to stay with the James L. Wainwright family in Prattville, near Montgomery, Alabama.*

MOBILE AUG 15 64.

Dear Lizzy:

There is nothing new yet— and I can make no better guess as to what will "turn up" than the day you left. King is not home yet and I hope that you will see him before he starts from Prattville

There is a story going about and generally believed that the Yanks will open on us to-morrow

Another street "grape vine" telegram says that the Fort Gaines prisoners will be exchanged at New Orleans Thursday, in that case they will be home about Saturday.

I hope that your trip up the [Alabama] river was not so irksome as you anticipated when you left

I have heard not a word of my case yet, and will to-morrow apply for a court of inquiry

Williams

MOBILE AUG 18, 1864

Dear Lizzy:

There is a pause in the Yankee operations, what will be the plan of the enemy no one can tell yet: There is a frantic effort on our part to get ready, and it may be that something will be accomplished.

Ladies and children are leaving in great numbers— the boat yesterday was crowded, I am so glad that you got off before the column started, I look for a letter from you to-day. . . .

Nothing has been done yet in my affair. I commenced yesterday pushing it up and will not rest until I have it thouroughly investigated— of course there is no doubt that my course will be vindicated— Now that I have you out of range of Yankee shells I have recovered from the gloomy feelings that have oppressed me so long, and but for my absence from you I would be as light hearted and happy as you could wish

Williams

MOBILE AUG [20] 1864

Dear Lizzy =

I didn't think I would have to write my fourth letter without being able to say that I had procured an investigation of my Fort Powell affair— but it is so. I am trying hard to have the matter attended to at once, but so far have not succeeded in effecting anything.

The Yanks like me appear to be in status quo, and have not developed their plans or intentions— it is still believed that they will not remain quiet many days more

I have dined— supped— and spent part of the evening with Mr R D Williams— He has been soldiering at the redoubts for ten days—[18]

I have not yet heard from you and am quite anxious for your first letter. . . .

Give my love to Mrs. Wainwright and write often, to your disconsolate

Williams

MOBILE [FRIDAY] AUG 26 64

Dear Lizzy:

Today has been the fourth occupied in the investigation of my affair— Everything has shown conclusively that I did my duty, and I have no doubt that the Court will fully sustain me The trial will close about Monday and by next Monday I expect to be returned to my command with my name unstained—

I have had two letters from you— but could not find the spirit to write while I had nothing cheering to say— the prosecution closed to-day— a complete

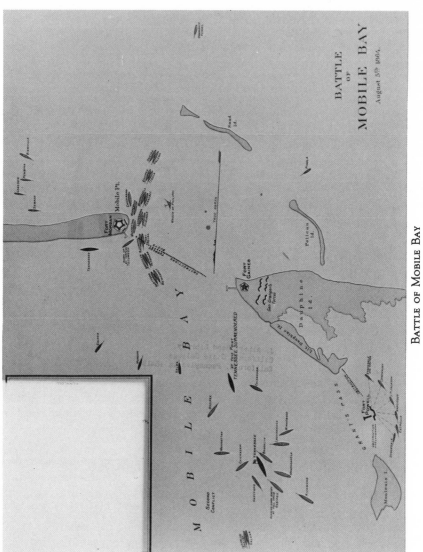

Battle of Mobile Bay

EXPLOSION AND RUINS OF FORT POWELL. SKETCHES BY E. B. HOUGH (FRANK LESLIE'S ILLUSTRATED NEWSPAPER, SEPTEMBER 24, 1864)

failure— and my defence as I said before will occupy until Monday noon

You have heard doubtless of the fall of [Fort] Morgan on the 23d The strong fort held out but 18 days— home generals say I could have held an open work without so much as a parapet 30 days! The proposition is ridiculous and eventually bring[s] into disgrace those who have endeavored to ruin me—[19]

Rest easy that I am "all right" The Enemy are landing below the city about thirty miles, and will doubtless soon attack— I only hope they will wait until I am returned to duty— and placed again at the head of my brave boys— They are even more impatient than I for my return to them[20]

I am so glad that you are safe among kind friends while Mobile is under a cloud . . .

Williams

MOBILE [WED.] AUG 31, 64

Dear Lizzy:

Your letter of 26th came yesterday— I received one of the same date from Mr Wainwright at Montevalo [Alabama]— he very cheerfully extends to me the hospitalities which I was forced to claim so suddenly and unceremoniously— I am so glad that you find your new friends so kind and self sacrificing, and I hope that you will not long be compelled to impose on their kindness—

My case closed Monday and I suppose the result will be published about the first of next week— of course there was nothing in the case that reflected the slightest discredit on me as a soldier and officer and I will be fully sustained in my course— The trial shows that I did my whole duty and more— A high officer who was present through the whole investigation remarked yesterday that it showed that Col Williams had done nothing but what was right and that it was evident that there was not a more gallant officer in the Confederate service— of course I only write this for your eye my darling!

I have a letter from Mr Osborne he offers you a home whenever you will desire or be compelled to accept it— . . . I expect to go back to my command about Monday don't know where I will be stationed and don't care so there is a chance for a fight

The Yanks are still landing troops at Cedar Point—

Williams

MOBILE SEPT 2, 64

Dear Lizzy:

It is all over and as I always assured you I have been acquitted of all blame in the Fort Powell affair—[21]

I return to my command to-day—

All are well
Williams

MOBILE SEPT 6, 64

Dear Lizzy:

I wrote to you hastily a day or two ago to tell you that the Military Court had sustained me and that I was returned to duty— I sent you the papers of the 3d— Do you see the Mobile papers regularly? if not I can send them to you

Everything remains quiet yet— but I feel now almost certain that there will be some active operations here before long— If the Yankees don't attack us we will them—

I was disappointed in the result at Fort Morgan— that Fort could I believe have held out for a long time   it was the only complete and strong work on the Line— . . .

I am stationed on the line of entrenchments and have command of Three Redoubts and a Battery— my line is nearly a mile long— I may be moved in a few days[22]

I have a letter from Mr Osborne in which he offers you a home if you will go to Augusta— That however you cannot do now— or until some success is gained by Hood[23]   I am pleased to hear that you are so pleasantly situated—

I long to see you and George again— How much you can't imagine . . .
Williams

MOBILE SATURDAY SEPT 10, 64

Dear Lizzy:

Mobile is still quiet   one or two slight affairs have occurred around the obstructions— but nothing of importance. I am in charge of Redoubts 4, 5, and 6, and Battery K   they are on the line of intrenchments back of the new graveyard [Magnolia Cemetery]— a good location for a soldier who is anxious for Christian burial— a weakness that I do not have however to any great extent— I wouldn't much prefer a lot in the consecrated ground to any hasty field trench! I don't mean to require either very soon, I feel like surviving this war even if it should last a score of years— I'll take George on my "staff " as soon as he is old enough! You must "teach the young idea how to shoot"— literally— . . .

You can probably do one thing for me that is quite urgent, that is procure me two or three pairs of socks The Ft Powell misfortune has left me almost destitute. . . .

I intend to write home [to Iowa] in a day or two by flag of truce— . . .
Williams

Williams's acquittal had been met with keen disapproval in the headquarters of the District of the Gulf. Therefore, Maury reported his own displeasure to Confederate headquarters in Richmond on September 14. General Richard Taylor, Maury's superior, suspended Williams from command "until a decision from the War Department can be had." On September 17, appealing directly to Secretary of War James A. Seddon, Williams reviewed the charges, the results of the court-martial, and pleaded "in the name of Justice, and as a soldier of the Confederacy, whose honor is dear to him, and who has no other resort" for a speedy revision of his case.[24]

MOBILE SEPT 28, 1864

Dear Lizzy:

I have not written for several days as I expected to have started for Prattville

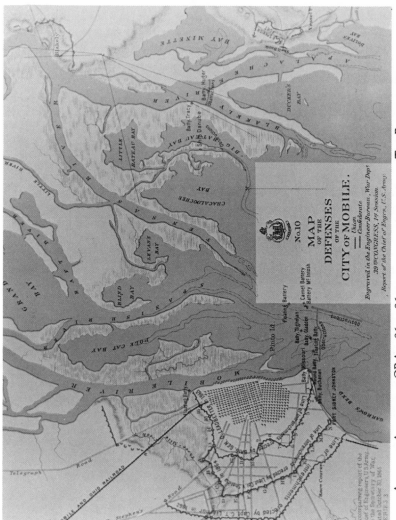

ATLAS TO ACCOMPANY ORA, 1861–1865, VOL. 2, PLATE 71, N. 13. THE BLAKELEY AND
APALACHEE RIVERS ARE REVERSED ON THIS MAP.

last evening, at the last minute I learned that my application for leave of absence was disapproved— you cannot imagine the depth of my disappointment, and all the bad words and thoughts it inspired— I think that is very— very hard that while I am idle for a month I cannot be permitted to visit my darling wife and boy— but in the life of a soldier many such things will occur and we can only learn to be patient and cheerful even under what appears to be injustice on the parts of our superiors— The disappointment was all the more cutting as I had no expectation of such a result, and thought that so reasonable and opportune a request would be granted immediately and cheerfully— My application is not yet returned and I do not know on what ground it is refused . . .

The Yanks are busy in the Bay— but what at no one seems to know. I begin to think they are making preparations for an attack upon our inner line— our authorities are working hard to repair the oversights of the past and I begin to hope that the attack will find us in a creditable state of preparation

The [steamboat] Coquette is laid up for a short time— when she resumes her trips [up the Alabama River] I will send you word.

It rains here every day— I am not yet entirely without hope of getting off to see you— I can tell when I see the endorsement of Gen Maury on my application. . . .

Kiss George for me

Williams

MOBILE OCT 3, 64

Dear Lizzy

I have not heard from you since the day which I had fixed for my departure— and I imagine that it is because you have been expecting me in   My disappointment has been very great; and it is with a very bad grace that I have reconciled myself to the harder orders that require me to remain idly in this city while I might be enjoying the society of my lovely wife and boy away off at Prattville. It seems long long years since I saw you and I often feel a sort of wonder as to how you look now   George too will be growing out of all likeness to the handsome little portrait that is treasured up in my memory— I expect to be ordered back to duty in about three weeks— I board with King and Bassett at the "Property" and manage to pass my time tolerably though sometimes when I think of you I cannot help chafing my bonds a little.

Williams

MOBILE— OCT 10, 64

Dear Lizzy:

. . . The weather is quite cold and suggests thoughts of cold comfort in store for me next winter, if I should be in the field or under the necessity of bivouacking any where.

John Pippin who has been quite sick for a long time is recovering and I had the pleasure of meeting him on the street to-day. He does not look the hearty jovial John of old days, but is in a fair way to be himself again—

I heard yesterday that Mr [Joel H.] Snow (the music man) has had two congestive chills and is very low— Col Robert Stirling one of my Fort Morgan friends died of congestion a few days ago at Mr Savages here in the city— He was buried with military honors— Tom Savage took every necessary care of him, and had him buried— Stirling was a fine man and a brave and distinguished soldier.[25]

John [King] and George [Bassett] have rented a house in another part of the city and in a few days will remove from the "Property" to their new quarters—
. . .

J Williams

Mobile Oct 11, 64

Dear Lizzy:

Time drags along heavily enough, these days— . . .

In a day or two we will commence moving to our new house, I dread the job very much, but its ugly features cannot be avoided—

Mrs [Sarah] Bond was at Mrs Turner's last night— she looks broken down very much— poor woman she has had some severe trials within the last few months— Judge [George W.] Bond was there too, and is the same old Judge of old— . . .

Williams

Mobile Oct. 12. 1864

Dear Lizzy:

. . . A fleet is reported to be assembling in the lower Bay— and as the Yankees are giving out very carefully that they do not intend to continue the operations against this city at present: I am very much inclined to think that they will attack us very soon. I hope they will, I am tired of this inactive life and long to hear the music of fire-arms again— It will rouse up the stagnant feelings that oppress me heavily—

I have not heard from Richmond and probably will not for three weeks or a month yet. What troubles me more is that I have not heard from you, and yet you must have written.

My men have been suffering generally with chills and fever. part of them have been brought into town and placed on provost duty, which will enable them to recover their health— I am anxious to resume command so that I can get them to-gether again, and take care of them: I have the vanity to think that I can take better care of them and do more with them than any-one else. . . . [26]

Williams

Mobile Oct. 13. 1864.

Dear Lizzy:

I have a horse buggy and harness at my disposal now and can take a ride as well as you— the horse is a very fine one for a buggy and I intend to commence operations with it this afternoon, I wish I had George here to drive out every day— the little fellow would be delighted as much as you and I— I am you know— and have long been anxious to go into the field in our own proper branch of service, light-infantry, many of my officers and men have expressed the same wish and I intend as soon as possible to try to have my command ordered to field duty— They will probably winter here and take the field in the spring— that is if we dont have a winter campaign at our own doors which I think is almost certain, As soon as the winter comes the operations in north Georgia Tennessee and Virginia will naturally be checked, and the enemy can then spare plenty of men for the attacks on Mobile and Charleston.

I will ride out to Mr Conning's to-day and see if he has not some letters for me in his pocket, he is so very careless and thoughtless, that he may have taken one or more from the office and forgotten it entirely: I have known him to do such things before.

I am rejoiced that we are about to move on account of a young ladies school that has been established next door: they are like so many mag-pies when not at study, and we cant move without attracting the attention of a dozen or so who have nothing better to do than to watch through the windows all that is going on in the neighborhood

An amusing circumstance occurred last week that illustrates the "depravity of human nature"— Mr King bought some potatoes and ordered them to be sent here on a dray— No potatoes arriving he went the next day to inquire about it, they had been sent and the drayman went to the wrong house,— a lady(?) there said that it was Mr King's house, and that she was "Mrs King" and received the potatoes!

Williams

An advertisement appears in one of the city papers for a "Wet Nurse" and directs application to be made at the "south west corner of Claiborne and St Anthony Sts"— that is our house and we have had quite a laugh at the blunder—

I have written home to my mother by flag of truce, by to-day's mails.

All well at No 91

MOBILE MONDAY OCT 17, 64

Dear Lizzy:

I will write you a line while "waiting for the wagon" in which all our household goods will "take a ride" to the new house: King and Bassett have gone to make arrangements for the immediate breaking up of our camp, while I am in charge and awaiting orders— if nothing happens we will accomplish the change of base to-day— The new house is not quite so roomy as this one but in other respects is better   a lot attached which will be used as a kitchen garden is not the least of the advantages it offers. This moving is a dreadful business, and when the necessity for it arises I always think that the less property one has on such an occasion the better for his peace of mind— The best possible condition is that of the soldier who with his knapsack and blanket, moves the very personification of independence with his house upon his back.— He is happy and cares for nothing, but the lovely wife and babe far away— or it may be the sweet heart who should remember him in the dangers and hardships that he makes so light— Too many, alas! forget the brave fellows who for years have cheerfully faced the foe with their lives in their hands, and have filled the place of the uncouth hero with some miserable gilded coward who remains in the rear to fatten like a hyena over the grave of his country. How are the mighty fallen— the extortioner moves about the streets in all the pride and costume of a gentleman— the admired of the ladies— while the soldier in his ragged uniform passes by unnoticed and despised— the first is really beneath the notice or even contempt of the good and fair— the other a glorious hero worthy to rank beside the demi-gods of chivilrous romance. Time will yet turn the tables, and the day is not far distant when a man will be ashamed to hold up his head and say that he did not "serve in the wars"— Money will not shield him from the contempt that is the portion of a coward. . . .

The Yankee fleet is increasing down the Bay— a land force is assembling at Pensacola and I think the indications are that the enemy will move upon us before very long, say within a month: The result of the campaign pending in Georgia may modify or alter their plans, but I believe their present intention is to attempt to reduce this city—[27] Some think the attack will be made on the eve of the Yankee [presidential] Election, and others that it will not be made at all for several months.

It is probable that the paymaster will have money by the last of this month, I fear that you are needing it now—

My shoes are almost played out, if you can have a pair made in the country and cheaper than they are here in the city ($150.) I wish you would have it done— Have them made 6½ in length, high instep and narrow in the sole. Write me whether or not you have ordered them to be made so that I will know what to do.

It is one month to-day since I wrote to the Secretary of War, I expect to hear from him and return to duty in two or three weeks from this time, that is about the first of next month.

I have been writing half an hour and the wagon has not yet appeared   I hope it will come to-day for I would like to finish the unpleasant [moving] job now that my mind is made up to it. I intend as I told you in a former letter to apply for leave to visit you as soon as I am ordered back to duty— if the enemy are not then in motion I may possibly be permitted   At any rate the effort will do no harm— even in its failure. I get quite angry when I think that in this time of my Idleness I cannot be with you and George— There is still some hope of that part of my regiment which was at Fort Gaines being soon exchanged   My old company [A] was with Gen Page at Fort Morgan and will be sent North according to the papers and the letters received from New Orleans by flag of truce—

Williams

MOBILE OCT. 22. 1864.

Dear Lizzy:

Another letter from you enclosing another from your uncle is received this morning: it is dated the 19th   I have also one from the Hon. Secretary of War which I will copy here: it is dated the 7th

"Colonel":

In reply to your letter of Sept. 17*th* 1864 I am instructed by the Hon. Sec. of War to inform you that the Court having acquitted you there is no necessity or propriety in reviewing the record of the court

Gen. Taylor, being your commanding officer, has the right to relieve you from command when in his discretion the good of the Service requires it.

I am "Colonel Very Resp'y &c&c"

So you see he declines to interfere to do me the act of justice which I claimed at his hands: and as I have no other recourse I must await the movements of those whose interest it is to injure me, that their own crimes and errors may not be known— This changes the aspect of my affairs this much that I no longer hope to be immediately returned to duty— and as I cannot obtain leave to visit you except upon terms humiliating to me; I think that you had better not wait for me at Prattville: but as soon as you are ready you had better go to Pike Co.— Indeed I find that in case I do obtain leave to visit you I can go to Brundidge as easily as to Prattville: I may not be returned to duty for months— and I will not resign, so I will tug it out— I am coming to have a perfect contempt for the corrupt and imbecile administration of our military department here: and shall do nothing to in any way detract from the impression which my quiet and reserved manner has created— I will remain here where public opinion sustains me, and appreciates the causes of my persecution— It don't worry my mind a particle, I rarely give it a thought, and really enjoy myself very well indeed— Don't show this letter to any one except it be to your uncle or some prudent friend. I am very much pleased with your uncle's manner of writing— and hope that before long I may be able to meet him.

It is quite a relief to hear that you can probably get me a pair of shoes for $100. Do not think of sending me any money: I can get along until I am paid, which, I hope, will be within a few weeks, I am glad to know that you are not suffering for the want of it, as the thought has troubled me a good-deal.

I hope and believe that you will feel at home with your new found relations, and that you see the dawn of happier days— it will nerve my arm in the hour of danger, to think that my wife and boy are among those who will care for and protect them, let what may happen to me. . . .

I had the pleasure(?) of meeting Mattox— or Maddox— last evening— he wears a Major's star, and is an irrepressible ass— He arrived last evening and entered the parlor with "How de-do Mrs Parrott! Here I am just from the front!" "Front"— indeed! front of a pile of bacon! He never smelled gun-powder nor ever will if he can help it— Yes! Here he is just from the front! Oh! you ineffable donkey! You should be sent to the front on a blind Jackass with your face to the tail and a placard on your back emblasoned with the inscription "Here I am! Just from the rear!

Williams

MOBILE OCT. 23. 1864

Dear Lizzy =

Mr. King says that Mr. Hazen will soon be sending him a package and if you have no other opportunity you can send my socks with it— The Coquette does not run to this city now but the "Virginia" does; and if you will leave them with the warehouse man at your landing marked "care of Mr Woodruff on steamer "Virginia," they will come soon: I need them very much as also the shoes—

As soon as there is the least hope of success I will apply for leave to visit you: I want to see you and George so much that I am occasionally tempted to accept the humiliating terms upon which I can obtain a leave— but no I can't do it—

Williams

MOBILE OCT. 30. 1864

Dear Lizzy:

Your letters of 16th and 23d came day before yesterday. I have not written for several days, partly because I had as now no news for you, but principally on account of the immense ammount of "unusual labor" that I have performed. I turned in last week to help King in his work, and worked very closely all day long taking only time for my meals— when night came I had all my "running about" to do, which from your numerous allusions to it in your letters I make no doubt you consider no small item: and are now wondering how I could do it all in the evenings between supper and bed time. I hardly know myself how I managed to go through with it all— but I did— and am proudly conscious that it was all accomplished satisfactorily to myself

Dr. Paine's brother died yesterday— he was a private in the [Mobile] Cadets [Company K]: I will attend his funeral this afternoon.[28]

At Mrs Turner's there is nothing new to tell you of— I believe I mentioned that she has sub-let the house next to Mrs [M. L.] Parmby's for [$]2400— furnished— she keeps the other half herself and has six or eight boarders, and appears to be doing very well indeed

. . . It is believed that the 21st will be home [from prison] within ten days— write often as you can

Williams

MOBILE NOV. 2, 1864.

Dear Lizzy:

Your shoe arrangements are satisfactory, and I can get along until the "week from next Saturday" pretty well   do not worry about them but as soon as they can be conveniently sent, see that they come— I'm not quite barefooted yet, though not so many removes from it as could be desired. I have as usual been hard at work all day assisting King, and write this at night feeling quite tired and very much under the influence of the bad spirits engendered by an ugly cold that has given me such a sore throat as I never had before, I believe— I will take some medicine for it to-morrow if the surgeon thinks proper to administer it— George is not only growing out of his shoes but away from my recollection I suppose— I wish that I could see him— with his stick and black playmate, I often think of him as you describe him, and in the indulgence of such reveries spend many an hour that might be worse employed.

. . . I have received another letter from your uncle in which he says he has written to you that he will meet you at Troy, or at another place which I cant now recall— whenever you inform him that you are coming

Williams

MOBILE Nov 9. 64

Dear Lizzy:

The shoes, socks, &c came last night, they are very acceptable and were needed very much. The shoes do very well, they are rather large but comfortable and good enough for a Confederate Soldier   I wish every one of my militant brethren had each such a pair—

Do not worry yourself to make me any more clothing   I have enough for present wants, and I dont want to accumulate anything to be lost at the next move of the military chess board.

It is odd that I never am unwell when I am exposed to the weather while here with a warm house— fire— bed and good fare I am the victim of a bad cold— the second that has annoyed me since I left the Fort.

I will send you five hundred dollars as soon as I am paid, but when that will be is still a very uncertain matter: I am sorry that you need money now and hope that before many weeks I will be able to give you "most" all I get from Jeff [Davis] for three or four month's work, and submission to the injustice of the old granny that I find over me here.

Williams

MOBILE MONDAY NIGHT Nov 21. 64

Dear Lizzy:

Hearty as a buck; tired as a soldier on a long march = forlorn as Crusoe = poor as a church-mouse = dirty as a mechanic; cold as a Laplander = cross as two sticks = Sleepy as Miss Phe at 11. P.M.: fond as Romeo = barren of news as last year's almanac = and nearly as bad off for breeches as "Brian O'Linn." . . . [29]

Havent heard from you— which I partly believe is chargeable to the fact that I have not been able to get into Connings for a day or two— its shut up While Taylor visits some of his friends out of town— send your letters hereafter care of Dr Miller Medical Purveyor

Williams

MOBILE SATURDAY NIGHT NOV 26. 1864.

Dear Lizzie:

I had not heard from you for a long time— and had concluded that you were moving to Pike. Co. but yesterday I received two letters dated 6th and 14th; . . . you may know when you send to the office and find no letter that I am moving along quietly in the life that I have so often described and that my whole mind is engaged in making money— King is in admiration at the change— he delights to see me interested in money getting and forgetful of "glory"— I have not forgotten "glory" as he calls it but as I am compelled to desist from the persuit of it for the time being I don't think of it or fret myself and occupy myself with the next best thing that is left to me

Williams

DEC 5— MOBILE [1864]

Dear Lizzy =

I am out of paper to-night— I have just received the above very kind and cordial letter from Mr Wainwright[30] and send it to you for your benefit   You will determine for yourself what is best to do— I will try and borrow some money for you and send it by next mail if successful—

There is nothing new and I am busy

Williams

Williams returned to his command in early December.

BATTERY HUGER DEC 19 64

Dear Lizzy:

Since I returned from the expedition after the raiders of which I gave you accounts, I have been ordered to this place and have been placed in command of Batteries Huger and Tracy, each of which is about as much of a Fort as Powell I feel at home again now that I find myself behind the ramparts of a Fort bristling with Brooke guns and Columbiads. I regret very much that my work [in Mobile] is stopped so soon but I take so much delight in my duties as a soldier that I am wonderfully consoled whenever I look out on the works around me and the brave comrades who wait for the approach of the Yank's to perform their grand Southern symphony on the big guns— The next time I go to the city I will send you Gen Maury's [reinstatement] letter for safe keeping. My batteries are the two known as the Appalachie [Appalachee] Batteries and are about fifteen miles from Mobile—[31] send my letters to Mobile as you have been doing and Mr. King will see that they are sent to me.

I am in a fine duck region now— have sent for my ammunition and will have a good time—

I feel that I will certainly be disappointed in my hopes of meeting you Christmas as the enemy appear to be threatening the city— The town is full of rumors and until these quiet down I could not succeed in obtaining leave of absence from so important a command   I will watch the indications and as soon as there is a ghost of a chance for success—

Among other things at which I am in a good humor about is the fact that you are safely away from the excitement and distress which [will] come upon Mobile whenever the enemy open upon it— You have heard that the enemy advanced on Pollard and destroyed the Bridges &c   there has been some fighting over there the last week.[32]

Williams

Battery Huger Dec 20, 1864

Dear Lizzy:

I forgot to mention in my letter yesterday that I wrote you two letters one about the 5th inst the other the 7th   in the first I enclosed $10. in the other $100. I have not heard yet that you received them, but hope so.

It is with a very bad grace that I am making up my mind to the necesity of foregoing, for a time, the promised pleasure of making you a visit during the holidays— I had come to look upon it as certain— but it is equally certain now that until the present apprehensions excited by the Yanks subside a little it will be useless to make an application for leave even if I would do so: but you know that I am so wedded to my pride and my duty, that I would not leave my forts while a fight appeared imminent, even to visit you and George— The cloud may blow over in a week or so, and when it does I will go to see you at once

It has been a long long time since I saw you and now that I cannot go I feel more anxious than I ever was to fly away from Mobile to Kiss you and George a Happy Christmas kiss—

We expect to have a grand dinner on corn bread and bacon for Christmas and will make as few wry faces over it as we can—

It is getting dark. I have no lights—

Good night

Williams

Mobile Jan 2, 1865

Dear Lizzy:

. . . I was ordered back to the city to-day with my command— Col Taylor the commandant of the post [of Mobile] applied for them, and so came the order— It is possible that I may leave my men here and go back to the batteries— I would like to do so— Report says again that our prisoners are exchanged and will be here in a few days— Major Currell the agent tells me that there is no doubt of it this time and that they will arrive here in a few days *certain* I hope so—[33] but have been disappointed so often that I am skeptical   I believe that I might now obtain two weeks leave of absence, but haven't the money to go— and dont know how I am to get it— I am very anxious to see you, and if I had the money would try the fate of an application to-morrow— Ten dollars is the ammount of my "Confed" at present. . . .

I enclose you a scrap from the [Mobile] Advertiser & Register of the 31st— you will see that Mr Forsyth has at last set himself right towards me— and (this is a secret which you must keep) I'll tell you what opened his eyes— I challenged him— or rather sent him such a letter as usually precedes a challenge   he saw that he must apologise or fight and so— this article— I accepted it and now that its all over and I am in no danger of being killed in a duel I tell you of it— I wish that you would send the slip to your uncle as I have no more— . . .

New Years like Christmas was a dull day for me— and devoted to homesickness— . . .

Yours Williams

I send John King alone— take care of him!

MOBILE JAN. 11, 65

Dear Lizzy:

I write in a hurry to send this letter by Lt Tell— I have just received a letter from you— the first in a long time: glad you have the $100— I am well and very busy ever since the prisoners returned— am quartered at Verona Warehouse not far from Mrs Turners— She and family are well— Mrs T has been disappointed and is not yet started on her trip— You have heard of Maj. Johns[t]ons treachery— it is disgraceful and we all feel humiliated by it very much[34]

I have borrowed $350 which I am selfish enough to use for myself— as I cannot let the opportunity pass to buy good clothing from the State which I need so badly that I can hardly appear at church

I think it likely that we will remain in the city, and from what I heard this morning in Gen Maury's office I expect to be put on heavy artillery duty again in a few days— I hope so for I like the big guns— . . .

Williams

MOBILE JAN 14. 65

Dear Lizzy:

Yesterday I moved from the city, where I was doing provost duty to this battery [C]. it is about two and a half miles from the post office on Stone street— Nearly all the prisoners exchanged have been furloughed for fifteen and twenty days— so that until they return my command will be small. Col Anderson and his officers are under arrest— when they will be tried or returned to duty I can't tell— it will probably not be for several months, I sent you a letter by Lieut Tell who promised to visit you if he could while on his Montgomery trip. I hope he will. When he returns if I am not unlucky I will have the clothing which I have so long needed— Street rumor says that the paymaster will have some money for us very soon— as soon as I can draw I will send you by express all that remains after paying the $100 borrowed for you and the $350 which I borrowed to buy clothing. . . .

I have miserable quarters but don't mind that half as much as some of my junior officers.

When you go to Montgomery any time have your ambrotype and George's taken together and send it to me— you may use the case which contains one of mine if you wish to save expense— get it for me if you can Lizzie for I am very anxious to receive it— if you haven't the money now I must wait until I can send you some— I have not heard from your uncle for a long time—

I cant give you any of the town talk or scandal— I never will learn to post myself up on such subjects— and even what I hear goes in at one ear and out at the other,— . . .

Williams

On Jan. 19, 1865, Grant ordered Maj. Gen. Edward R. S. Canby, commanding the Military Division of West Mississippi, to move against Mobile from Pensacola, Pascagoula, or Mobile Bay with Selma and Montgomery as secondary objectives. To prevent any reinforcements from being sent to Maury from central Alabama and Mississippi, a large cavalry force was organized near Florence, Alabama. Commanded by Bvt. Maj. Gen. James H. Wilson, the expedition's primary objective was Selma. In a lightning campaign beginning March 22, Wilson captured Selma on April 2.[35]

BATTERY C. NEAR MOBILE FEB. 8, 65.

Dear Lizzy:

I wrote you yesterday— This is number four of the new series—[36] I will visit Mrs. Wainwright this evening if nothing unexpected occurs to prevent. . . .

My clothes came in good time, and I have hardly laid off my overcoat since it came. It looks very nice and is comfortable as a good— good— well I dont know what to compare it with— I was going to say a good wife— but that is not so— for there is nothing in the world so good and comfortable as she.

My present quarters are much better than those that I have been occupying at Batteries A and B. They are in a large unoccupied dwelling in the rear of Battery C. This letter is written from it and a party of officers are chatting vivaciously around a scanty fire, and if I were not accustomed to the confusion I would be distracted.

Two of our young officers that returned from prison (the brothers Poellnitz) have died of small pox at their home in Clarke Co.[37]

I saw an officer last night who has just returned from a scout in the neighborhood of Pascagoula: he says that the Yankee force there has all reembarked. The last man left last Wednesday— That looks like a promise of a few days more quiet here. I did think last week that we would have a fight in a few days— I wish that I was certain of the "impunity" of our lines for twenty days and that Gen. Maury would give me leave of absence for that time— I would borrow the money and visit you, much as I would grudge spending money that you need— But it cant be yet and I must be patient.

I occasionally spend the night in the city with John [King], but generally I sleep on the floor of my quarters rolled up in my blanket with a coat for a pillow— and dream of Lizzy and George.

Williams

When I last wrote I was under the impression that it was likely that we would be soon ordered away from the city— I don't know whether I mentioned this to you or not— but from the tone of an order received today I think that we have to make up our minds to stay here a while longer

MOBILE FEBRUARY 11, 65

Dear Lizzy:

I sent $200 by express to-day to Capt E. R. Spalding Montgomery for you— Capt S. is one of our officers residing in Montgomery during his arrest; and I have requested him to forward it to you, or if he has no opportunity to do so, to drop you a note— I hope that you will have received it before this letter reaches you as the express is quicker than the mail.

All is quiet at present. You must excuse my short letter I am worried to day with a general aching of all my teeth caused I think by a slight cold— I am therefore as fidgety as possible—

Williams

No 6

HD QTS 21ST ALA. MOBILE FEBY 22. 65

Dear Lizzy:

. . . I have drawn to-day pay to the amount of $1020.00 and as soon as I repay the money borrowed to send to you, and that which I used to buy clothing from the State, I will send you the ballance by express. (— I am now paid up to the "First of February")— that is if I think it will get through safe from the Yankee raiders—

All is quiet here yet, but as you see by the papers the enemy have movements on foot that appear to have Mobile for their object. I suppose and hope too that you will before long hear of exciting times in this Department— I want to hear the music of battle again six months rest has made me impatient again.

I am drilling my men daily as skirmishers and they can now manuervre very well by the sound of the bugle— When the enemy comes I will either be sent back to my big guns, or will be put on skirmish duty with my sharpshooters—

Williams

MOBILE FEBRUARY 24. 1865

Dear Lizzy:

We are in the midst of what appears to be the rainy season; drills and fatigue duty are "easy", streets and crossings a loblolly— spirits partake of the gloom of the weather and gold goes up in proportion— a weeks good weather would enliven us so much that I would not be surprised if it brought gold down five hundred. Our officers are still under arrest and the powers that be don't seem to be in any hurry to bring them to trial. It makes the duty bear pretty heavily on the few who have it to perform— and I have never been so closely confined as I find myself now-a-days— It is a good thing for us perhaps to be forced to exert ourselves more than we are disposed to do, we wont be so confined in habits of laziness when the war is over— I didnt number my last letter   it was the *"ninth"*—

I believe that I have told you that my camp is at Eslava warehouse on the corner of Water and Congress streets and consequently but a few blocks from Mrs Turner's—

If the Yanks should become quiet in this Department I will try to get a leave of absence for a couple of weeks to visit you cost what it may: in a few days I think we will be able to see what their present intentions are— I however do not believe that my request will be granted so long as Col Anderson and the other officers are in arrest. I will only "try, try again"

In paying off my debts I discovered or rather remembered one or two hundred dollars borrowed from John Werthman nearly a year ago, which has quite spoiled my calculations— I have paid as follows out of my $1020.00—
$320 for clothes
 30 mess bill
200 borrowed from Werthman
300 to send to you
$850 = which leaves for you only $170

Williams

12. Mobile [Thursday] March 2, 1865

Dear Lizzy:

The bad weather has doubtless impeded the operations of the enemy and we are still in peaceful possession of our lives— I am confident that we will have to fight for them however in a few days— My reg't will I suppose act as sharpshooters and my orders require me to march to the front at the first alarm, where I will probably have the honor of participating in the opening ceremonies of the fight for Mobile: I have my ideas as to the fighting programme but it would not be proper to "trust them to paper"— I hope and believe that I will have a fair opportunity to do services of which you will be proud.

The military authorities are seizing all the cotton in the city and storing it together so that in the event of disaster it can be destroyed, and so saved from the Yankee maw.— The revelations made by this search for the leaven of the Pharisees are disgraceful and sometimes amusing— Every house in the city is being rigidly searched and cotton is discovered where no one suspected its existence— many a patriotic— war-meeting— "loyal Confederate" citizen has had a score of cotton bales tumbled from the doors and windows of his private residence into the street   In some cases it has been found under floors or buried in cisterns— I heard of one who had a single bale disguised as a bed— covered with sheets and blankets with an innocent pillow at the head—

It is a great shame for any one who has cotton secreted cannot be loyal in his heart— and as I said many of our loud mouthed war citizens have been made to disgorge.

Miss Ophelia is quite well again   I am very well and have received another letter from you since writing.

I had the pleasure of sleeping out in the rain on picket duty last Tuesday night— and find that it still comes natural for me—

I am thinking of sending you all the clothing that I can dispense with— not much to be sure, but it may be the means of saving it from loss in case the coming campaign should be disasterous to our army—

Good bye, and dont get discouraged if our communications are cut off— my star is a lucky one and I will come out all right.

Williams

Spanish Fort March 13. 65

Dear Lizzy:

Spanish fort is on the eastern shore two miles from my old battery Huger— and six miles below Blakely— I came over here with my regiment[38] day before yesterday; on that day a large fleet appeared before the city and people suppose that a fight is certain to occur within a few days— I am not so certain of it, and think that they will pass by Mobile and march direct on Selma— If there is any fighting about Mobile I look for it however on this side of the bay. A few days will tell; and before you receive this letter you may know more than I can guess now.

I had been quite ill for a day or two before leaving the city, and yesterday I feared that I would be really sick, but thanks to fortune, the doctor and the proximity of the enemy I am quite well and strong this morning— The approach of the Yanks always cures me of any little ailments very quick— You remember how effectually they cured me at Powell a year ago of a disease that had resisted the surgeons for several months.

I might make this an interesting letter for you by giving you a description of our fortifications and forces and sketching off a fancy picture of the fight that may be impending— but those things cannot be "trusted to paper" and you must wait for the developments of time

A great many people have charged me to remember them to you   I can think of— Capt [John F.] O'Connor, The Holcombe's— John Pippen— Commodore [Ebenezer] Farrand— [First Lieutenant George] Vidmer— and half a dozen of B. Co (The Montgomery Guards) and of course King & Bassett.[39]

We have some little cabins for quarters which will keep of[f] wind and rain to some extent— I will write to you whenever I have the opportunity— but you need not be alarmed if communications should be cut off for a time.

Williams

Spanish Fort Mar 17. 65

Dear Lizzy:

Since I left Mobile I have received your letters of Feb 25 and Mar 11— Have written twice— when we left Mobile a fight appeared imminent, but now it seems more of an uncertainty every day— The Maj Gen Commanding who has by some been irreverently dubbed the Lord of Panic issued his battle order, and for the last time as he probably supposed, cleared his decks for action; yet we still possess our lives in quiet— The Yankee force at Pensacola is said to be much less than at first reported, and the waters are so high that it cant advance; . . .

I haven't given up as you imagine my intention of visiting you but I have given up all hope of being permitted to do so for some time to come   While the enemy is in front I could not get leave of absence even if my pride would suffer me to apply for it.

I have one slight hope— that is as I am and have been for more than a week about half sick with diarrhoea— if I should get worse I'll try for a sick leave— . . .

Williams

Spanish Fort March 18, 65

Dear Lizzy:

I write just to be before you again: without a word of news to add to my barren letter of yesterday. The sun, for a wonder is shining to-day, but the clouds portend rain again before night; when the clerk of the weather pleases to dry up for a week or ten days, I think it not improbable that we and the Yanks will celebrate the occasion by a small fight on this side [of] the bay; but until then there will be little to do or to write about from this stronghold.[40]

Last Teusday we had a military execution— I had charge of it and commanded the brigade which was ordered out to witness it— the particulars I omit as I have no doubt that they would not interest you as much as they do some people— Two more will be shot here during the next week or ten days— they are deserters from my regiment.[41]

You would be amused to see our barber-shop this morning— the officers are shaving each other all round, and it makes quite an amusing tableaux—

I long very much to go up to see you, and I am not always so unselfish in this desire as to forget that if I was there I would be partaking daily of your good country fare in place of the corn bread and bacon which we have lived on so long that the mere mention of it takes away my appetite anytime.

Master George does not occupy so much space in your letters as I would wish, I never can hear enough of his doings to satisfy my fondness— . . .

Williams

Spanish Fort March 19, 1865

Dear Lizzy:

I am no better and no worse, a boat is coming at an unusual hour and I take advantage of the opportunity to drop you a hurried letter,— Remember I am not much sick, I wish I was "bad enough off " to get a furlough to go and see you—

I don't think that my future crown of laurels is growing on the hills of this fort, so I would hail with pleasure any order to move elsewhere— My men are returning slowly   many are absent without leave and I feel the loss of the officers who are in arrest very much— I need their services every day. Rumor says that we are ordered or will be in a few days back to Mobile— I dont believe it—

Respy
Yr
Obdt
Sevt
Williams

SPANISH FORT MARCH 22, 65

Dear Lizzy:

At last I have something to tell you that is interesting— it is a God-send!

The enemy are reported in force in the neighborhood of Point Clear, about twelve miles from us; They have a good road all the way up, and may be in our front in a few hours if they are so disposed— Keep up your old fashioned Navy Cove courage and dont be alarmed about me, even if you dont hear from me for some time; The newspapers from Mobile will each one of them be as good to you as a letter from me for if I should be unfortunate they will publish it, and if they say nothing about me you may rest assured that I am "all right" and not hurt— There is no certainty yet that an attack will be made— The very latest report, received this moment, is that the enemy's force is very small— There are plenty of rumors all the time, a new one is born every minute, but no-body is excited— half my men are working in the trenches and nearly all the other half are playing marbles before the quarters like so many school boys. If the Yankees don't come this time I will be vexed— for I want to see them in front of my boys once more— However as I know that you are not of the same mind I will try to console myself, by being pleased on your account

The boat is coming and as I have told my story I'll pause for the present— with a God bless you and George

Williams

On March 23, Maury ordered Brig. Gen. Randall L. Gibson to take his brigade and report to Liddell at Blakeley. Liddell ordered Gibson to dispute Canby's moves above Fish River. On March 25, however, Maury, with only 4500 men, became aware of the magnitude of the Federal thrust. He ordered Liddell to fall back to Blakeley and Gibson to Spanish Fort. While doing so, on March 26, the Twenty-first Alabama surprised the Eighty-first Illinois Regiment with a volley from 400 yards on the north side of Bay Minette Creek. Canby immediately began the investment of Spanish Fort, and it was completed on March 27.[42] As the Confederates retreated toward Blakeley, the Twenty-first (now in Liddell's command) fought a six-hour skirmish on March 27 at Bay Minette.[43] The next day, March 28, Liddell ordered the Twenty-first down to Spanish Fort in exchange for Thomas's Reserve Regiments. By April 1, Gibson informed Maury that he could not defend the works with "only 1,400 infantry, with two corps d'armée in my front pressing up night and day." (Richmond was evacuated the next day.) Thomas's brigade was soon relieved, but the Twenty-first Alabama remained at Spanish Fort in Brig. Gen. James T. Holtzclaw's brigade. Despite extensive pressure from the Union seige forces, the garrison was not evacuated until the evening of April 8. The picket line and artillery were left to be captured. They walked silently without shoes along a narrow treadway about 18 inches wide and 1,200 yards long to waiting boats that took them to Battery Huger, and from there in steamers to Blakeley. The next day, Sunday, April 9, they were transported to Mobile. On that day Blakeley was taken by assault and Lee surrendered at Appomattox Court House. The war was ending.

Taylor ordered Maury's command, including the Twenty-first Alabama (numbering about 4,500) to evacuate Mobile on April 11–12. They went north on the Mobile and Ohio Railroad to Meridian, Mississippi and then east a few miles to Cuba Station, Alabama, on the Alabama and Mississippi Railroad. Generals Taylor and Canby agreed to a truce on April 30 and the formal surrender was agreed to on May 4.[44] On May 3, Williams had the regiment sign its last roster in a small four-by-six-inch notebook. There are 207 signatures and marks.[45] Williams and his men received their paroles on May 10, 1865, in Meridian, Mississippi.

NOTES

INTRODUCTION

1. The James Madison Williams Collection is in the possession of Mrs. Louise Williams Chamberlin, Williams's granddaughter, in Mobile, Alabama. See the elder Williams's advertisements in the *St. Clairsville Gazette*, 1838–52, passim, especially Feb. 28, 1847, and Jan. 15,1852; Williams's obituary, ibid., Feb. 11, 1903; *Journal of the Proceedings of the Thirty-Fourth General Convention of the New Church in the United States* (Boston: Otis Clapp, 1852), p. 75. The biographical data for John H. Williams was furnished by his great-granddaughter, Doris Williams Ekstrom, of Duncombe, Iowa, 1976. See John Kent Folmar, ed., "Pre–Civil War Sentiment from Belmont County: Correspondence of Hugh Anderson," *Ohio History* 78 (Summer 1969):202–3.

2. The newlyweds arrived in Mobile on the morning of Dec. 17. This personal information is from letters written 1858–60 to Williams from his father, mother, and sister Bella in Iowa; his grandfather Hugh Anderson and cousin W. H. Rudolph, in Ohio; his cousin Rachel Jackson, in Philadelphia; and James Conning; and a scrapbook marked "Private, J. M. Williams, Choctaw Bluff," Williams Collection. Lizzy's parents had migrated south from Newburgh, New York. Conning's career is outlined in Sidney Adair Smith, *Mobile: Silversmiths and Jewelers, 1820–1867* (Mobile: Historical Mobile Preservation Society, 1935), [p. 3].

3. Prior to Alabama's secession on Jan. 11, 1861, Governor Albert B. Moore had ordered the seizure on Jan. 4 of Fts. Morgan and Gaines at the entrance to Mobile Bay, and the federal arsenal at Mount Vernon, thirty miles north of Mobile. For Alabama's secession, see Walter L. Fleming, *Civil War and Reconstruction in Alabama* (New York: Columbia University Press, 1905), pp. 49–56.

4. John Pippin to Williams, Aug. 12, 1861. Pippin, Conning's brother-in-law, sent his condolences to the Williamses from an "entrenched camp" near Norfolk. Pippin had enlisted in the original Mobile Cadets, which became Company A of the Third Alabama Regiment, Volunteers. Organized in Montgomery in April 1861, it entrained immediately for Virginia. In October he was elected second lieutenant of Company H, in the newly organized Twenty-second Alabama Regiment, Volunteers. He served through the Shiloh campaign and was discharged July 19, 1862, because of poor health.

5. Col. James Crawford, a wealthy commission merchant in Mobile, entered state service in April. He had been attempting to organize the Second Alabama Regiment since mid July. Advertisement for recruits appeared almost daily in the Mobile *Advertiser and Register* after early September. On Sept. 20, the editor wrote that Crawford's Second Alabama would be mustered into Confederate service in a few days, "to be stationed on the coast in the neighborhood of our city." The regiment was mustered into Confederate service as the Twenty-first Alabama Regiment, Volunteers. Crawford was its colonel until March 1, 1862, when he resigned because of ill health.

The best secondary source for Alabama's Civil War military units is Willis Brewer, *Alabama: Her History, Resources, War Record and Reminiscences, from 1540 to 1872* (Montgomery: Barrett and Brown, 1872), pp. 589–705. The compiled service records for Alabama's Confederate officers and enlisted men are in Microcopy 311, War Department

Collection of Confederate Records, Record Group 109, National Archives Building, Washington, D.C., hereafter referred to as CSR, RG 109, NA. Most of the old and new companies which were organized in the Mobile area are listed, with their original rosters, in the Mobile *Daily Herald,* Nov. 15, 1904.

Not only did the prospects of service on the coast near his wife offer Williams an inducement to enlist, but also Conning agreed to continue his salary. The Washington Light Infantry was the second Mobile company to have that designation; the first outfit had gone to Virginia with the Third Alabama Regiment, Volunteers, in April. On Aug. 21, 1864, the editor of the Mobile *Advertiser and Register* wrote that the "Twenty-first [was] a duplicate of the veteran Alabama Third, or formed from old volunteer organizations and did not go to Virginia; soon raised new companies, with same names as old, with II added for distinction from old. Mostly younger brothers and relatives of [those in] the original companies. From the first and still are 'of the best blood in Mobile.' "

6. Undated application to the Raphael Semmes Camp of Confederate Veterans, Mobile, Williams Collection; Mobile *Advertiser and Register,* Oct. 13, 1861. The ten original companies of the Twenty-first, eight of which were from Mobile County, were: A (Washington Light Infantry, #2), B (Montgomery Guards), C (Witherspoon or Marengo Rifles, Marengo County [north of Mobile]), D (Battle Guards), E (Chamberlain or Woodruff Rifles), F (Baldwin Rifles, #2, Baldwin County [across the bay]), G (Spanish Guards), H (French Guards), I (United Rangers), and K (Mobile Cadets, #2).

7. John Kent Folmar, "Post–Civil War Mobile: The Letters of James M. Williams, May–September, 1865," *Alabama Historical Quarterly* 32 (Fall and Winter 1970):191.

8. Mobile *City Directory,* 1870–99; Kennedy and Lyons to Williams, June 8, 1869, Williams Collection.

9. Mobile *City Directory,* 1873, 1891.

10. Ibid., 1891; *Confederate Veteran* (Nashville, Tenn.) 3 (March 1895):79; 4 (April, June, 1896): 121, 265; 5 (July 1897):370; 6 (July 1898):321; newspaper clipping, n.p., n.d., Williams Collection.

11. *Can't-Get-Away Club: Their Works in 1897* (Mobile: George Matzenger, 1878), pp. 1–27, in Local History Section, Mobile Public Library; Mobile *Press Register,* Oct. 17, 1948.

12. Powell was Mrs. Louise Williams Chamberlin's father. He named his only son Powell Williams, Jr. Mrs. Chamberlin told me that when her father enrolled in school as a youngster, he thought that his real name was Fort Powell. He later said that he should have kept that name.

CHAPTER I

1. The new camp, located about ten miles south of Mobile, was a training site as well as an outpost against any Union movement from the Gulf coast.

Effective Sept. 12, 1861, Mobile's defenses became a part of the District of Alabama, which included Alabama and the Mississippi coast east of Pascagoula. Brig. Gen. Jones M. Withers, a prominent merchant and politician in Mobile both before and after the war, was the district's first commanding officer. A graduate of West Point, he was the first colonel of the Third Alabama Infantry. When promoted, he was transferred from Virginia to Mobile. On Oct. 7, Maj. Gen. Braxton Bragg, who had commanded Confederate troops at Pensacola, Florida, was named commander of the newly created Department of Alabama and West Florida. Withers continued to command the District of Alabama with headquarters in Mobile. *War of the Rebellion: Official Records of the Union and Confederate Armies* (Washington: 1880–1901), Series 1, 7: 738, 751–52, hereafter referred to as ORA. Biographical data for generals is from Willis Brewer, *Alabama: Her History, Resources, War Record and Reminiscences, from 1540 to 1872*; Ezra J. Warner, *Generals in Gray: Lives of the Confederate Commanders* (Baton Rouge: Louisiana State University Press, 1959); Ezra J. Warner, *Generals in Blue: Lives of the Union Commanders* (Baton Rouge: Louisiana State University Press, 1964); and Mark M. Boatner, III, *The Civil War Dictionary* (New York: David McKay Co., 1959).

2. Q.M. Sgt. Matthew Chester had previously served in the Governor's Guards in Selma. Discharged in May 1862, he later became a secret detective officer searching for deserters. He worked out of the Provost Marshal's office in Mobile at least through Sept. 1864.

3. Lizzy lived in Mrs. Eliza P. Turner's boarding house, which was located on the corner of St. Louis and Jackson Streets. Mrs. Turner was George W. Turner's wife. The Census of 1860 and the Mobile City Directories for 1859 and 1861 were useful in identifying James's nonmilitary acquaintances.

4. The camp was temporarily named for Alabama's "secession" governor, Albert B. Moore. He served two terms, 1857–61.

5. Turner was Fifth Sergeant of Company A until detached to work as a nurse in the Mobile General Hospital. He received a medical discharge Jan. 11, 1862.

6. Dog River flows into the bay eight miles south of Mobile on the western shore. Two prewar masonry forts, thirty miles south of Mobile, protected the entrance to Mobile Bay. The larger of the two, Ft. Morgan, was on Mobile Point, near the main channel. Ft. Gaines was on the eastern tip of Dauphin Island, three miles to the west. In late October, while feverishly preparing the coastal defenses, Bragg determined that Ft. Gaines's function would be to prevent a landing on Dauphin Island. Also, a small work at Grant's Pass between Dauphin Island and Cedar Point was being constructed to prevent any movement into the lower bay through the Mississippi Sound. ORA, 6:755–57; James L. Nichols, "Confederate Engineers and the Defense of Mobile," *Alabama Review* 12 (July 1959):181–94.

7. Williams is concerned about the huge naval and land expedition (77 ships and 12,000 troops) commanded by Flag Officer Samuel F. DuPont and Brig. Gen. Thomas W. Sherman. When it sailed from Hampton Roads, Va., on Oct. 29, there was great uncertainty in the South as to where it would strike. Fts. Walker and Beauregard at Port Royal Sound, S.C., fell to the combined force on Nov. 7, 1861. *U.S. Official Records of the Union and Confederate Navies in the War of the Rebellion* (Washington: 1894–1922), Series I, 12: 228–30, 261–65, hereafter referred to as ORN.

8. Williams is probably referring to the Nineteenth Alabama Infantry, which was organized in Huntsville in August and ordered to Mobile. It is listed in the Dec. 2, 1861, district field return, ORA, 6:772.

9. Capt. John F. Jewett, Company A's first commanding officer, mustered into state service, April, 1861. He resigned, effective May 12, 1862.

10. 2d Lt. Nathan Whiting also entered state service in April. When he resigned April 20, 1862, Williams was elected to succeed him.

11. Mrs. Malissa Wainwright was, apparently, the wife of James L. Wainwright, a tinner in Prattville, Ala.

12. The blockading vessels on station were the sailing frigate U.S.S. *Potomac* and side-wheeler steamer U.S.S. *Water Witch. ORN*, 16:769. The lighthouse was on Sand Island at the entrance to the outer channel. Used as a federal lookout post, it was

destroyed on Feb. 23, 1863, by engineers led by 1st Lt. John W. Glenn. Caldwell Delaney, *The Story of Mobile* (Mobile: Gulf Printing Co., 1953), p. 114; Glenn to Brig. Gen. Danlille Leadbetter, Engineer Bureau, Ft. Gaines, Feb. 24, 1863, Binder 20, Dabney H. Maury Collection, Museum of the City of Mobile, Mobile, Ala.

13. *Childe Harold's Pilgrimage*, part 179, canto 4.

14. Pvt. George H. Bassett, a close friend of Williams's was soon detached as a clerk in General Withers's headquarters. In Sept. 1863, he was assigned to the Medical Purveyor's Office in Mobile as an orderly and druggist.

15. Tommy Traddles, a school friend of David Copperfield, often referred to his wife, Sophy Crewler, as "the dearest girl in the world." See Charles Dickens, *David Copperfield* (1850).

16. The "regulars" were members of the First Alabama Battalion of Artillery. Recruited at Mobile, Montgomery, Selma, and Eufaula, it became a part of the "Army of Alabama" in early Feb. 1861. Assigned to Fts. Morgan and Gaines, it was transferred to Confederate service as "regulars." Brewer, *Alabama*, p. 623. The district field return for Ft. Gaines, Dec. 2, 1861, listed 61 officers and 991 men present for duty. ORA, 6:772. The Dec. 1861 regimental muster roll for the Twenty-first Alabama indicates that 838 men were present. This is the only muster roll by company in CSR, RG 109, NA.

17. Franklin (1786–1847), an English explorer, led four expeditions to the Arctic between 1819–47.

18. Pvt. John A. King was another personal friend. After suffering a severe wound in the battle of Shiloh on April 6, 1862, King later rejoined Williams at Choctaw Bluff.

19. The Confederates won the battle of Manassas, Va., (Bull Run) on July 21. The battle of Belmont, Mo., was fought on Nov. 7. Confederates from Columbus, on the Kentucky side of the Mississippi River, participated in the battle.

20. This was a fight between the C.S.S. steamer *Florida* (a converted packet) and the blockading steamer U.S.S. *Montgomery* at Horn Island Pass near Ship Island, in which the Confederate ship had the better of a two-hour duel. The *Florida's* name was changed to *Selma* in Sept. 1862. ORN, 16:808–9; Naval History Division, Navy Department, *Civil War Naval Chronology, 1861–1865* (Washington: Department of the Navy, 1971), 6:300–301.

21. George Taylor, an employee of Conning's, apparently lived at Mrs. Turner's.

22. 2d Sgt. John F. Cothran, another close friend, ultimately succeeded Williams as captain of Company A. On Dec. 7, General Order No. 10 designated the troops at Ft. Gaines the Second Brigade. Noted on Dec. 1861 regimental roster.

23. On Dec. 9, the *Potomac* fired a rifled gun to attract the attention of the steamer U.S.S. *Huntsville* after rescuing one of five blacks who had escaped in a boat from Ft. Morgan to Sand Island. The *Huntsville* fired the practice-round shot toward the beach. Log Books, Records of Bureau of Naval Personnel, Record Group 24, NA; ORN, 16:813.

24. Lt. Col. Andrew J. Ingersoll began his state service in July. He resigned his commission May 27, 1862, because of illness. He had already been appointed Provost Marshal of Mobile on May 26, 1862.

25. Williams is alluding to a Confederate surprise night attack from Pensacola against Union troops outside Ft. Pickens (Santa Rosa Island, Florida) on Oct. 9, 1861, in which Col. William Wilson's Sixth New York Zouaves were routed. ORA, 6:438–63, passim.

26. This "magnificent" fight between the C.S.S. *Florida* and the *Huntsville* is described in ORN, 17:11–13.

27. Ophelia ("Miss Phe") was Mrs. Turner's eighteen-year-old daughter.

28. The two additional "sea-leachers" were probably the *Water Witch* and the flagship U.S.S. *Niagara. ORN,* 17: 14–15, 23.

29. Maj. Frederick Stewart entered state service in July and was the Twenty-first's first major. He resigned, effective March 31, 1862, but before the resignation's acceptance he led the regiment on April 7, the second day at Shiloh.

30. Entering state service in April, Lt. Frederick V. Cluis was elected first lieutenant of Company A in October. In March 1862, he became the regimental commissary. Later in 1862, he was named post commissary at Ft. Morgan.

31. Pvt. Robert G. Wier was in Company A until July 3, 1862, when he was detached as a hospital nurse in Mobile. He was later promoted to sergeant and appointed hospital steward and wardmaster.

32. For the federal occupation of Biloxi, see *ORN,* 17:33–34.

33. Frank D. Snow was a friend of Williams's. He enlisted May 10, 1862, as a musician in Company K, Twenty-second Alabama Regiment, and received a medical discharge Feb. 11, 1863. His father, Joel H. Snow, owned a music store in Mobile.

34. 3d Sgt. William B. Campbell received a disability discharge May 9, 1862.

35. 4th Sgt. Abram Sellers soon procured a substitute and received a discharge.

36. Pvt. Robert H. Ward was wounded and captured at Shiloh on April 7, 1862. Exchanged in September, he was detached in Jan. 1863 as a clerk and special messenger in the Quartermaster Department until captured at Ft. Morgan on Aug. 23, 1864. He was a prisoner of war at Elmira, N.Y., until the war's end.

37. Cpl. Harry M. Gazzam was also captured at Shiloh and exchanged. Promoted to second lieutenant of Company A, he, too, was captured at Ft. Morgan, and imprisoned at Ft. LaFayette, N.Y., and Ft. Warren, Mass.

38. *The Household of Bouverie; or the Elixir of Gold: A Romance by a Southern Lady,* 2 vols. (New York: Derby and Jackson, 1858–60).

39. The Dec. 1861, muster roll listed 74 enlisted men present in Company A.

40. The vessels assigned in the Mississippi Sound were the *Water Witch* and the steamers *Massachusetts* and *New London.*

41. The schooner's crew did burn her, as reported by the U.S.S. *Huntsville's* captain. *ORN,* 17:83.

42. On Jan. 27, 1862, Withers's command was designated the Army of Mobile, which included the Gulf defenses from the Perdido to the Pascagoula Rivers. The Twenty-first Alabama is listed, for the first time in the *ORA,* as a part of his command. 6: 815, 819. This letter is written after Williams returned from a brief furlough to Mobile.

43. In state service since April 1861, Jr. 2d Lt. John W. Mann resigned his commission on March 30, 1862.

44. Federal forces under Brig. Gen. U. S. Grant captured Ft. Henry on the Tennessee River, Feb. 6. Ten days later Ft. Donelson, on the Cumberland River, fell. This forced the Confederates to evacuate western Kentucky and Nashville, Tennessee. Their concentration on the "Tennessee line" led to the battle of Shiloh.

45. The blockade runner *Magnolia,* loaded with cotton, was chased eastward from the Mississippi River by the U.S.S. *Brooklyn* and *Mercedita.* The U.S.S. *South Carolina* joined the chase until the *Magnolia* was hit and abandoned south of Dauphin Island. *ORN,* 17:140–48. It is unlikely that the lightly armed *Magnolia* returned the Federal fire.

46. Christopher G. Memminger, of South Carolina, was the Confederate Secretary of the Treasury. The Twenty-first's sudden move was precipitated by the War Department's order to Bragg, on Feb. 18, that "all the Confederate forces in Mobile, as well as those in

Pensacola, are to be moved as rapidly as possible to the Tennessee line [near Corinth, Mississippi]." *ORA*, 6:82. Corinth, in northeastern Mississippi, was the point of concentration, because there the strategically significant east-west Memphis and Charleston railroad crossed the north-south Mobile and Ohio Railroad. Robert C. Black, *The Railroads of the Confederacy* (Chapel Hill: University of North Carolina Press, 1952), pp. 139–40.

47. Williams apparently means that Lieutenant Cluis is acting captain, in Jewett's absence.

48. A distinguished veteran of the Mexican War, Brig. Gen. Adley H. Gladden took the First Louisiana Regulars to Pensacola, where, in Sept. 1861, he was promoted to brigadier general. The Twenty-first was assigned to his brigade, but not by this date. Lt. Col. W. K. Beard was not the assistant adjutant general for the brigade; he commanded the First Florida Regiment. *ORA*, 6: 849, 857.

49. Bragg ordered Pippin's regiment (Twenty-second Alabama) with the Eighteenth Alabama and the First Louisiana to Corinth on Feb. 26. Ibid., p. 836.

CHAPTER II

1. Beauregard's command was designated the Army of the Mississippi on March 5, 1862. *ORA*, 7:915; 10, Pt. 2: 299–300.

2. Apparently Lizzy thought that she was pregnant again.

3. An engineer, Sgt. George E. Dixon received a severe wound at Shiloh. After recovering, he was promoted to first lieutenant of Company A, and served with the regiment until he volunteered to help develop the *H. L. Hunley* sub-torpedo boat project in Mobile and Charleston. R. J. Cocke was first corporal of Company A.

4. On March 13, 1862, learning that the enemy had landed troops at Pittsburg Landing, Tennessee, on the Tennessee River, Beauregard ordered a concentration at Bethel Station, Tennessee, which was about twenty miles north of Corinth on the Mobile and Ohio Railroad. *ORA*, 10, Pt. 2: 318–19.

5. On March 29, Gen. Albert Sidney Johnston, commander of the Western Department, combined the armies of Kentucky and of the Mississippi into the Army of the Mississippi, which numbered around 40,000. There were four corps (with Beauregard second in command): Bragg commanded the Second Corps and Withers was assigned the Second Division. Williams got his wish and the Twenty-first was brigaded with the Twenty-second, Twenty-fifth, and Twenty-sixth Alabama Regiments, the First Louisiana Regulars, and Capt. Felix H. Robertson's Battery under Gladden's command. Ibid., p. 370–71.

6. Maj. Gen. William J. Hardee, commander of the Third Corps of Johnston's Army, wrote *Rifle and Light Infantry Tactics* in 1855, while still an officer in the U.S. Army. His book was the standard drill manual for both sides in the Civil War.

7. Pvt. George Van Antwerp, Company A, was often detached as a druggist at the Mobile Hospital through 1863.

8. Capt. Isadore P. Girardey's Battery (Washington Light Artillery) was attached to the Second Division, Third Brigade, Brig. Gen. John K. Jackson commanding. Lt. J. J. Jacobus was killed at Shiloh on April 6. *ORA*, 10, Pt. 1: 383, 565–66.

9. By the evening of April 2, Johnston decided to attack Grant's army at Pittsburg Landing before it could be reinforced from Nashville by Maj. Gen. Don Carlos Buell's Army of the Ohio. *ORA*, 10, Pt. 2: 388–89.

10. Capt. Stuart S. W. Cayce, the Twenty-first's adjutant, succeeded Ingersoll on March 30. He led the regiment at Shiloh on the first day until injured, captured, and subsequently rescued. Maj. Frederick Stewart led the regiment on April 7, the second day of the battle. Cayce resigned May 9, 1862. He was soon assigned to the Provost Marshall's office in Mobile. In Oct. 1864, he commanded the City Battalion, Post of Mobile. ORA, 10, Pt. 1: 541; 45, Pt. 1: 1233; see Williams's letter, Aug. 25, 1862.

11. King survived; we read more of him later. Plum was captured on the second day, April 7, and exchanged Sept. 18, 1862. At the war's end, he was a clerk in Company K. After recovering, Chevalier was detached as a druggist and later as a hospital steward in Mobile. Severely wounded in the hand, Gilsinan was detached in late 1862 to the Engineering Department in Mobile, where in 1864 he was a ship's carpenter. Hays was in Company A until Ft. Morgan's garrison surrendered, Aug. 23, 1864. He, too, was imprisoned at Elmira, N.Y. John Keith was severely wounded in the forehead and knee and captured April 7. Exchanged in September, he was again captured at Ft. Morgan. Promoted to sergeant in Company A, Milligan was also taken prisoner at Ft. Morgan. Paroled in March 1864, he was third sergeant of Company K when the regiment surrendered. Shay was also captured at Ft. Morgan. Werthman was furloughed and discharged, Oct. 31, 1862. Westermeyer apparently died in August. Captured on April 7, White was exchanged Sept. 18. Detached as a clerk in the Quartermaster Department of Mobile, and later as a special messenger, he was also captured at Ft. Morgan. Both Skates and Eldridge were in Company K. Eldridge received a discharge on July 24, 1862. Dixon's sweetheart had given him the twenty-dollar gold piece when he left Mobile. The bullet was embedded in the coin. See details in Mobile *Daily Herald*, Nov. 15, 1904.

12. Ward, Gazzam, Treat, and Junius F. Williams were captured on April 7. Junius Williams was exchanged and subsequently promoted to corporal. Captured at Ft. Morgan, he was imprisoned at Elmira, N.Y.

13. Originally placed in Bragg's second line of attack, Gladden's brigade of Withers's Division was placed in the first line when it was discovered that Hardee's Corps did not extend to the Union left. The regiments' order of advance, from left to right, was the First Louisiana, the Twenty-sixth, Twenty-fifth, Twenty-second, and Twenty-first Alabama Regiments. Gladden was mortally wounded early in the heavy fighting, and Col. Daniel W. Adams (First Louisiana) led the brigade until wounded in midafternoon. Col. Zachariah C. Deas (Twenty-second Alabama) then assumed command. He, too, was wounded, but remained in command. ORA, 10, Pt. 1: 465, 470; Thomas Lawrence Connelly, *Army of the Heartland: The Army of Tennessee, 1861–1862* (Baton Rouge: Louisiana State University Press, 1967), pp. 161–65, 170. See Wiley Sword, "The Battle of Shiloh," *Civil War Times Illustrated* 17 (May 1978):1–50.

14. Brig. Gen. James R. Chalmers's brigade was soon placed on Gladden's right. Gladden's brigade was in the day's hottest fighting during the efforts to dislodge the Union defenders at the "Hornet's Nest" in the center of the line. ORA, 10, Pt. 1: 533. General Johnston was mortally wounded at 2:30 P.M., and Beauregard assumed command.

15. Reinforced with Buell's army during the night, Grant ordered a counterattack early the next day. Fighting continued all morning and into the afternoon. The Twenty-first Alabama was temporarily brigaded with the Nineteenth Alabama and Second Texas Regiments, Col. John C. Moore commanding. Ordered to attack in conjunction with troops commanded by Maj. Gen. John C. Breckinridge's Reserve Corps, they were severely beaten back. Learning that expected reinforcement from Arkansas under Maj. Gen. Earl Van Dorn would not arrive in time to affect the battle, Beauregard ordered a

retreat toward Corinth. Grant did not pursue the defeated Confederates. *ORA*, 10, Pt. 1: 467, 535–36, 556–57; Connelly, *Army of the Heartland*, pp. 173–75.

16. Pvt. Samuel Allen, a clerk, was discharged April 11, 1862, for defective eyesight.

17. Cayce reported on April 13 that the Twenty-first lost 198 killed, wounded, and missing, including five color-bearers. Williams was mentioned in the report as being "particularly active in the discharge of [his] several duties." He wrote his father that the regiment lost 217 men of 550 engaged. Withers reported that Gladden's Brigade lost 129 killed, 597 wounded, and 103 missing. *ORA*, 10, Pt. 1: 535, 541.

18. Pvt. A. B. Bradford was apparently wounded and hospitalized. He was captured with Company A at Ft. Morgan. Williams wrote this letter on the back of a letter from his wife, dated April 3, in which she noted that "Mrs. Turner gave me Miss Phe's gown to make you a pair of drawers."

19. Col. Joseph Wheeler commanded the Nineteenth Alabama at Shiloh. Here he led a demi-brigade that made up the rear of Breckinridge's command, which was in turn the rear guard of the army. In July, Wheeler was named chief of cavalry for the Army of the Mississippi. Monterey, Tenn., is about eleven miles north of Corinth.

20. Pvt. John Crimmins received a discharge on July 7, 1862. Sgt. Charles L. Tell enlisted as a private on Oct. 13, 1861. On Aug. 30, 1862, he succeeded Dixon as second lieutenant and on May 16, 1864, succeeded Dixon as first lieutenant of Company A. He was not at Ft. Morgan when it capitulated and he served until the end of the war.

21. Col. John H. Morgan commanded the Second Kentucky Cavalry. His later exploits became legendary. The skirmish at Monterey, Tenn., occurred on April 17.

22. On April 16, the Confederate Congress enacted the Enrollment Act, which extended the one-year volunteers' enlistments for two additional years and made liable for the draft all white men between the ages of eighteen and thirty-five unless they volunteered or were legally exempt. Albert B. Moore, *Conscription and Conflict in the Confederacy* (New York: MacMillan Co., 1924), pp. 12–17.

23. Dr. R. H. Redwood was captured on April 7 while tending the wounded. Released on June 25, 1862, he served for the balance of the war.

24. On April 28, Jackson's Third Brigade, Withers's Division, included, besides the Twenty-first, the Seventeenth, Eighteenth, and Twenty-fourth Alabama Regiments; his own Fifth Georgia, and Burtwell's (Ala.) Battery. *ORA*, 10, Pt. 2: 461.

25. The Twenty-second Alabama remained in the First Brigade of Withers's Division, Brig. Gen. Franklin Gardner commanding.

26. *Hamlet*, act 3, sc. 1, lines 79–80.

27. Pvt. Joseph C. Ackerman, Company A, was apparently ill. He received a disability discharge May 3, 1862.

28. 1st Lt. Gideon M. Parker (Company E) was captured on April 6 and imprisoned at Sandusky, Ohio. He was exchanged Nov. 8, 1862. Andrew J. Witherspoon was also captured, imprisoned at Sandusky, and released Aug. 3. He resigned April 23, 1864.

29. Company K's commanding officer, Charles S. Stewart, entered state service in April 1861. He was appointed major on May 1, and lieutenant colonel on May 16, 1862. He was killed at Ft. Morgan on April 30, 1863, when a cannon exploded. Williams succeeded him.

30. The Clinch Rifles of Augusta were now Company A, Fifth Georgia Regiment.

31. Preliminary to moving on Corinth, the Union army, now numbering over 100,000, occupied Monterey on the morning of April 29, 1862. *ORA*, 10, Pt. 1: 798–800.

32. Samuel Butler, *Hudibras*, canto 3, part 1, lines 1–2.

33. Williams wrote most of this letter on the back of an undated morning report. Only 184 were present in the regiment, excluding Companies I and K.

34. Herman G. Whiting was Chief Musician in Company A, Fifth Georgia Regiment.

35. Henry J. Osborne, Jr., commanded a company in the Thirty-ninth Georgia Regiment. See John Kent Folmar, ed., "Augusta, Georgia, 1860–1861: As Seen in Three Letters," *Georgia Historical Quarterly* 53 (Dec. 1969):526.

36. Pvt. Robert W. Welch, Company A, was apparently en route home, since he received a discharge for "general bad health" on May 3.

37. A "Peter Funk" was the contemporary nickname for bogus bidders at auctions.

38. On May 6, Bragg was appointed commander of the Army of the Mississippi. He immediately ordered all twelve-month volunteer units to hold reorganization elections as allowed by the Enrollment Act. Beauregard continued to command the Confederate forces around Corinth. *ORA*, 10, Pt. 2: 500–501; Moore, *Conscription and Conflict*, p. 14.

39. This action was near Farmington, four miles east of Corinth. *ORA*, 10, Pt. 1: 812–31, passim; Connelly, *Army of the Heartland*, p. 176. Note that two letters are dated May 10.

40. Maj. Gen. Ormsby M. Mitchel commanded the Third Division, Army of the Ohio.

CHAPTER III

1. On Friday, May 30, Beauregard ordered the evacuation of Corinth. He termed it "a complete surprise to the enemy." The army retreated down the Mobile and Ohio Railroad and finally halted at Tupelo, fifty-two miles to the south. The Booneville raid was executed by the Second Iowa Cavalry, twenty-two miles south of Corinth. *ORA*, 10, Pt. 1: 762-65, 861–64; Thomas Lawrence Connelly, *Army of the Heartland: The Army of Tennessee, 1861–62* (Baton Rouge: Louisiana State University Press, 1967), p. 177.

2. Maj. Gen. Henry W. Halleck, the Union commander, did not follow the retreating Confederates in force. *ORA*, 10, Pt. 1: 668.

3. Elected junior second lieutenant of Company A on May 8, 1862, William S. Badger was elected first lieutenant of the "new" Company H in March 1864. Captured at Ft. Gaines Aug. 8, 1864, he was exchanged at Ship Island, Miss., on Jan. 5, 1865.

4. Williams is referring to Maj. Gen. Thomas J. "Stonewall" Jackson's Shenandoah Valley Campaign of May–June 1862, which was a strategic diversion against Maj. Gen. George B. McClellan's unsuccessful Peninsular Campaign toward Richmond.

5. The word *contraband* was, by this date, a slang word for slaves. It implied that slaves were property that could be seized by Union forces.

6. Van Dorn's Army of the West, recently defeated at Pea Ridge, Ark., arrived a few days after the battle of Shiloh. Maj. Gen. Sterling Price commanded a division in that army. *ORA*, 10, Pt. 2: 462.

7. Company G (Spanish Guards) and Company H (French Guards) were, in fact, transferred to the First Louisiana. Six of their officers including Muths were ordered discharged by Bragg, effective June 27, 1862. The two replacement "conscript" companies were not organized until March 1864.

The two new "conscript" companies, G and H (Capts. Edward R. Spalding and Algernon S. Carrington commanding, respectively), were organized in March 1864. Spalding was appointed captain on March 24, 1864. Taken prisoner at Ft. Gaines and subsequently exchanged, he was captured by Union cavalry on April 19, 1865. Carrington entered state service Sept. 21, 1864, as second lieutenant in the Chamberlain Rifles, which became Company E on Oct. 13, 1861. He was promoted to first lieutenant on May

8, 1862, and to captain of Company H on March 24, 1864. Captured at Ft. Gaines, he was exchanged and served in the regiment until the war's end.

8. When the war began, Charles D. Anderson was a first lieutenant of artillery in Texas. He was appointed Captain of Artillery in the Confederate regular army on April 12, 1861. Promoted to major on Dec. 9, he served with the Twentieth Alabama in Knoxville. On Feb. 15, 1862, he was detached to serve on Gladden's staff in Mobile and was his acting assistant adjutant general at Shiloh. When the regiment was reorganized, he was elected to command the Twenty-first Alabama.

9. Daniel Stirling was later promoted to sergeant. Second Lt. Henry Sossaman was elected captain of Company E during the regimental reorganization in May 1862. He served with the regiment until the end of the war.

10. Thomas G. Barrett was first lieutenant of Company C, Fifth Georgia Regiment until promoted to captain in May 1862, when he was assigned, initially, to the Seventeenth Alabama Regiment, and, in mid-May, to ordnance officer in Jackson's Brigade. Col. James Strawbridge commanded the First Louisiana Regiment.

11. Williams is referring to Maj. Gen. Benjamin F. Butler's Order No. 28 to treat females in New Orleans as women of the streets for insulting, in any manner, officers of the United States. This led to a great public outcry in the South.

12. July 16 was the date that the conscript exempts were to be discharged. However, their enlistments were extended for three months.

13. In the first battles of the Seven Days' Battle near Richmond, Gen. R. E. Lee had forced McClellan's army to fall back toward the James River. On June 27, Bragg replaced Beauregard as commanding general of the newly designated Department No. 2. He subdivided the department into the Districts of Mississippi and the Gulf. ORA, 15:771; 17: 112, 626, 636.

14. It is important to note that Bragg's old Second Corps troops are expressing a sentiment that few other soldiers in that army ever uttered. See Grady McWhiney, *Braxton Bragg and Confederate Defeat*, vol. 1, *Field Command* (New York: Columbia University Press, 1969):253–55, 258–60.

15. Charles B. Johnston is the correct spelling of his name. He entered state service in April 1861 and was elected captain of Company B (Montgomery Guards) in Oct. He succeeded James as regimental major on April 30, 1863. Captured at Ft. Gaines Aug. 8, 1864, he refused to be exchanged and took the oath of allegiance.

16. The only regimental roster for 1862, dated July 3, lists 250 men present for duty of 321 "effectives"; 23 men were detached for extra duty and 47 were sick. RG 109, NA.

17. Lauderdale, where there was an officer's hospital, is fifteen miles north of Meridian, Miss. The road to which Williams refers is the Mobile & Ohio Railroad.

18. On July 4, Bragg ordered Withers's Division "without delay" to Saltillo, eight miles north on the Mobile & Ohio Railroad. ORA, 17, Pt. 2: 638.

19. Pvt. Jerome S. Cartwright was in Company A until captured at Ft. Morgan. He took the loyalty oath and was released March 20, 1865.

20. Pvt. Francis H. Reynolds, Company A, was detached in June as a foundryman.

21. Promoted to surgeon in July 1862, Dr. John F. Y. Payne was transferred Aug. 5, 1864.

CHAPTER IV

1. The Department of Western Alabama and West Florida was discontinued in July and merged with the Western Department. Brig. Gen. John H. Forney commanded the newly created District of the Gulf, which extended from the territory east of Pearl River

to the Appalachicola River in Florida, and north to the thirty-second parallel. *ORA*, 17, Pt. 2: 655–57, 659; 15: 770–71.

2. Williams's brother, twenty-year-old John H. Williams, enlisted on Aug. 13, 1861, in Company G of the First Iowa Cavalry. By Nov. 1864 he was a sergeant. He mustered out at Memphis, Tenn., on June 13, 1865. CSR, RG 94, NA.

3. Second Lt. Augustus P. Dorgan was elected captain of Company K (Mobile Cadets) on April 16, 1862. He resigned Aug. 3, 1864.

4. Williams received the coveted promotion five days after writing this letter, on Aug. 30, 1862.

5. The *Yorktown* did get through the blockade safely but sprung a leak and foundered off Ship Island. The crew escaped and the letter must have been returned to Williams. *ORN*, 19:238–40.

6. Because rough weather often prevented boats from landing at the fort's wharf, in Oct. 1861 Bragg had ordered another wharf constructed and a railroad built to it at Navy Cove, three miles east of the fort on Bon Secours Bay (notwithstanding the present-day maps, Bon Secours was the correct spelling at that time). It was, by this date, a thriving little community. *ORA*, 6:755.

7. Col. William L. Powell, a lieutenant in the U.S. Navy, resigned in July, 1861. He was named a lieutenant in the C.S. Navy in Virginia, then Captain of Artillery (regular), and colonel in the Provisional Army at Pensacola prior to being named brigade commander of the lower Mobile Bay defenses (the Second Brigade) on Dec. 15, 1861. He died Sept. 25, 1863, and on Oct. 23 Maury named the "defenses at Grant's Pass" Ft. Powell in his honor.

8. Capt. Douglas Vass was Post Quartermaster from Nov. 1861 until he was "relieved" Aug. 26, 1864.

9. General Lee also defeated Maj. Gen. John Pope at "Second Manassas," Va., on Aug. 29–30, 1862.

10. See troop organization for the district, Oct. 31, 1862, *ORA*, 15:850; Brigade Field Return, Oct. 31, 1862, RG 109, NA.

After the fall of New Orleans in April 1862, work began on these two batteries in order to prevent the navigation of the rivers by the enemy if Mobile fell. On Jan. 31, 1863, Leadbetter assigned Major Von Sheliha, a Prussian, as chief engineer at Choctaw and Oven Bluffs. He was promoted to lieutenant colonel and district engineer in Sept. 1863. Important shipyard and saltworks were located near Oven Bluff (misspelled Owen Bluff in *ORA* until May 1863). James L. Nichols, "Confederate Engineers and the Defense of Mobile," *Alabama Review* 12 (July 1959):185–91. Letters from the Engineering Dept., District of the Gulf, RG 109, NA; William N. Still, Jr., "The Confederate States Navy at Mobile, 1861 to August 1864," *Alabama Historical Quarterly* 30 (Fall and Winter 1968): 130–31, 135. There were numerous engineering problems on the river obstructions at these two locations. See district engineer's reports, *ORA*, 15: 963–64, 1012, 1015, 1029.

Von Sheliha considered the batteries at Choctaw Bluff to be a model for river defense. Viktor Ernst Karl Rudolph Von Sheliha, *A Treatise on Coast Defense: Based on the Experience Gained by Officers of the Corps of Engineers of the Army of the Confederate States* (London: E. and F. N. Spon, 1868), p. 42. A district troop report, dated Dec. 20, 1862, indicates that there were 244 effectives at Choctaw and Oven Bluffs. *ORA*, 15:903.

11. In a statement of troops for the district, dated April 1863, Anderson's First Battalion is listed as heavy artillery at Choctaw and Oven Bluffs in Brig. Gen. James E.

Slaughter's First Brigade of the Western Division, Brig. Gen. William W. Mackall commanding. Lieutenant Colonel Stewart's Second Battalion at Ft. Morgan is listed in the Third Brigade, Colonel Powell commanding. Maj. Gen. Simon B. Buckner commanded the district from Dec. 14, 1862, until replaced on April 27, 1863, by Maj. Gen. Dabney H. Maury. Ibid., 899–900, 1055–56, 1068.

12. Lieutenant Colonel Stewart's death occurred at Ft. Morgan on April 30. The officers of both battalions held separate meetings to honor Stewart's memory and signed a "Tribute of Respect" which was published in the Mobile papers.

13. Selma was the site of the important naval gun foundry and ordnance works. Frank N. Smith was second lieutenant of Company F until elected captain of Company C on Aug. 30, 1862. He was captured with the garrison at Ft. Gaines on Aug. 8, 1864, and exchanged Jan. 4, 1865. He led the company until the final surrender.

14. Williams received a brief furlough to Mobile, probably to be examined for promotion to lieutenant colonel. His promotion, which he does not allude to, was effective May 1, 1863.

15. Williams named his son George Dixon, after his good friend.

16. Michael Burke, first sergeant of Company B, was elected second lieutenant April 8, 1864. Captured at Ft. Gaines, he refused to be exchanged in Jan. 1865.

17. The Federal force under Grant's command was, on May 31, 1863, in the fourteenth day of the siege of Vicksburg, Miss.

18. There was a Pvt. John McCabe in Company B. He enlisted Sept. 11, 1862, at Ft. Morgan. Stockley and Scott were merchant tailors in Mobile.

19. Both steamers, the *James Battle* and the *William Bagley*, were captured after spirited chases by the blockaders. The *Bagley* was not captured until 11:00 P.M. They carried, according to the Federal report, over 1,300 bales of cotton. ORN, 20:397–98.

20. Augusta Evans Wilson, *Beulah* (New York: Derby and Jackson, 1859). The author lived in Mobile. On July 20, 1863, "the operations at Choctaw and Oven Bluffs were suspended until further notice." Leadbetter to Robertson, Letters from the Eng. Dept., District of the Gulf, RG 109, NA. The First Battalion of the Twenty-first Alabama was soon ordered back to the lower bay defenses.

21. Adm. David G. Farragut commanded the Western Blockading Squadron in the Gulf of Mexico. Federal ironclads had failed to reduce Ft. Sumter in Charleston harbor on April 7, 1863.

22. Dixon volunteered to accompany the sub-torpedo boat *H. L. Hunley* to Charleston after numerous failures in Mobile Bay. See Wallace Shugg, "Prophet of the Deep: The *H. L. Hunley*," *The Civil War Times Illustrated* (April 1973), pp. 4–10, 44–47; Mobile *Daily Herald*, Nov. 15, 1904, front page; *Civil War Naval Chronology*, 6:44–45.

23. On Aug. 10, the Second Battalion of the Twenty-first is listed in the district's returns as being at Ft. Morgan in Colonel Powell's brigade, which included Ft. Gaines and Ft. Grant (Grant's Pass). Four companies are listed for the defenses of Mobile, Brig. Gen. James Cantey commanding. ORA, 26, Pt. 2: 157. The company muster rolls in CSR, RG 109, NA for 1863 indicate that Companies E, I, and K were at Ft. Morgan from June to Oct. 31, and that Company D was at Ft. Powell from Aug. 21 to Dec. 31. Companies A and C were at Ft. Morgan from Aug. to Oct. 31, Company B was there from Sept. to Oct. 31, and Company F was ordered there from Point Clear, about halfway up the bay on the east shore, on Aug. 27.

24. Adm. Franklin Buchanan commanded the naval forces in Mobile Bay. The *Buckner* was, presumably, the captured blockade runner *General Buckner*, which, in a

report from the Confederate consul in Havana dated June 2, 1863, noted that she was "our best blockade runner, and has since been fitted out as a gunboat to operate against us." *ORN,* 20:828.

25. Maj. James T. Gee commanded the First Alabama Artillery Battalion prior to Lt. Col. Robert C. Forsyth's appointment on Feb. 13, 1862, and after his resignation on July 13, 1864. Gee was captured at Ft. Morgan, Aug. 23, 1864.

26. The U.S.S. *DeSoto,* in fact, captured the swift *Alice Vivian* at 7:40 P.M. on Aug. 16. Logbook, *DeSoto,* RG 24, NA.

27. On Aug. 3, Leadbetter ordered Robertson to Grant's Pass. Letters from the Eng. Dept., District of the Gulf, RG 109, NA. Leadbetter, in his engineering report for Sept. 1863, described the construction at Grant's Pass as "being enlarged so as to mount six heavy guns, and will contain a bomb-proof shelter for the garrison and stores. A large quantity of sand has been transported to the site, and a part of the bomb-proof shelter has become available. Four of the gun platforms have been laid." *ORA,* 26, Pt. 2:274–75.

28. Williams sent Company D to Grant's Pass.

29. Thomas J. Savage was promoted to first lieutenant of Company D on Aug. 30, 1862. On Aug. 24, the gunboats U.S.S. *Genesee* and *J. P. Jackson* bombarded Grant's Pass at long range. Logbook, *Genesee,* RG 24, NA.

30. The *H. L. Hunley* sank twice while maneuvering in Charleston Harbor in late Aug. She was raised and refitted after each incident. Shugg, "Prophet of the Deep," p. 9.

31. Gen. Joseph E. Johnston commanded the Western Department, with headquarters in Meridian, Miss.

32. On Sept. 30, Williams is listed as commanding the "21st Alabama (battalion)," obviously at Ft. Morgan; however, the Third Brigade (as then designated) was now commanded by Brig. Gen. Francis A. Shoup. Anderson's First Battalion remained on detached duty in Cantey's Brigade, now designated the First Brigade. *ORA,* 26, Pt. 2: 275.

33. A small screw steamer-torpedo boat, the *Gunnison* had a torpedo attached to her bow. She was designed to attack the blockaders. The Union naval authorities soon knew about the plan and the expected attack did not occur. *ORN,* 20: 690, 697, 705, 848; 21:106; *Civil War Naval Chronology,* 6:244.

34. On Oct. 15, 1863, the *H. L. Hunley* sank again with all hands, including Horace L. Hunley, while practice-diving under a ship. Shugg, "Prophet of the Deep," p. 10; *Civil War Naval Chronology,* 6:245. On Dec. 14, Dixon was ordered to assume command of the *Hunley. ORA,* 27, Pt. 2: 553.

35. Davis had traveled to Chattanooga to confer with Bragg about serious internal command problems in the Army of Tennessee. While in the west, he made a tour of inspection through Selma, Meridian, and Mobile. Hudson Strode, *Jefferson Davis: Confederate President* (New York: Harcourt, Brace, and Co., 1957), pp. 486–87.

36. Col. George A. Smith, Williams's senior, commanded the First Confederate (Georgia) Regiment in the Third Brigade. *ORA,* 26, Pt. 2: 275, 402, 511, 562.

37. On Nov. 10, 1863, the department's troop organization report lists the Twenty-first Alabama, Anderson commanding, in Shoup's Third Brigade. On Dec. 17, Brig. Gen. Edward Higgins is listed as commanding officer of the Third Brigade. Ibid., 402, 511, 562.

38. As inspection and mustering officer, Williams had to tour the small cavalry camps within the brigade's jurisdiction. He could have written this letter from the picket outpost twelve miles east of Ft. Morgan. Camp Powell was one of the camps east of Camp

Anderson. On Aug. 10, 1863, the district troop report indicated that the Baldwin Rangers (106 effective total) were at Camp Powell. The May 1, 1863, troop report indicates that the same detachment was at the "Perdido River." On Nov. 23, 1863, Federal Brig. Gen. Alexander Asboth, commanding officer of the District of Pensacola, reported that one of the camps was "west of the Perdido River, near Neunces Ferry, on the Blakeley road." This camp, he continued, "about 300 strong, is constantly scouting up and down the river, guarding all crossings and ferries." Ibid., Pt. 1, p. 818. After discussions with local inhabitants, I determined that Camp Powell was located near the present-day village of Elberta, about fifteen miles northeast of Camp Anderson.

39. Camp Anderson, named for the Twenty-first's colonel, was located near the extensive salt works on both sides of Bon Secours River, where it flowed into Bon Secours Bay on the east shore of Mobile Bay. The works and the camp were destroyed by a U.S. naval force on Sept. 9, 1864. One report of that expedition suggests the size of the operation. There were "55 furnaces, averaging 18 pans or pots each, making a total of near 1,000. . . . The whole works covered an area of a square mile . . . [and] . . . averaged 2,000 bushels of salt per day." ORN, 21:631–38. These salt works are not mentioned in Ella Lonn, *Salt As a Factor in the Confederacy* (Tuscaloosa: University of Alabama Press, 1965).

CHAPTER V

1. The fort was built on a shellbank, partially submerged at high tide. The best technical description of the fort is in Viktor Von Sheliha, *A Treatise on Coast Defense: Based on the Experience Gained by Officers of the Corps of Engineers of the Army of the Confederate States* (London: E. and F. N. Spon, 1868), pp. 39–42. He considered it to be a "model" water battery in which sand was used to absorb the heavy bombardment in February.

2. On Feb. 12, 1864, Farragut ordered five mortar schooners from Pensacola—the U.S.S. *Port Royal, O. H. Lee, Orvetta, Henry Janes,* and *John Griffith*—and one mortar brig, the U.S.S. *Sea Foam,* to join the four steamers in the Mississippi Sound. They were to reduce Ft. Powell, enter the lower bay, and attempt to draw Confederate troops away from Maj. Gen. William T. Sherman's Vicksburg campaign to Meridian, Miss. (Feb. 3 – March 6). Maury soon knew of Farragut's tactical ruse. On Feb. 15, Maury reported to James A. Seddon, Secretary of War, that the defenses at Grant's Pass were "weak, and the difficulties of fortifying it are very great. . . . The line between Forts Morgan and Gaines is also very liable . . . to be forced. . . . The enemy will probably, therefore, be able to occupy the lower bay with his fleet of warships," ORN, 21: 91–95, 103–4.

In an ammunition report, dated Jan. 11, 1864, Ft. Powell's long-range armament included two 8-inch columbiads, and one 6.4-inch rifled columbiad. The garrison consisted of Companies D (Battle Guards) and K (Mobile Cadets) and part of Culpeper's (S.C.) Battery, i.e., 136 men. ORA, 32, Pt. 2: 547; ORN, 21:885; typescript letter, Francis Kierman to W. D. Whetstone, Sept. 12, 1910, Military Records Division, Alabama Department of Archives and History, Montgomery, Ala.; hereafter referred to as ADAH. Private Kierman was in Company K. Whetstone was the original fifth sergeant of Company D. He was promoted to third sergeant in Dec. 1862.

3. Shoals usually prevented the Union flotilla from getting any closer than two miles. The attack began on Feb. 16, when 165 shells were fired. Seven or eight hit the fort; two men were wounded slightly and the officer's quarters were knocked down. Mobile

Advertiser and Register, Feb. 18, 1864. See day-by-day Federal naval reports, ORN, 21:98–103.

The submarine *H. L. Hunley* sunk again, with the loss of all hands, on Feb. 17, 1864, with George Dixon in command, while exploding a torpedo under the blockader U.S.S. *Housatonic's* hull. Wallace Shugg, "Prophet of the Deep: the *H. L. Hunley*," *The Civil War Times Illustrated* (April 1973), pp. 44–47; ORA, 35, Pt. 1: 112–13; Mobile *Daily Herald,* Nov. 15, 1904, front page.

4. On Feb. 24, Capt. Percival Drayton, aboard the U.S.S. *Calhoun,* wrote in a light but objective vein to Capt. Thornton A. Jenkins, on the blockader U.S.S. *Richmond:* "We are hammering away at the fort here, which minds us about as much as if we did not fire—that is, the fort—for the men skedaddle as soon as the fire is at all brisk, although they will keep up anything like a fair fight, as they did with me for two hours yesterday in the *Orvetta,* and until the others commenced action, when they retired." ORN, 21:95.

5. On Feb. 27, Maury reported to Seddon that on Feb. 25, 470 shot and shell were fired at the fort, which sustained three casualties. ORA, 52, Pt. 2 (supplement): 631.

6. Maury ordered the gunboats *Huntsville* and *Tuscaloosa* and the ram *Baltic* to stand by near Ft. Powell. The last bombardment occurred on Feb. 29. The Mobile *Advertiser and Register* on Mar. 2 reported that over 500 shot and shell were fired at the fort, and the result was, literally, "nobody hurt." Three of the ships were hit and crippled, according to their informant. The *John Griffith* was struck six times. Logbook, RG 24, NA. On March 1, Farragut thought that he saw the ironclad ram C.S.S. *Tennessee* near Ft. Powell. (He probably saw the *Baltic,* since the *Tennessee* had not yet negotiated the Dog River bar.) Farragut immediately ordered the withdrawal of the flotilla "except for the two boats heretofore in the sound." ORN, 21:97–98; Caldwell Delaney, *The Story of Mobile* (Mobile: Gulf Printing Co., 1953), p. 129.

7. There was a district brigade headquarters near Pollard, Alabama, where the forty-five-mile-long Mobile and Great Northern Railroad, from Tensas Station, north of Blakeley, connected with the Mobile and Florida Railroad to Montgomery. Cavalry camps and outposts were located south and southeast toward Union-occupied Pensacola. Kierman to Whetstone, ADAH; ORA, 32, Pt. 3: 790, 816, 866, 872; 52, Pt. 2 (supplement), 661. The company muster rolls, RG 109, NA, indicate that the regiment was at Pollard on April 4 and 16, 1864. Telegraph Book I, Ft. Morgan, Richard L. Page Collection, University of North Carolina Library, Chapel Hill. On April 30, the brigade included the First Alabama Battalion Artillery, Thirtieth Louisiana, First Tennessee Heavy Artillery, and four companies of the Seventh Alabama Cavalry. ORA, 32, Pt. 3: 861; 39, Pt. 2: 752.

8. On May 2, Davis reported to the opening session of the Second Confederate Congress that "a naval attack on Mobile was so successfully repulsed at the outer works that the attempt was abandoned." *Journal of the C.S.A., 1861–1865,* 7 (Washington: Government Printing Office, 1905):11.

9. On Apr. 12, Von Sheliha ordered Capt. L. J. Frenaux, Engineer in Charge of Lower Bay Line at Ft. Gaines, to give first priority to the construction of redoubts at Ft. Powell. On June 2, Frenaux reported to Maury that 182 workers, primarily blacks, were at the fort (more than at Fts. Gaines and Morgan combined), yet he recommended 100 more. ORN, 21: 893, 900–901.

10. A Federal raiding party boarded and burned the blockade-runner *Ivanhoe* in the early morning of July 6, 1864. The cargo was saved, however, by an expedition from Ft. Morgan. ORN, 21: 353–57, 905.

11. An internationally known socialite, Madame Octavia LeVert was the leader of Mobile's social life during the 1850s. Delaney, *Story of Mobile,* pp. 109–10.

12. The monitor *Manhattan* arrived off Mobile on July 20. Farragut was anxiously awaiting three additional monitors and troops in order to beseige Ft. Gaines, run past Ft. Morgan, and attack the Confederate fleet in the lower bay. *ORN,* 21: 381, 387.

The pictoletter is deciphered as follows:

Headquarters Fort Powell
July 23, 1864

Dear Lizzy:

You failed to write the name of your post office plainly in your last letter, and as I cannot make it out you must excuse my apparent neglect—This epistle will be awaiting you at home three or four days before you return; you can blame no one but yourself for the delay.

A soldier is making palmetto braid for Mrs. Parrott   I have promised to send it flying on the *Crescent* soon—Don't you want some too?

I have a hearty desire to escape for a few days from duty when you return to the city, but fear that I am doomed to be disappointed—The general is preparing for an attack which he thinks the enemy will make very soon—I pray for it to come quick so that we can obtain leaves of absence again once in a while.

There is nothing new or exciting to tell you of our life here. a monitor lies off Morgan, but it frightens nobody

13. After months of delay, the *Tennessee* finally got over the Dog River bar on May 22 and anchored near Ft. Morgan. *ORN,* 21:935.

14. The monitors *Manhattan* and *Winnebago* were now joined by the *Chickasaw. ORN,* 21:396.

15. Lt. Cmdr. James C. P. deKrafft commanded the flotilla in the Sound. Farragut had planned to enter the bay on Aug. 4; however, the monitor *Tecumseh* did not arrive from Pensacola until the evening of Aug. 4. This delay worked to the Union's advantage because on Aug. 3, additional troops were ordered to Ft. Gaines. These troops were captured with the garrison. *ORA,* 39, Pt. 1: 429; *ORN,* 21: 405, 416, 502–4; *ORA,* 52, Pt. 2: 716.

16. The *Chickasaw,* hit thrice by the Brooke rifle, succeeded in destroying the water tank and towing away the construction barge *Ingomar. ORN,* 21:500–501; *ORN,* 39, Pt. 1:441–42.

17. *ORA,* 39, Pt. 1:442. On May 1, 1890, Williams took exception to Maury's report and wrote on the margin of his personal copy of Commodore Foxhall A. Parker's *Battle of Mobile Bay . . .* (Boston: A. Williams and Co., 1878), p. 126: "the east side of the fort besides being strewed with lumber had one gun disabled and they both stood on the pinacle of their foundations—nine feet above the terreplain—you could not reach up to the muzzle." Mobile *Advertiser and Register,* Jan. 22, 1903. John Forsyth, in a series of editorials in the Mobile *Advertiser and Register,* was very critical of Williams's surrender of Ft. Powell. On Aug. 9, he termed it a "disgraceful surrender." The next day he wrote that if an escape to Cedar Point had not been so easy, "Ft. Powell would still be in our possession." Commodore Parker, in his analysis of Williams's action, wrote (p. 50): "There can be no doubt that he acted wisely and prudently; for . . . the monitors and the light-draught gunboats . . . crossing their fire with DeKrafft's flotilla . . . would have

forced a surrender in less than twelve hours." See Folmar, "Lt. Col. James M. Williams and the Ft. Powell Incident," *Alabama Review* 17 (April 1964):125–31.

On Aug. 6, the *Winnebago* attacked Ft. Gaines from close range, and Granger's artillery was in place the next day. Anderson surrendered the fort on Aug. 8. Maury, very critical of Anderson's action, reported that the garrison consisted of 600 troops; however, Granger reported 818 prisoners. Maury also reported that there were six companies of the Twenty-first Alabama there, but an analysis of the last unofficial "roster" in the Williams Collection, dated May 3, 1865, indicates that seven companies surrendered: B, C, E, F, G, H, and I. *ORN*, 39, Pt. 1:410. For the controversy concerning Anderson's surrender, see ibid., pp. 417–19, 426–29, 436–38; and the Mobile *Advertiser and Register*, Aug. 9, 10, 16, and Sept. 4, 22, 24, 1864.

18. Pvt. Richard D. Williams was in Company D, then Company E of the First Regiment, Mobile Volunteers, Local Defense. On Sept. 22, 1864, John Forsyth printed in his paper an extract from a letter sent to him by "J. L.," written by Colonel Anderson on Aug. 18 to his wife. It read, in part:

"As soon as the fleet ran in, Col. Williams . . . retreated with his command, and therein acted more sensibly than any of us. The whole line ought to have been prepared for the same thing. . . . I did not consider Mobile in danger, for the enemy had evidently not come prepared for anything except to gain a harbor for a safe anchorage, and as a preliminary step towards further operations in the fall."

19. ORA, 39, Pt. 1: 418–19, 438–41. Concerning the surrender of Fts. Morgan and Gaines, Commodore Parker wrote in *Battle of Mobile Bay*:

"If there had been a Confederate *army* marching to the relief of Mobile, it would undoubtedly have been the duty of General Page and Colonel Anderson to hold their forts to the last extremity; but . . . Maury . . . was at that very time sending reinforcements to [Mississippi]. . . . Page would have done well had he blown up Fort Morgan . . . and marched his troops to Mobile; . . . Anderson's duty to his soldiers . . . required him to act . . . as he did." (p. 50)

Fort Morgan's surrendered garrison included Williams's old company, A, John Cothran commanding. He was imprisoned at Ft. LaFayette, N.Y., until the end of the war.

20. Six Federal regiments and a battery occupied Cedar Point on Aug. 25. ORA, 39, Pt. 1: 422. Williams is referring to Companies D and K as his "brave boys." Two strong defensive lines protected Mobile from a land attack. A third, outer line was no longer operative. The Dog River bar, torpedoes, obstructions, and water batteries prevented any immediate naval effort against the city. In addition, the delta system to the east prevented any Federal movement except by a tortuous water route up the Apalachee River (as indicated on Civil War maps) to Blakeley, down the Tensas River, up the Spanish River, and, finally, down the Mobile River to the city. To prevent this move, the Confederates obstructed the rivers and built batteries Tracy and Huger. Fortifications at Spanish Fort and Blakeley protected the land approaches to the river system.

21. In the margin of Parker's *Battle of Mobile Bay* (p. 128), where Maury is quoted as approving Williams's court-martial, Williams wrote: "The result of the court-martial was a long opinion reviewing my position which fully approved my action and closed with the declaration that in the opinion of the court I had 'acted with sound discretion and in obedience to the letter and the spirit of his orders.' "

22. Williams's command was a portion of the Right Wing, Center Division. Endorsement, Williams to Seddon, Sept. 17, 1864, Williams's Personal Service Record, RG 109, NA, hereafter referred to as WPSR.

23.Gen. John B. Hood commanded the Army of Tennessee in Georgia. After a siege of six weeks, he abandoned Atlanta to Sherman on the night of Sept. 1–2, 1864.

24. WPSR, NA. Williams wrote, May 1, 1890, in the margins of Parker's *Battle of Mobile Bay*, pp. 125–27:

"The fact which does not appear in the record is that a scapegoat had to be provided to bear the load of sins, which left our position an easy prey for Farragut. The bay side of Fort Powell had been left unprotected while our engineers were engaged in many absurd works, and some which deserve a worse name—such as the construction of batteries near fort Morgan for no other purpose than the protection of blockade runners in the swash channel. That the staff of the general commanding was interested in this money-making business was an open secret. While I commanded at Fort Morgan I repeatedly called attention to the fact that we could not successfully oppose an attempt to pass the fort unless the channel was effectively closed with torpedoes—No attention was paid to this as to do so would stop the blocade runners—Such torpedoes as were placed were carefully buoyed. My opinions . . . were shared by every intelligent officer who was familiar with the position. Sergt. Wm. Demoney who made the copies of my monthly reports . . . once asked me, if I did not fear to give offence at headquarters, by repeating each month, in the same language, my suggestions as to the necessity of torpedoes. I am very well satisfied that I did give offence, and but for the independent integrity of the Court Martial . . . I would have been ruined and disgraced by the speculative gentlemen who were unfortunately my superiors."

Before becoming sergeant major of the regiment, Demoney was first corporal, then second sergeant of Company K. He was promoted to second lieutenant of Company G on March 24, 1864, captured at Ft. Gaines, and exchanged. He commanded the company during the last weeks of the war.

25. Lt. Col. Robert Sterling (Williams misspells his name) had commanded the First Tennessee Heavy Artillery at Ft. Morgan.

26. The company muster rolls for Oct. 31, 1864, indicate that Company D (76 present, 2d Lt. John D. Cogburn commanding) was at Battery Huger, and that Company K (107 present, 1st Lt. John Bond commanding) was at Barron's Warehouse in Mobile. Another muster roll dated Aug. 31 – Oct. 31 lists Captain Sossaman's Detachmant (81 – men present), 1st Lt. Charles Tell commanding. In a district troop report, Nov. 1 and 20, 1864, the 21st Alabama (detachment), Capt. B. Frank Dade commanding, is in Col. Thomas H. Taylor's Post of Mobile command. ORA, 39, Pt. 3: 876; 45, Pt. 1: 1232–33. Dade was elected first lieutenant of Company F in Oct. 1861, and captain May 8, 1862. Cogburn was promoted to second lieutenant Aug. 30, 1862. Bond was formerly a lieutenant in Company B.

27. By this date, Hood was moving into northern Alabama en route toward Nashville, Tennessee, in an attempt to force Sherman to follow him. On Dec. 15–16, 1865, George H. Thomas's Army of the Cumberland defeated Hood's army at Nashville. The remnants of the Army of Tennessee were pursued into northern Alabama. Some of the surviving units were ordered to the District of the Gulf.

28. Bailey C. Paine enlisted at Ft. Morgan on Nov. 22, 1863. He died of meningitis at Ross Hospital, Mobile.

29. Brian O'Linn was a stock Irish character in mid-nineteenth-century verse.

30. Williams wrote his brief note on the bottom of Wainwright's letter, dated Dec. 1. Wainwright wrote from Selma, suggesting that Lizzy should not go to Pike County. "I do not think," he continued, "that what they eat will break me yet awhile & even if it

should I will only be in the fix that many of my fellows are at the present time. I feel that I ought to be doing something for those that are sacrificing every thing for their country."

31. Commanded by Brig. Gen. John W. Davidson, the "raiders" were, apparently, the cavalry column of about 4,000 men that moved in early December from Baton Rouge, La., toward Mobile. There was a skirmish at Chickasawha River in Mississippi on Dec. 10, and the column turned south toward Pascagoula. *ORA*, 45, Pt. 1: 787–90. The two batteries were 1000 yards apart, about two miles above Spanish Fort on the eastern shore. They were designed to command Blakeley River. Huger had four bastions and eleven guns, and Tracy, and enclosed bastioned work, had five guns. C. C. Andrews, *History of the Campaign of Mobile, Including the Cooperative Operation of Gen. Wilson's Cavalry in Alabama* (New York: D. Van Nostrand, 1867), pp. 70–71. Williams later wrote in the margin of Parker's *Battle of Mobile Bay*, p. 128, that the two batteries were "the key of the new line of defense opposite Spanish Fort."

32. An expedition from Ft. Barrancas (near Pensacola), consisting of the Ninety-seventh Colored Infantry, Col. George D. Robinson commanding, occupied Pollard, Ala., on Dec. 16. Public property, the depot, and several railroad bridges were destroyed. *ORA*, 44:449.

33. James R. Currell was the Assistant Agent of [Prisoner] Exchange in Mobile. Union officials had agreed to exchange the Ft. Gaines prisoners since Nov. 5, 1864. *ORA*, Series 2, vol. 7: 1095, 1202.

34. The Ft. Gaines prisoners were exchanged at Ship Island, Miss., on Jan. 5, 1865. Johnston refused to be exchanged and took the oath of allegience on Dec. 23, 1864.

35. *ORA*, 48, Pt. 1:580; 49, 355, 781, 851, 869; John Kent Folmar, "The War Comes to Central Alabama: Ebenezer Church, April 1, 1865," *Alabama Historical Quarterly* 26 (Summer 1964):187–202.

36. A number of letters are obviously missing in February and March.

37. Edwin Poellnitz, formerly first sergeant of Company C, was elected second lieutenant in Aug. 1862. His brother, James A. Poellnitz, of the same company, was promoted from private to first sergeant by June, 1863, and elected second lieutenant Nov. 20, 1863. The last regimental roster in RG 109, NA, was signed by Williams on Jan. 19, 1865, at Headquarters, Battery "A," Right Wing Defenses of Mobile. He noted that "the papers and regimental books having been lost at Ft. Gaines and most of the officers being now absent with leave it is impossible to make out the above roster more accurately."

38. On March 10, 1865, the depleted Twenty-first Alabama, with Williams commanding, is listed in the district's last organization of troops as being in Brig. Gen. Bryan M. Thomas's Alabama Reserves Brigade, which included the First and Second Alabama Reserves. The latter two regiments consisted of "old men," according to a deserter from Maury's headquarters. *ORA*, 49, Pt. 1: 1046; *ORA*, 49, Pt. 2: 226.

39. O'Connor was elected first lieutenant of Company B on May 8, 1862, and captain May 1, 1863. An L. L. Holcombe was in Company K. Farrand commanded the naval forces at Mobile. Vidmer, a corporal in Company F (Baldwin Rifles), was seriously wounded at Shiloh on April 6. Promoted to first lieutenant and regimental adjutant on June 20, 1862, he was captured at Ft. Gaines and exchanged. He was wounded again at Spanish Fort.

40. On March 17, Canby, with an army of 32,000, ordered the Thirteenth Corps (Granger commanding) to march from Ft. Morgan around Bon Secours Bay toward a ferry landing on Fish River, the point of concentration with the Sixteenth Corps, Maj.

Gen. Andrew J. Smith commanding. The Sixteenth Corps was transported from Dauphin Island across the bay on March 20–22. Heavy rains delayed the completion of movement until March 24. Both brigades then moved up the eastern shore toward Spanish Fort and Blakeley. In addition, on March 20, Maj. Gen. Frederick Steele led a cooperating 3,000-man expedition from Pensacola to Pollard, which he occupied on March 25. The command then turned west toward Mobile Bay and participated in the investment of Blakeley. ORA, 49, Pt. 1: 92–93, 790.

41. The two deserters, Pvts. Thomas Elam and Elijah Wynn, of Company F, were shot in front of the brigade at Blakeley on March 31, 1865. Elam enlisted Oct. 13, 1861, and Wynn on Feb. 23, 1863. Both were Baldwin County natives and deserted with their equipment at Point Clear on Sept. 11, 1863. Hdq. to James M. Williams, March 15, 1865, Blakeley, Eastern Division, Dist. of the Gulf, in Letters Sent, March–April, 1865, RG 109, NA; Brig. Gen. St. John R. Liddell to Col. Garner, March 31, Blakeley, Eastern Division, Dist. of the Gulf, in Telegrams Sent, March 8 – April 8, 1865, RG 109, NA.

42. Blakeley's investment was delayed until Steele's force arrived on April 1. B. L. Roberson, "Valor on the Eastern Shore," (unpublished paper in Local History Section, Mobile Public Library: Mobile, 1965), pp. 1–22; Kierman to Whetstone, ADAH; Richard Taylor, *Destruction and Reconstruction: Personal Experiences of the Late War* (Waltham, Mass.: Blaisdell Publishing Co., 1968 [1879]), pp. 220–26. Brig. Gen. Christopher C. Andrews, who commanded the Second Division of the Thirteenth Corps, is the authority for the volley by the Twenty-first on Bay Minette Creek. He also wrote that the Twenty-first Alabama consisted of 225 troops and that Gen. Smith, the corps commander, barely escaped. Andrews, *History of the Campaign of Mobile,* p. 51. ORA, 49, Pt. 1: 94, 313–15.

43. Williams's command lost seven killed and fourteen wounded during the siege of Spanish Fort. Newspaper clipping, May 12, 1891, pasted in the back cover of Williams's copy of Parker's *Battle of Mobile Bay;* Williams's undated application for membership in "Raphael Semmes Camp of Confederate Veterans;" Roberson, "Valor on the Eastern Shore," pp. 22–33; Liddell to Gibson, Blakeley, March 28, 1865, Telegrams Sent, Eastern Div., Dist. of the Gulf, March 8 – April 8, 1865, RG 109, NA; Kierman to Whetstone, ADAH; ORA, 49, Pt. 2: 311, 1184–87, 1219.

44. ORA, 49, Pt. 2: 1225, 1231, 1275, 1282–84.

45. The final roll consisted of Company B (14 men, and Company D, 12 men, Capt. Melville C. Butt, commanding); Company C (27 men, Capt. Smith); Company E (20 men, Capt. Sossaman); Company F (15 men, 1st Lt. George B. Gwin); Company G (22 men, 2d Lt. Demoney); Company H (19 men, Capt. Carrington); Company I (27 men, 1st Lt. Murdock McInnis); and Company K (45 men, 1st Lt. William J. Brainard). On Oct. 10, 1861, Gwin was elected second lieutenant of the Battle Guards, which became Company F three days later. He was elected first lieutenant on May 8, 1862, and captain August 30, 1862. McInnis enlisted as a private in Company I and was elected first lieutenant Aug. 10, 1862. Brainard, the original fourth corporal of Company K, was elected second lieutenant on May 8, 1862, and first lieutenant July 4, 1863.

Bibliography

Andrews, Charles C. *History of the Campaign of Mobile; Including the Cooperative Operation of Gen. Wilson's Cavalry in Alabama.* New York: D. Van Nostrand, 1867.

Black, Robert C. *The Railroads of the Confederacy.* Chapel Hill: University of North Carolina Press, 1952.

Boatner, Mark M., III. *The Civil War Dictionary.* New York: David McKay Company, 1959.

Brewer, Willis. *Alabama: Her History, Resources, War Record, and Reminiscences, from 1540 to 1872.* Montgomery: Barrett and Brown, 1872.

Can't-Get-Away Club: Their Work in 1897. Mobile: George Matzenger, 1898.

Confederate Veteran. Nashville, Tennessee. 40 vols.

Connelly, Thomas Lawrence. *Army of the Heartland: The Army of Tennessee, 1861–1862.* Baton Rouge: Louisiana State University Press, 1967.

Delaney, Caldwell. *The Story of Mobile.* Mobile: Gulf Printing Company, 1953.

Ekstrom, Doris Williams. Interview. Duncombe, Iowa, 1976.

Fleming, Walter L. *Civil War and Reconstruction in Alabama.* New York: Columbia University Press, 1905.

Folmar, John Kent, ed. "Augusta, Georgia, 1860–1861: As Seen in Three Letters." *Georgia Historical Quarterly* 53 (December 1969):523–27.

———. "Lt. Col. James M. Williams and the Ft. Powell Incident." *Alabama Review* 17 (April 1964):123–36.

———. "Post–Civil War Mobile: The Letters of James M. Williams, May–September, 1865." *Alabama Historical Quarterly* 32 (Fall and Winter 1970):186–98.

———. "Pre–Civil War Sentiment from Belmont County: Correspondence of Hugh Anderson." *Ohio History* 78 (Summer 1969): 202–10, 229–30.

———. "The War Comes to Central Alabama: Ebenezer Church, April 1, 1865." *Alabama Historical Quarterly* 26 (Summer 1964):187–202.

Journal of the Congress of the Confederate States of America, 1861–1865. 7 vols. Washington: Government Printing Office, 1905.

Journal of the Proceedings of the Thirty-fourth General Convention of the New Church in the United States. Boston: Otis Clapp, 1852.

Log Books. Records of Bureau of Naval Personnel. Record Group 24. National Archives and Records Service. Washington, D.C.

Lonn, Ella. *Salt as a Factor in the Confederacy.* Tuscaloosa: University of Alabama Press, 1965.

McWhiney, Grady. *Braxton Bragg and Confederate Defeat.* Vol. 1, *Field Command.* New York: Columbia University Press, 1969.

Maury, Dabney H., Collection. Museum of the City of Mobile, Mobile, Alabama.

Military Records Division. Alabama Department of Archives and History, Montgomery, Alabama.

Mobile *Advertiser and Register,* 1861, 1864–65, 1903, 1908.

Mobile *City Directory,* 1859–99.

Mobile *Daily Herald,* 1904.

Mobile *Evening News*, 1864.

Mobile *Press Register*, 1948.

Moore, Albert B. *Conscription and Conflict in the Confederacy*. New York: MacMillan and Company, 1924.

Naval History Division. *Civil War Chronology, 1861–1865*. Washington, D.C.: Department of the Navy, 1971.

Nichols, James L. "Confederate Engineers and the Defense of Mobile." *Alabama Review* 12 (July 1959):181–95.

Page, Richard L., Collection. University of North Carolina Library. Chapel Hill, North Carolina.

Parker, Foxhall. *The Battle of Mobile Bay and the Capture of Forts Powell, Gaines, and Morgan, by the Combined Sea and Land Forces of the United States, under the Command of Rear Admiral David Glasgow Farragut, and Major General Gordon Granger, August, 1864*. Boston: A. Williams and Company, 1878.

Record Groups 94 and 109. Service Records Division. National Archives and Records Service. Washington, D.C.

Roberson, B. L. "Valor on the Eastern Shore." Typewritten. Mobile, Ala.: Local History Section, Mobile Public Library, 1965.

St. Clairsville *Gazette*, 1838–52, 1903.

Shugg, Wallace. "Prophet of the Deep: The *H. L. Hunley*." *The Civil War Times Illustrated* (April 1973): 4–10, 44–47.

Smith, Sidney Adair. *Mobile: Silversmiths and Jewelers, 1820–1867*. Mobile: Historical Mobile Preservation Society, 1935.

Still, William N., Jr. "The Confederate States Navy at Mobile, 1861 to August 1864." *Alabama Historical Quarterly* 30 (Fall and Winter 1968):127–44.

Strode, Hudson. *Jefferson Davis: Confederate President*. New York: Harcourt, Brace and Company, 1957.

Sword, Wiley. "The Battle of Shiloh." *The Civil War Times Illustrated* 17 (May 1978):1–50.

Taylor, Richard. *Destruction and Reconstruction: Personal Experiences of the Late War*. Waltham, Mass.: Blaisdell Publishing Company, 1968 [1879].

U.S. *Bureau of the Census*. 1860–1890. Washington: Government Printing Office.

U.S. *Government. Atlas to War of the Rebellion: Official Records of the Union and Confederate Armies*. 2 vols. Washington: Government Printing Office, 1885–95.

U.S. *Government. Official Records of the Union and Confederate Navies in the War of the Rebellion*. Series 1, 27 vols. Washington: Government Printing Office, 1894–1922.

U.S. *Government. War of the Rebellion: Official Records of the Union and Confederate Armies*. Series 1, 53 vols.; series 2, 8 vols.; series 4, 3 vols. Washington: Government Printing Office, 1880–1901.

Von Sheliha, Viktor Ernst Karl Rudolph. *A Treatise on Coast Defense: Based on the Experience Gained by Officers of the Corps of Engineers of the Army of the Confederate States*. London: E. and F. N. Spon, 1868.

Warner, Ezra J. *General in Blue: Lives of the Union Commanders*. Baton Rouge: Louisiana State University Press, 1964.

———. *General in Gray: Lives of the Confederate Commanders*. Baton Rouge: Louisiana State University Press, 1959.

Williams, James Madison, Collection. Mobile, Alabama.

Index

Ackerman, Joseph C., 167 (n. 27)

Adams, Daniel W., 166 (n. 13)

Alabama and Mississippi Railroad, 159

Alabama Gold Insurance Co., xv

Alabama Militia (postwar): First Regiment, Alabama State Troops, xv; First Infantry Battalion, Volunteer Militia, xv

Alabama Port, 156

Alabama River, 110, 137, 143

ALABAMA TROOPS

artillery: First Battalion, 101, 120, 163 (n. 16), 174 (n. 7); Burtwell's Battery, 167 (n. 24); Felix H. Robertson's, 165 (n. 5)

cavalry: Seventh, 174 (n. 7)

infantry: First, 43; Second, 43; Third, 160–61; Seventeenth, 129, 167 (n. 24); Eighteenth, 165 (n. 49), 167 (n. 24); Nineteenth, 162 (n. 8), 166 (n. 15); Twentieth, 169 (n. 8); Twenty-first, see Twenty-first Alabama Infantry; Twenty-second, 57, 88, 160 (n. 4), 165 (n. 49), 166 (n. 13), 167 (n. 25); Twenty-fourth, 61, 167 (n. 24); Twenty-fifth, 165 (n. 5), 166 (n. 13); Twenty-sixth, 165 (n. 5), 166 (n. 13); Twenty-ninth, 129

local defense: First Regiment, Mobile Volunteers, 176 (n. 18)

Alice Vivian, blockade runner, 120, 172 (n. 26)

Allen, Samuel, 55, 63, 167 (n. 16)

Anderson, Charles D., 88, 96–97, 99, 103–04, 108, 110, 112, 114, 120, 122, 124, 131, 135–36, 152, 155, 169 (n. 8), 172 (nn. 32, 37), 176 (nn. 17, 19)

Anderson, Mrs. Charles D., 110, 113, 136

Anderson, Eleanor Frances (mother), xi, 102, 116

Anderson, Hugh, xi, 102

Andrews, Christopher C., 179 (n. 42)

Apalachee River, 176 (n. 20)

Appalachee Batteries, 150, 178 (n. 31). See also Batteries, Huger and Tracy

Appalachicola River, 170 (n. 1)

Asboth, Alexander, 173 (n. 38)

Atlanta: surrender, 177 (n. 23)

Augusta, xi, 72, 141

Badger, William S., 84, 87, 89, 168 (n. 3)

Bagaley, steamboat, 6

Baldwin Rifles. See Twenty-first Alabama Infantry

Baldwin Station, Miss., 80, 84–85

Baltic, C.S.S., 174 (n. 6)

Barnes, George T., 51

Barrett, Thomas G., 92, 169 (n. 10)

Bassett, George W., 6, 8, 21, 24, 54–55, 60, 69, 79, 81, 135, 143–45, 156, 163 (n. 14)

Baton Rouge, 178 (n. 31)

Batteries: Huger, 150, 156, 176 (n. 20), 177 (n. 26), 178 (n. 31); Tracy, 150, 176 (n. 20), 178 (n. 31)

Battle Guards. See Twenty-first Alabama Infantry

Bay Minette Creek, skirmish, 158 (n. 42)

"Bazaar" mess, xiii, 13, 19, 24–25, 28, 33, 36–37, 39–40, 46, 56–57, 60, 69

Beard, W. K., 41, 165 (n. 48)

Beauregard, P. G. T., 43, 52, 77–78, 165 (n. 5), 166 (n. 15), 168 (n. 38); evacuation of Corinth, 168 (n. 1), 169 (n. 13)

Belmont, Mo., battle, 163 (n. 19)

Bethel Station, Tenn., 48, 165 (n. 4)

Biloxi, Miss., 164 (n. 32)

Blakeley, xv, 156, 174 (n. 7), 176 (n. 20); seige, 158, 179 (nn. 40–42); surrendered, 159

Blue and Gray Veterans' Union, xv

Bond, John, 177 (n. 26)

Bond, Judge George W., 144

Bond, Sarah, 144

Bon Secours Bay, 170 (n. 6), 178 (n. 40)

Bon Secours salt works, 173 (n. 39)

Booneville, Miss., 80; raid, 168 (n. 1)

Bradford, A. B., 55, 167 (n. 18)

Bragg, Braxton, 91, 94, 95, 99, 101, 161 (n. 1), 162 (n. 6), 164 (n. 46), 165 (n. 5), 166 (n. 13), 168 (n. 38), 169 (n. 14), 170 (n. 6)

Brainard, William J., 179 (n. 45)

Breckinridge, John C., 166 (n. 15)

Brooklyn, U.S.S., 164 (n. 45)

Brundidge, Ala., 147

Buchanan, Franklin, 119, 171 (n. 24)

Buck, William A., 61, 62, 68

Buckner, Simon B., 171 (n. 11)

Buckner, U.S.S., 119, 171 (n. 24)

Buell, Don Carlos, 164 (n. 9)

Burke, Michael, 113, 171 (n. 16)